IMAGES
*of America*

# Warm Springs, Fremont

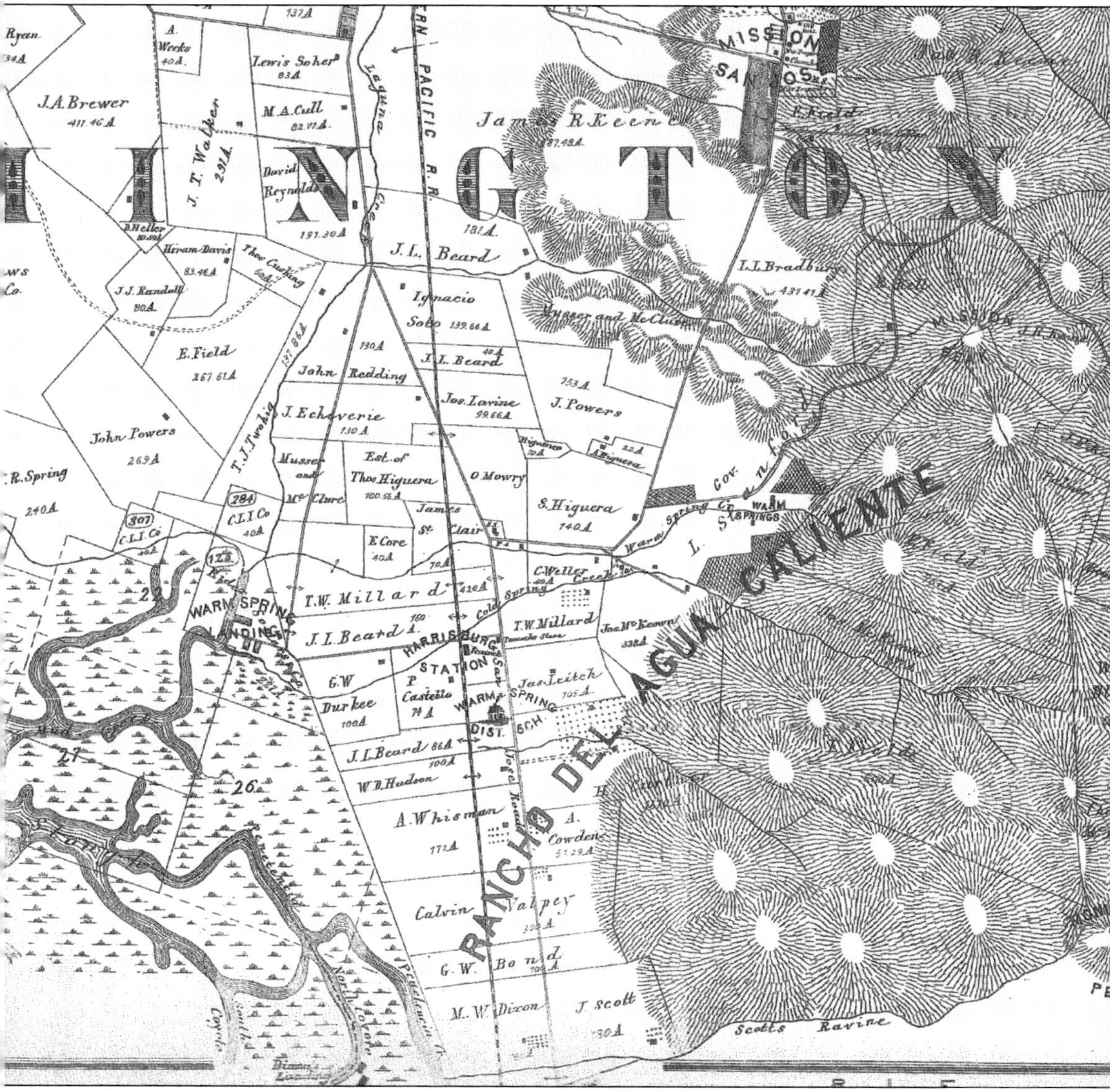


This 1878 map from the *New Historical Atlas of Alameda County* shows the boundary of Rancho del Agua Caliente, which includes most of the present Warm Springs area. It is bordered by Scotts Ravine to the south, Canada de Aliso to the north, Mission Peak and Monument Peak to the east, and Laguna Creek and the marshlands to the west. Harrisburg railroad station (later named Warm Springs) and Warm Springs District School are in the center of the map. The old Warm Springs Landing is to the left of center. The ghost town of Drawbridge was on Station Island between Mud Slough and Coyote Creek. (Courtesy Museum of Local History.)

**ON THE COVER:** This photograph of the first gasoline-powered water pump in Warm Springs was taken at the east end of the Antonio Alvernaz farm in a field of sweet peas, which were grown for seed, in 1918. From left to right are Mae Alvernaz (child), Elsuko Kita, Maria and Antonio Alvernaz, and Yoniko Kita. The Kitas were Japanese immigrants and were sharecroppers on the Alvernaz farm. (Courtesy Eleanor Alvernaz Currie.)

IMAGES
*of America*

# WARM SPRINGS, FREMONT

Philip Holmes and
Patricia Wipfli Schaffarczyk

ARCADIA
PUBLISHING

ISBN 978-0-7385-9663-1

Published by Arcadia Publishing
Charleston, South Carolina

Printed in the United States of America

Library of Congress Control Number: 2012948043

For all general information, please contact Arcadia Publishing:
Telephone 843-853-2070
Fax 843-853-0044
E-mail sales@arcadiapublishing.com
For customer service and orders:
Toll-Free 1-888-313-2665

Visit us on the Internet at www.arcadiapublishing.com

*Dedicated to Philip Brazil Jr.*

# Contents

# ACKNOWLEDGMENTS

We would like to thank everyone who gave their time and images to help put this book together. Gil Garza was always ready to research information and prepare photographs. Susan Vargas Murphy contributed many images and stories about the Vargas family and their descendants. Harry Avila shared many photographs and interesting stories and facts about living in Warm Springs. Lionel Goularte provided images and told stories of growing up in Warm Springs. Trish Nunes contributed images of Warm Springs School and information she collected about the town. Ted Klein gave his knowledge and images as a resident and photographer of the history of Warm Springs. A special thanks to our proofreaders, Lila Bringhurst, Susan Vargas Murphy, Gil Garza, and Jane Huber. Jan Giovanini-Hill and Adrienne Stephens helped us with community contacts and support.

Unless otherwise noted, the images are from the Museum of Local History, Robert B. Fisher Collection. Other images are noted for the following collections, all housed in the museum: US Fish and Wildlife Service, Don Edwards San Francisco Bay National Wildlife Refuge (DE); Doug Tavis and Barbara Melin (DT); Dino Vournas Collection (DV); Harry Avila (HA); Architectural Resource Committee, all photographs by Julianne Howe (JH); Jay Ball (JB); Gil Garza (GG); Herman and Bette Hebel (HBH); Museum of Local History Collection (MLH); Mollie Sinclair (MS); Philip Holmes (PH); Roan McClure (RM); Susan Vargas Murphy (SVM); Ted Klein (TK); Lionel Goularte (LG); Marlene Weibel (MW); and lithographs from *The Official and Historical Atlas Map of Alameda County, California*, Oakland, CA: Thompson & West, 1878 (TW).

In 1898, Josiah W. Stanford hired the San Francisco commercial photographers Andrews and Lange to create a photograph album of his estate's extensive gardens and buildings. The 1898 Andrews and Lange photograph album is part of the Robert B. Fisher Collection. Unless otherwise noted, the photographs in chapter four are from the 1898 photograph album.

Others who contributed to the book include Ed Bettencourt, Ted Brice, Evelyn Brown, Don Brown, Jacquee Cook, Regena Dennie, Jim Coehlo, Janet Cronbach, John Dutra, Larry Fudenna, Alberta Nunes George, Nancy Margherita, Gus Morrison, Donna Olsen, Wayne Sakuda, Paul Sethy, Jill Singleton, Tim Swenson, Frank Vargas, Josephine Wagner, and Marlene Weibel.

# INTRODUCTION

Native Americans who lived in villages around the bay first discovered the warm springs bubbling from the ground. They recognized the value of living near the warm mineral waters and established villages nearby. They were living in the area when the Franciscans founded Mission San Jose in 1797 and eventually piped the warm water for their use.

Pioneer Spanish families in the area used the "agua caliente" to wash their clothes. They knew that the water was very soft and that clothes washed in it came out white and soft without the use of harsh soap. Guadalupe Vallejo, who lived with her family across the street from the mission, described a "wash day expedition" to get the family clothes washed. Josefa Higuera came once a month from Las Positas to wash their clothes.

Don Jose Jesus Vallejo came to Mission San Jose in 1836 with orders to sell the mission properties as part of the secularization process. The plan had been to distribute some of the mission property to the Native Americans, but most of the local land was granted as awards for service to loyal Spanish families. Rancho Agua Caliente was granted to Fulgencio Higuera. It contained more than 95,000 acres, covering the Warm Springs area from Mission Peak to the San Francisco Bay. Higuera had a large family. Several of his sons built adobe homes in the vicinity of Warm Springs and Agua Caliente Creek.

Higuera sold 3,000 acres of his best land in 1852. The Americans began to farm with improved machinery, and the land began to yield abundant crops under their management. Abram Harris bought some of the land, and the name Harrisburg was given to the settlement. The Southern Pacific Railroad built through in 1869 and named its station Warm Springs. Later, the name was also applied to the post office and town.

George Peacock erected a hotel and store in 1861, and the next year, he became the first postmaster. A school was opened in 1863 in a small shed, replaced a year later by a new school, and then finally replaced by a larger building in 1889.

The muddy waters of the bay came farther inland here than at any place in the southern part of what is now Alameda County. These waters provided ideal spots for landings where crops could be loaded on schooners and carried to markets in San Francisco.

Clement Colombet established a health resort at the springs. He piped water into buildings so his customers could enjoy its healing qualities. The resort became known all over the United States and even in Europe. A steady stream of customers came to gamble, drink, eat, and enjoy the medicinal water.

Leland Stanford, a railroad magnate who became governor of California and founded Stanford University, bought the resort in 1870. He planned to establish his main residence there, but his older brother, Josiah Stanford, ended up taking over management of the ranch, planting vines and enlarging the winery. By 1875, there were 50,000 gallons of wine being produced and distributed under the family name. Warm Springs was the second-largest wine producer in the country in 1876, with a yearly production of 100,000 gallons.

Josiah Stanford's son, Josiah Winslow Stanford, and his family lived at the residence for years and managed the property and winery. His 1899 Winton automobile was the first car in the area. The buildings that have survived are tangible connections to the history of the Colombet and Stanford era. In 1923, the property was sold to Lawrence Kelly, and in 1927, the Sisters of the Holy Names of Jesus and Mary purchased the property and used it as a retreat for the sisters as well as a summer camp for students. The property was then sold and divided into two parcels, one becoming the world-famous Weibel Champagne Vineyards, owned by Fred Weibel and family, and the other becoming Hidden Valley Dude Ranch, owned by the Goossen family.

Drawbridge is a ghost town with an abandoned railroad station on Station Island, at the southern end of the San Francisco Bay. Six miles south of downtown Fremont on the Union Pacific Railroad route, it was formerly a hunting village and has been a ghost town since 1979. It is slowly sinking into the marshlands.

From the 1920s to the 1960s, Warm Springs was a rural farming community with predominately Portuguese immigrants and their families. The community was close-knit, and social activities centered around family celebrations, house parties, church functions, and events at the school, including activities with the school board, the Parent-Teacher Association, Portuguese organizations, women's clubs, and the 4-H Club. Neighbors helped each other on their farms and volunteered for the fire department.

When General Motors established its huge plant there in the 1960s, Warm Springs began to grow rapidly. New housing, more schools, and two new freeways were built. Later, a significant number of high-tech and other business firms were established in the area, including an Apple computer plant to assemble the "new" Macintosh and, later, NeXT, a brainchild of Apple chief executive officer Steve Jobs. Teddy Ruxpin's Worlds of Wonder Manufacturing was another interesting factory.

Jose Higuera Adobe Park was constructed and the Curtner house was restored. The Don Edwards San Francisco Bay National Wildlife Refuge and Mission Peak Regional Preserve and city parks have set aside land for residents to enjoy the natural environment and to protect wildlife. Warm Springs is a unique place with a rich history and a promising future. Residents take pride in the area and feel privileged to live there.

# One

# Ohlone, Explorers, Missions, and Ranchos

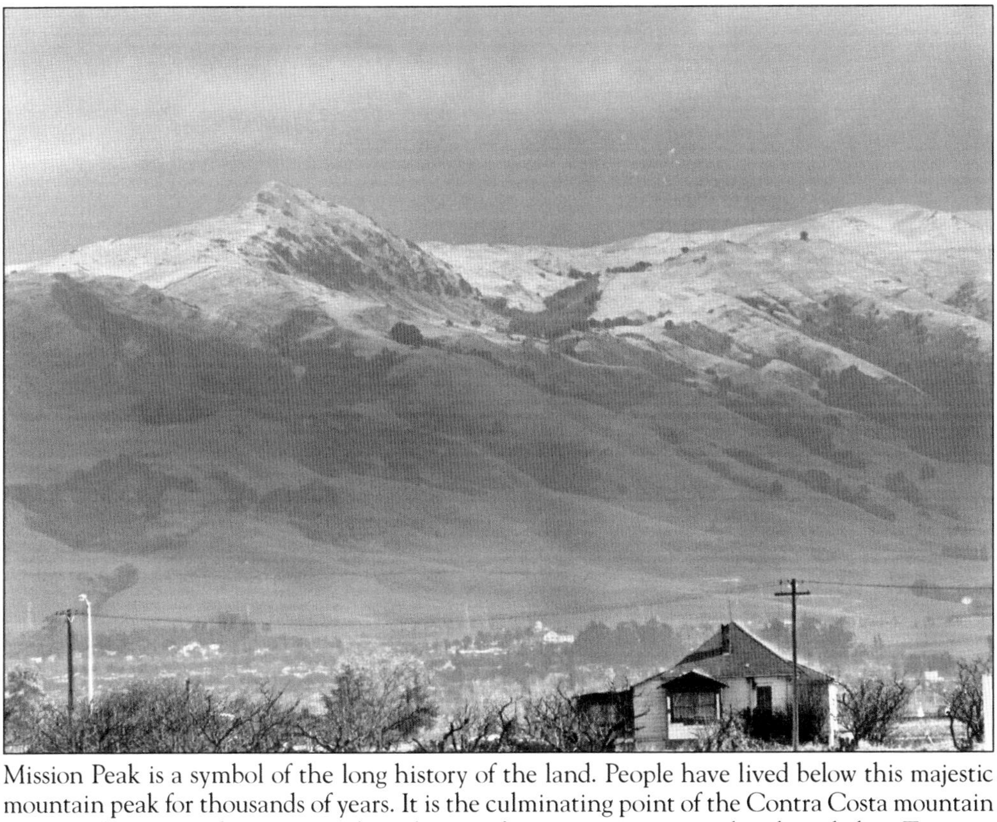

Mission Peak is a symbol of the long history of the land. People have lived below this majestic mountain peak for thousands of years. It is the culminating point of the Contra Costa mountain range. It dominates the region and can be seen from many points on the plains below. To some, it is a giant sentinel, forever on guard, a spire or steeple watching over those on the plateaus and broad valleys beneath its grand summit. It gives a dignity to the landscape and is there every day waiting to be photographed, climbed, and appreciated. Who could drive up Mission Boulevard and not be inspired by the wonder of this mountain? The peak is seen here, capped in snow, in 1999. (Photograph by Alwyn Silva.)

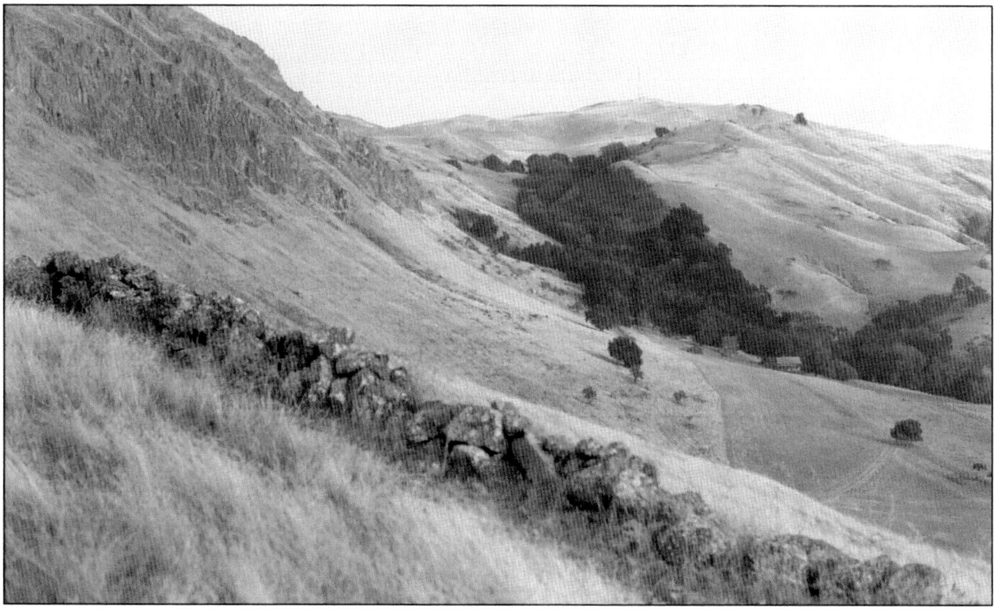

Throughout the hills of the East Bay, there are rock walls of unknown origin in various configurations. This rock wall is near the last steep pitch leading to the top of Mission Peak. They are a reminder of past civilizations. (Photograph by Philip Holmes.)

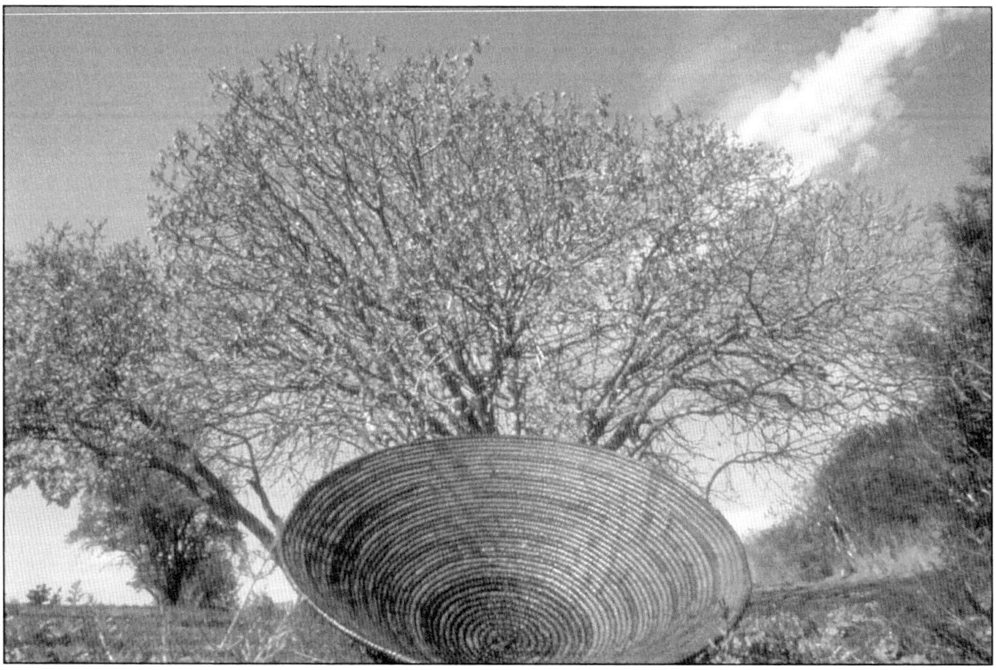

For thousands of years, descendants of Penutain-speaking migrants lived in numerous tiny tribal territories below Mission Peak. This photograph of an oak tree and gathering basket is a symbol of the hunting and gathering life of the Ohlone. One of the most important food items was the acorn, which the women ground, leached, and made into mush or bread. They also collected nuts from the California laurel, hazelnuts, and buckeyes. (Courtesy *The Galindo-Higuera Adobe: A Perspective*.)

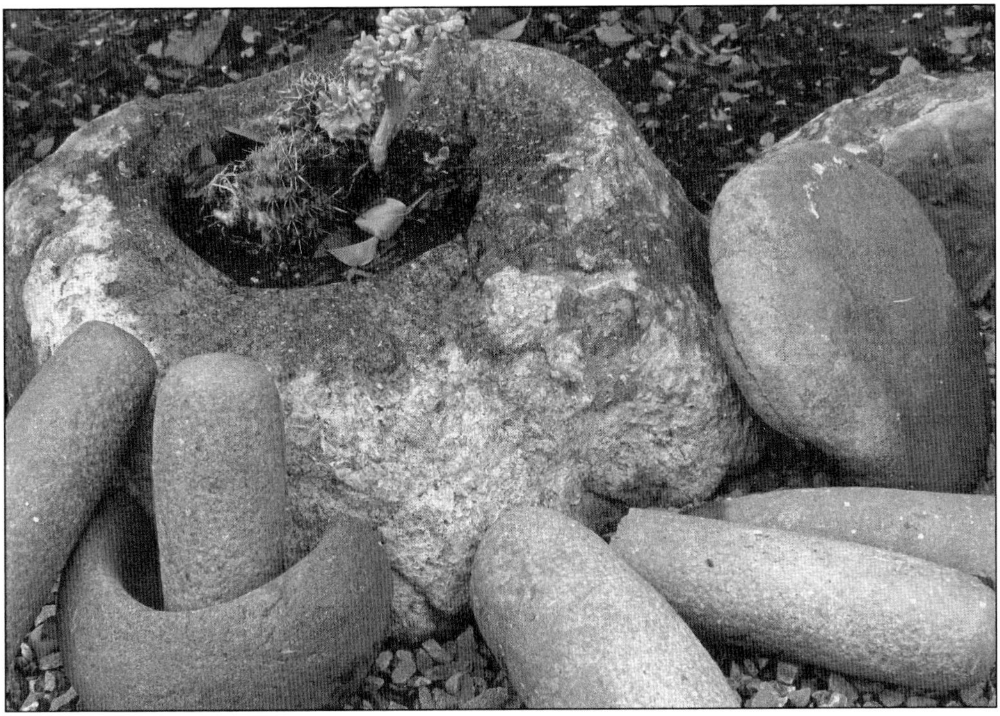

There were two types of mortars: portable mortars that could be moved as needed, and bedrock mortars, which were created and used where the seeds and nuts were gathered. The bedrock mortars are found throughout the hills below Mission Peak near creeks, as water is necessary during the grinding. The mortars and pestles above are from the Ohlone village site at what is now the corner of Mission Boulevard and Curtner Road. (Photograph by Julianne Howe, courtesy Historical Resources Collection.)

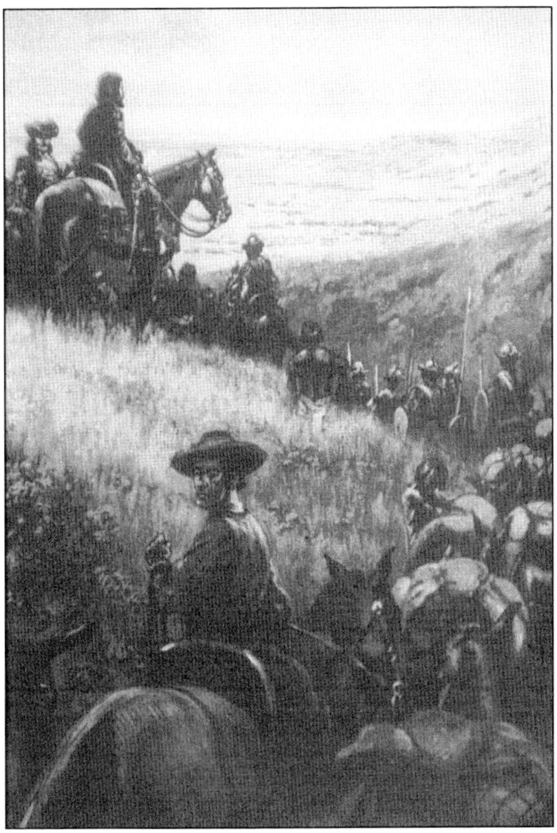

The first expedition to the Bay Area by the Spanish was led by Don Gaspar Portola, seen here. The expedition halted and camped near the present town of Palo Alto in November 1769. Portola sent his scout, Sgt. Jose Francisco Ortega, and eight soldiers to try to get around the bay. Sergeant Ortega forded the present Guadalupe River and continued northeast of the bay to what is now the Alameda Creek area, surely passing Warm Springs.

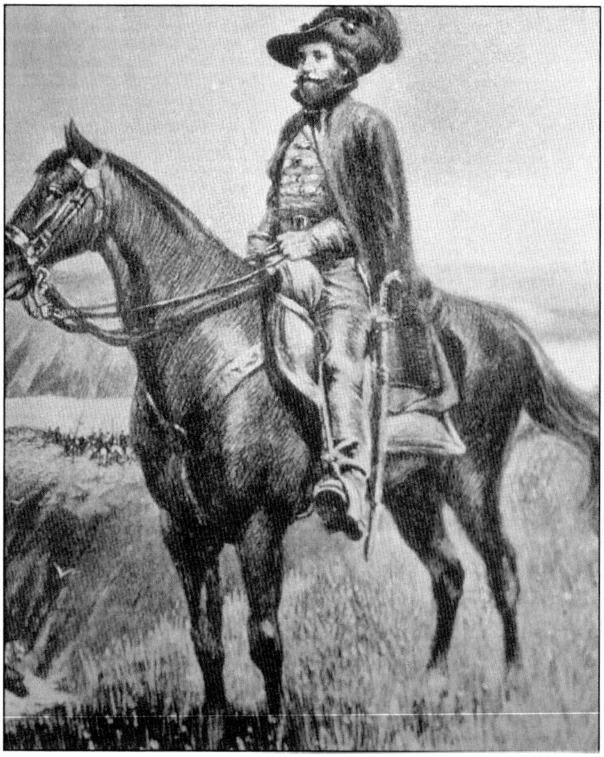

Col. Juan Bautista de Anza, seen here, led the famed expedition from Mexico to colonize Monterey and San Francisco in 1776. He spent two days laying out sites for Mission Dolores and the San Francisco Presidio and set out to explore the east bay. On March 31, 1776, the expedition celebrated mass at its camp near the Guadalupe River and then forced its way through sloughs and marshes to higher ground at the foot of the hills, going through the Warm Springs area.

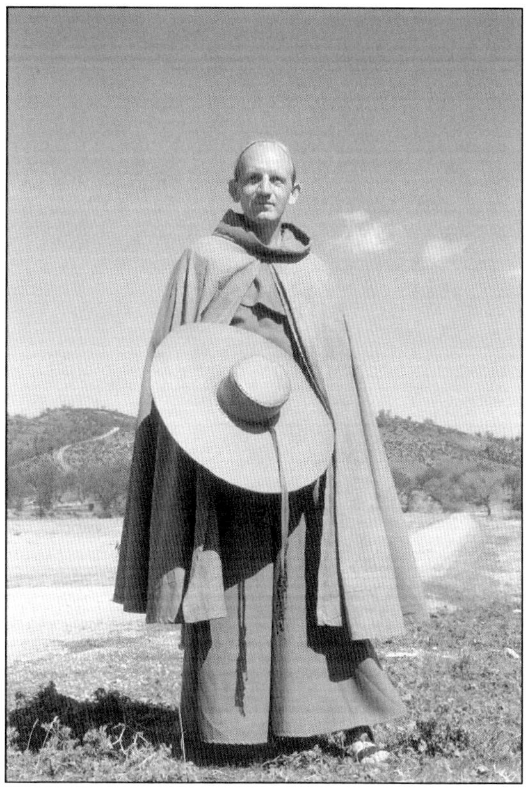

The Ohlone must have been startled when they saw explorers on horses with all their strange clothing. The Franciscan padre's habit was described as gray, full-skirted, full-sleeved, with a rimmed, low-crowned hat, a white cord around the waist, and a rosary of beads draped down the left side from the girdle. This photograph was taken in 1976 as part of the bicentennial celebration. (Photograph by Philip Holmes.)

This watercolor depicting the founding of Mission San Jose in 1797 is one of a series created by Harold "Hal" Booth as a cover for the book *Two Centuries at Mission San Jose, 1797–1997.* The founding of the mission brought Christianity, the mission system, building, industry, farming, and vast herds of cattle and horses, completely changing the way of life of the thousands of Native Americans who lived in the places where missions were established.

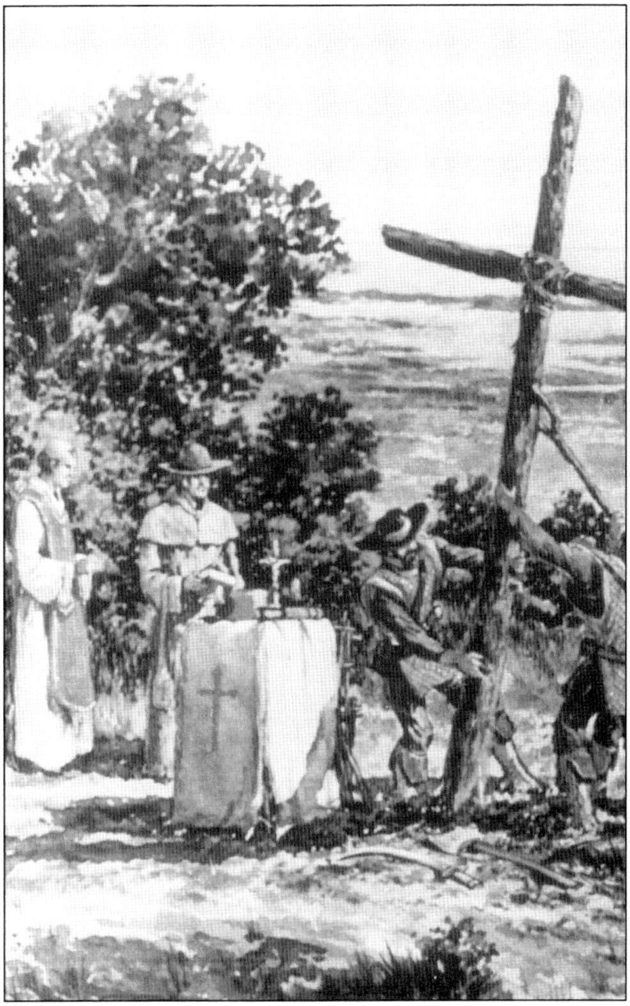

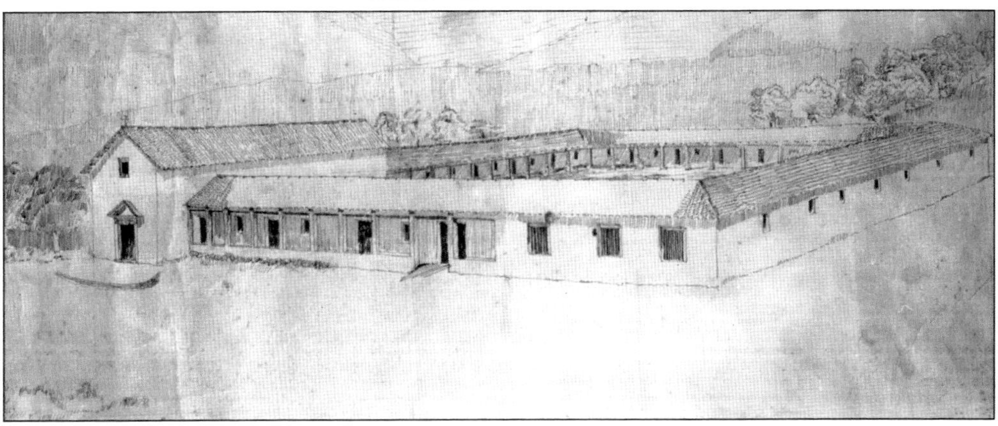

This illustration of the mission compound was drawn by A.L. Sunderer, a cobbler and architect in Mission San Jose, which was one of the most successful missions from the point of view of the Spanish founders. It was a busy, self-sustaining community where some 2,000 converts lived, growing the food and manufacturing the products needed by the Spanish and the church community.

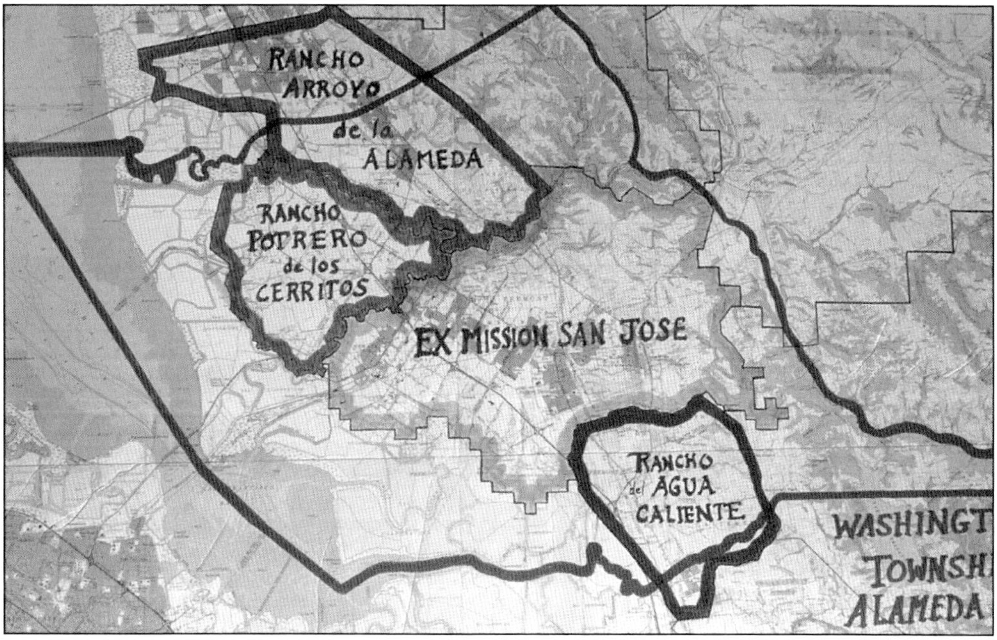


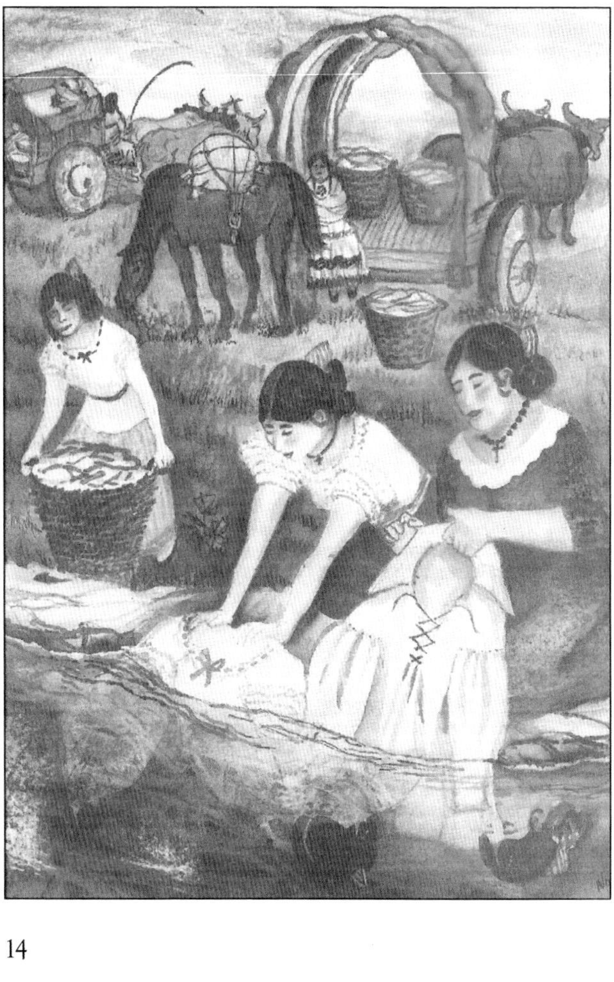

In 1833, after 36 years, Mission San Jose was secularized and large swaths of land were given to a select number of loyal families. In the Rancho Era, between 1833 and 1850, local citizens were called Californianos. The map above shows the ranchos in Washington Township. Rancho Aqua Caliente (now Warm Springs) is bordered by the former Mission San Jose lands to the north and Rancho Tularcitos (now Milpitas) to the south. Washington Township (the Tri-Cities area) is the larger outlined area.

Guadalupe Vallejo described a washday expedition from her home near the mission to the warm springs, where women washed clothes with homemade soap in the warm water. This scene is from a watercolor painting by Nancy Pratt, a Newark artist, depicting this oft-repeated event. (Courtesy Nancy Pratt.)

Jose Higuera was *mayordomo*, or general manager, of Mission San Jose in the 1820s. He built an adobe near the warm springs and occupied nearby land claimed by the mission. Higuera had no title to the land, but the mission padres paid him for his service in cattle, horses, sheep, and use of the land by his grazing animals. His son, Fulgencio Higuera (right), built an adobe near his father's and continued to run his herds on land owned by Mission San Jose.

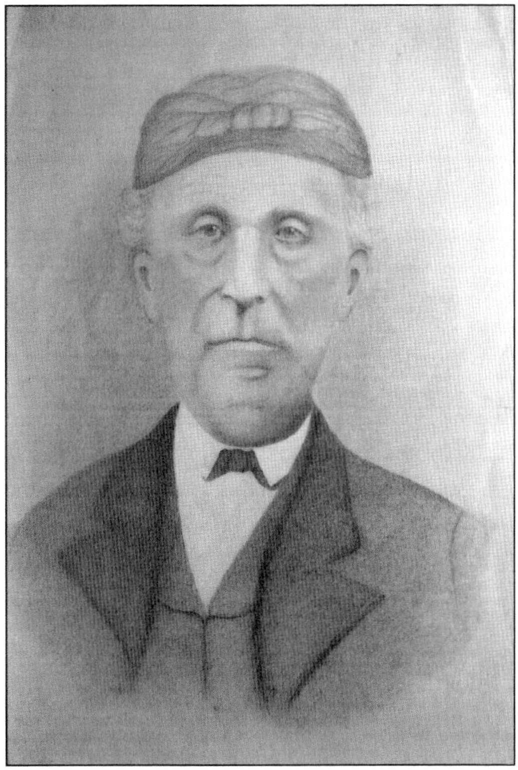

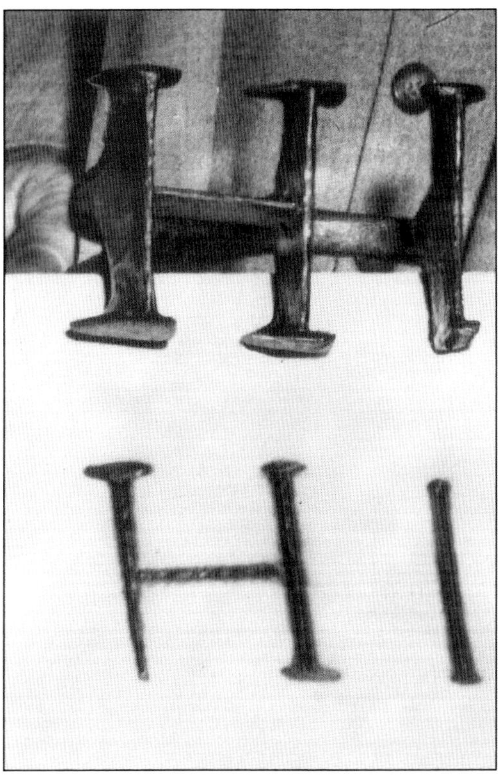

After the secularization of the mission lands, Fulgencio Higuera was given a grant of more than 9,000 acres called Rancho del Agua Caliente in 1836. The branding iron at left belonged to Fulgencio Higuera.

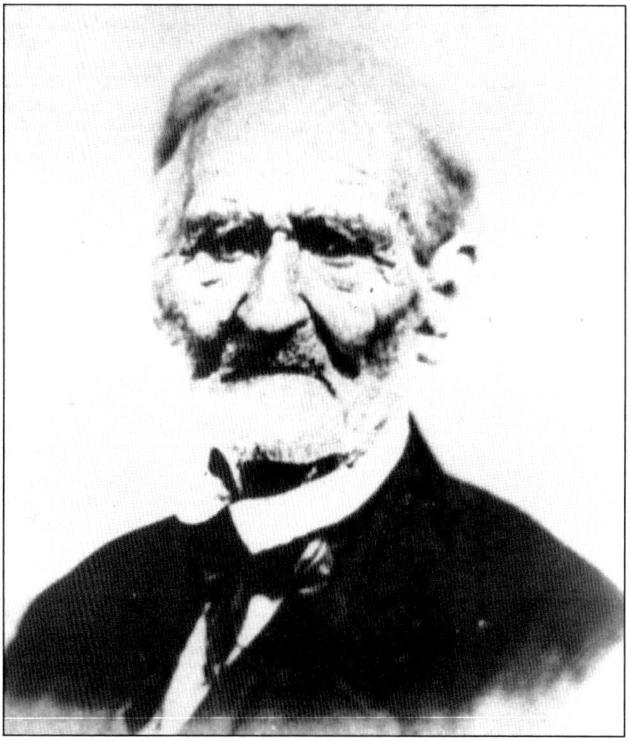

Of the seven adobe homes built by the Higuera family on Rancho del Agua Caliente, the only one that survived was later restored as the Galindo-Higuera Adobe. Juan Crisostomo Galindo, seen here, reportedly resided in that adobe. He was born at the San Francisco Presidio in 1783. His parents, Nicolas Galindo and Maria Teresa Pinto, were members of the De Anza Expedition.

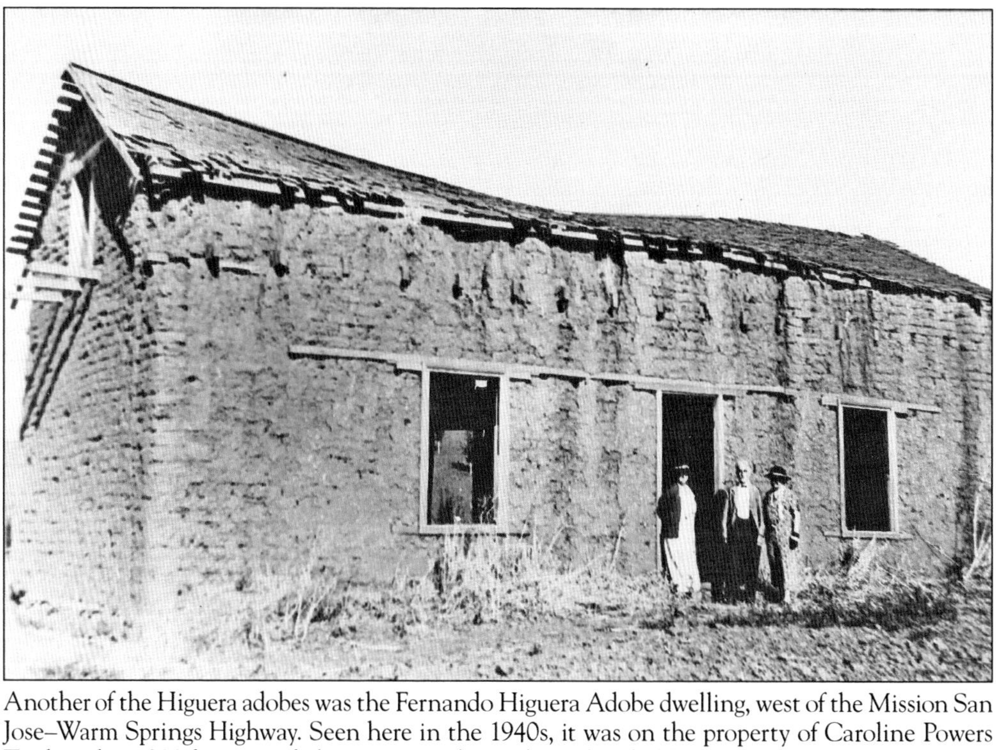

Another of the Higuera adobes was the Fernando Higuera Adobe dwelling, west of the Mission San Jose–Warm Springs Highway. Seen here in the 1940s, it was on the property of Caroline Powers Twohig, about 300 feet west of a large spring. The roof was already falling and the house was in decay. The people, from left to right, are Mrs. Thomas Powers, Joseph Thane, and Laura Whipple.

# *Two*

# WARM SPRINGS RESORT

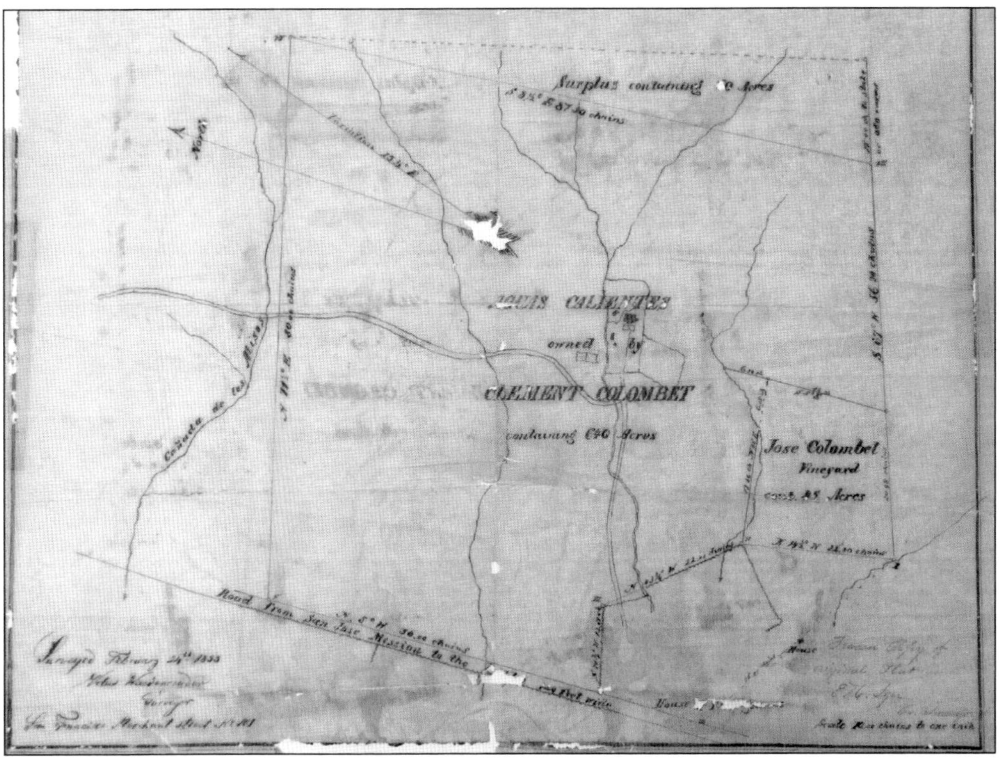


The earliest efforts to develop premium wines in Northern California from European vines were made by the French immigrants who moved into the area around Santa Clara and Warm Springs. Clement Colombet was born in France in 1817 and came to California in 1844. By 1851, he had moved to Mission San Jose and opened a hotel and general store in a building that he moved from San Jose. In 1850, he purchased 640 acres to establish vineyards and a hotel complex, which he named the Warm Springs Resort. The complex included four hotels, a hospital, two wine cellars, barns, and stables. This original 1855 survey map shows Colombet's original hotel compound and vineyard on Agua Caliente Creek.

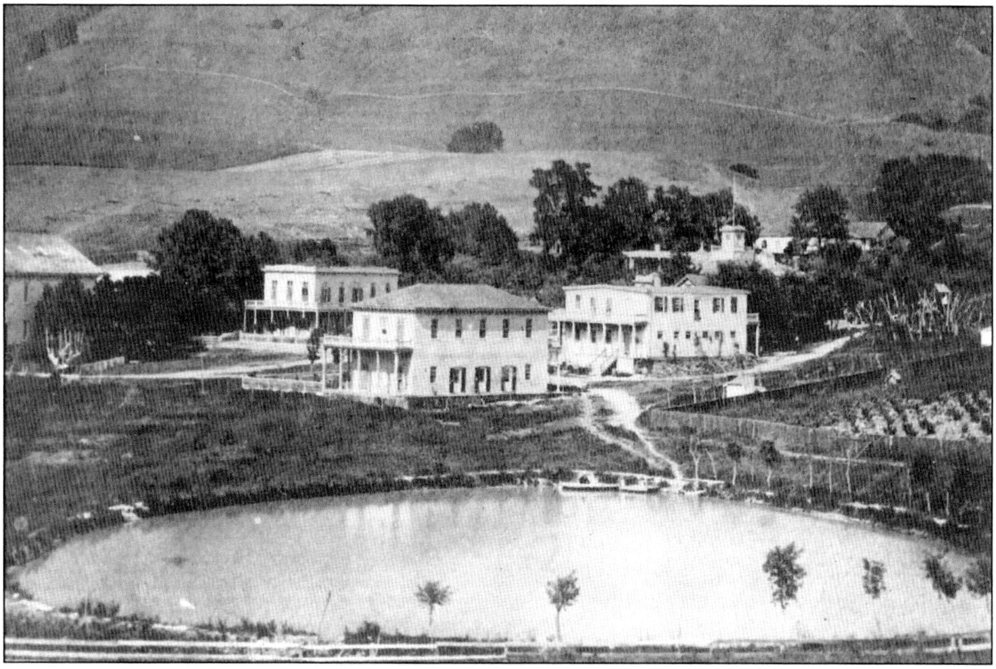

This rare stereoscopic view of the Warm Springs complex and lake was taken in 1865. The resort was a famous watering place situated in the foothills of Mission Peak and having a delightful climate, beautiful scenery, and fine drives, together with the well-known medicinal property of its water, making it the most desirable place for a resort in the state, both for the invalid and the pleasure seeker.

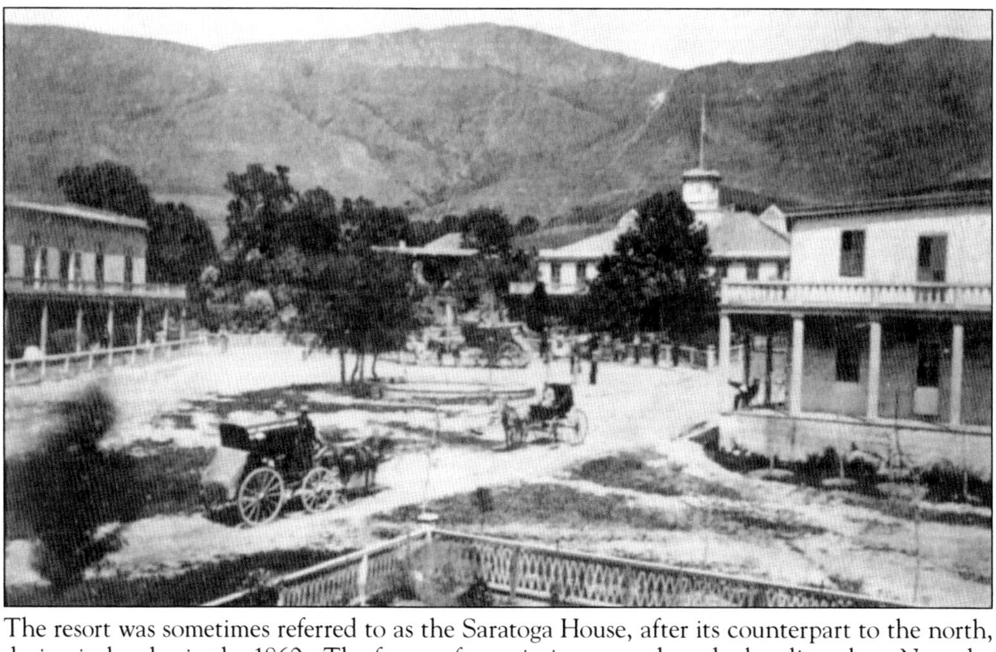

The resort was sometimes referred to as the Saratoga House, after its counterpart to the north, during its heyday in the 1860s. The famous fountain is centered on the bustling plaza. Note the Wells Fargo stagecoach arriving with guests. The resort was so widely known throughout California that it was unnecessary to advertise its advantageous features.

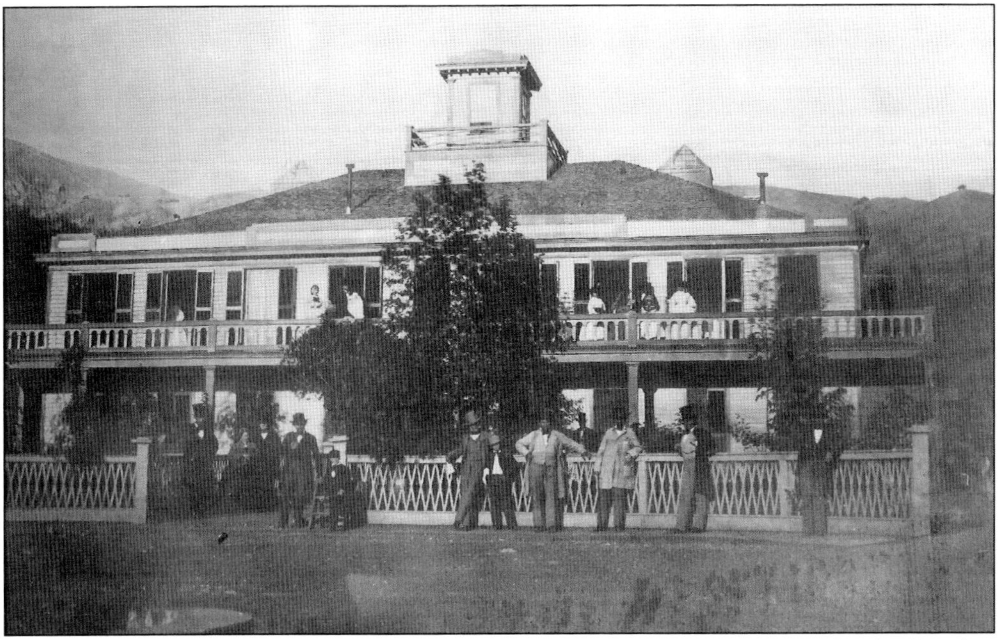

Colombet apparently leased the resort to various operators, as newspapers of the day listed as many as six different proprietors in nine years. Mr. J. David announced, in May 1861, that he had enlarged and renovated the resort and was ready to welcome visitors by the day, week, or month. W. Redding and Co. advertised the resort in 1863. This building was later the home of the Josiah Stanford family.

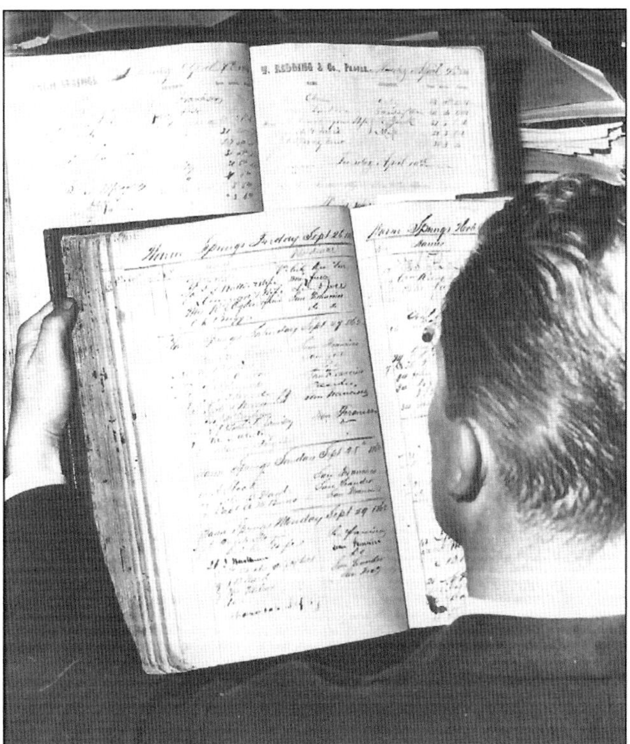

Visitors to the Warm Springs Hotel signed their names in the hotel registers. The registers were presumed lost, but Helen Stanford had given them to her attorney, who passed them on to the California Historical Society in San Francisco. Famous guests included Pio Pico, the last Mexican governor of California; Sen. George Hearst, of the Hearst newspaper empire; Domingo Ghirardelli, of the chocolate family; and Adolph Sutro, the mayor of San Francisco.

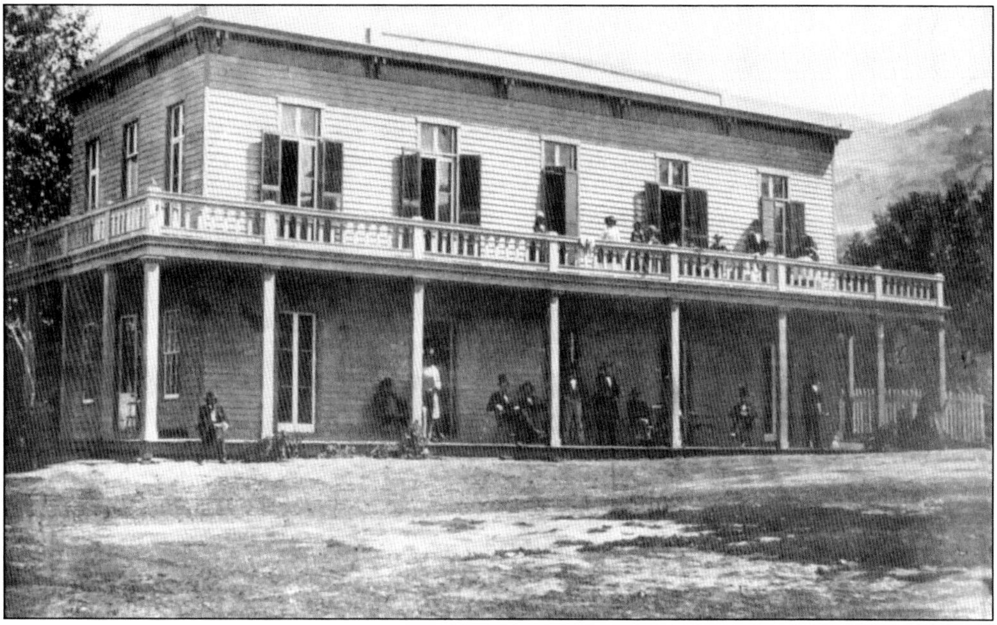

The photograph above shows a typical Warm Springs Hotel scene with guests lining the porch. People came from all over the state to enjoy the hotel's pleasures. An advertisement in *Alta California* in 1863 beckoned visitors to the Warm Springs Hotel: "This well known watering place having changed hands and been leased for a term of years by Messrs. Lee and Redding will be reopened June 13 for the reception of visitors."

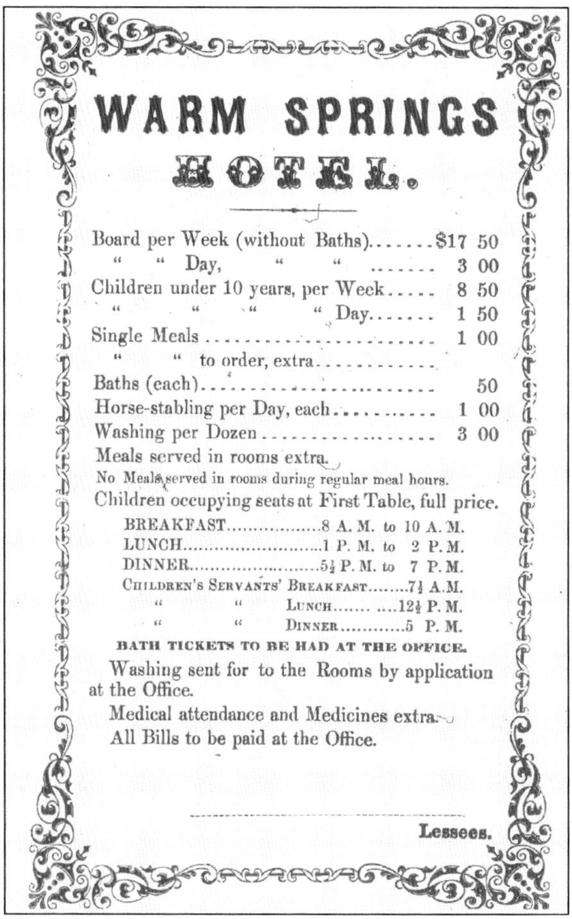

WARM SPRINGS

HOTEL.

| | |
|---|---|
| Board per Week (without Baths)....... | $17 50 |
| " " Day, " " ....... | 3 00 |
| Children under 10 years, per Week..... | 8 50 |
| " " " " Day....... | 1 50 |
| Single Meals ........................ | 1 00 |
| " " to order, extra............. | |
| Baths (each)......................... | 50 |
| Horse-stabling per Day, each........... | 1 00 |
| Washing per Dozen.................. | 3 00 |

Meals served in rooms extra.

No Meals served in rooms during regular meal hours.

Children occupying seats at First Table, full price.

| | |
|---|---|
| BREAKFAST.................. | 8 A. M. to 10 A. M. |
| LUNCH........................ | 1 P. M. to 2 P. M. |
| DINNER....................... | 5½ P. M. to 7 P. M. |
| CHILDREN'S SERVANTS' BREAKFAST........ | 7½ A. M. |
| " " LUNCH....... | 12½ P. M. |
| " " DINNER........... | 5 P. M. |

BATH TICKETS TO BE HAD AT THE OFFICE.

Washing sent for to the Rooms by application at the Office.

Medical attendance and Medicines extra.

All Bills to be paid at the Office.

Lessees.

This price list and daily schedule includes the prices for board per week, board per day, board for children under 10, meals, baths, horse stabling, and more. Children occupying seats at the First Table were charged full price. Childrens' servants' breakfast was served at 7 1/2 a.m. instead of 7:30. Medical attendance and medicines were extra.

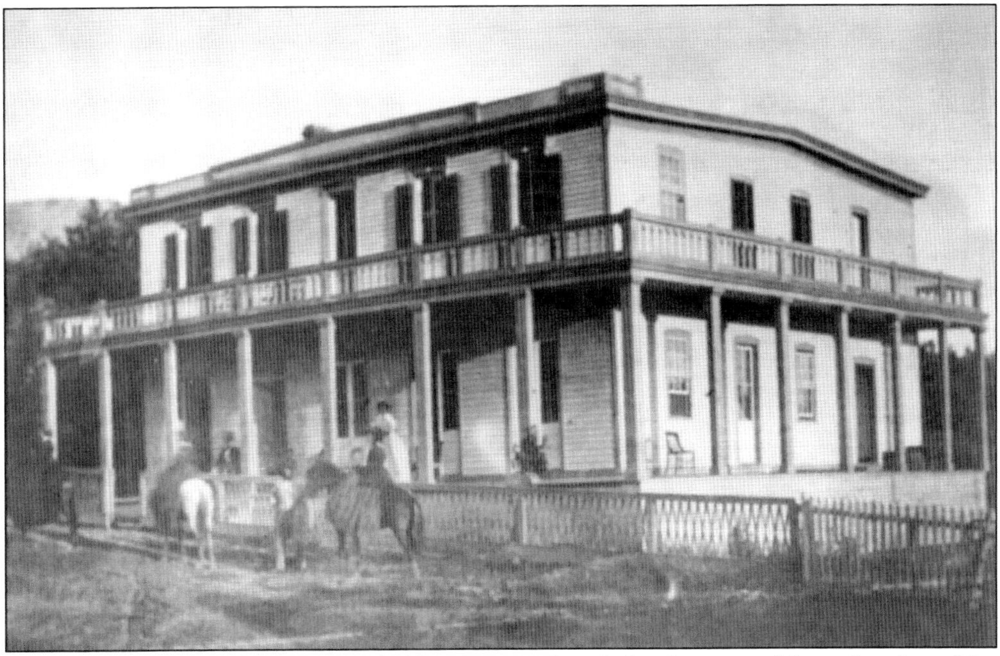

This other hotel building was much like the one that Colombet moved from San Jose. The horses are a reminder that the resort offered a variety of horse-centered entertainment, including horseback riding. Other drawing cards included a bar, billiards, swimming, hiking, hunting, trout fishing, boat racing on the artificial lake, bowling, and gambling.

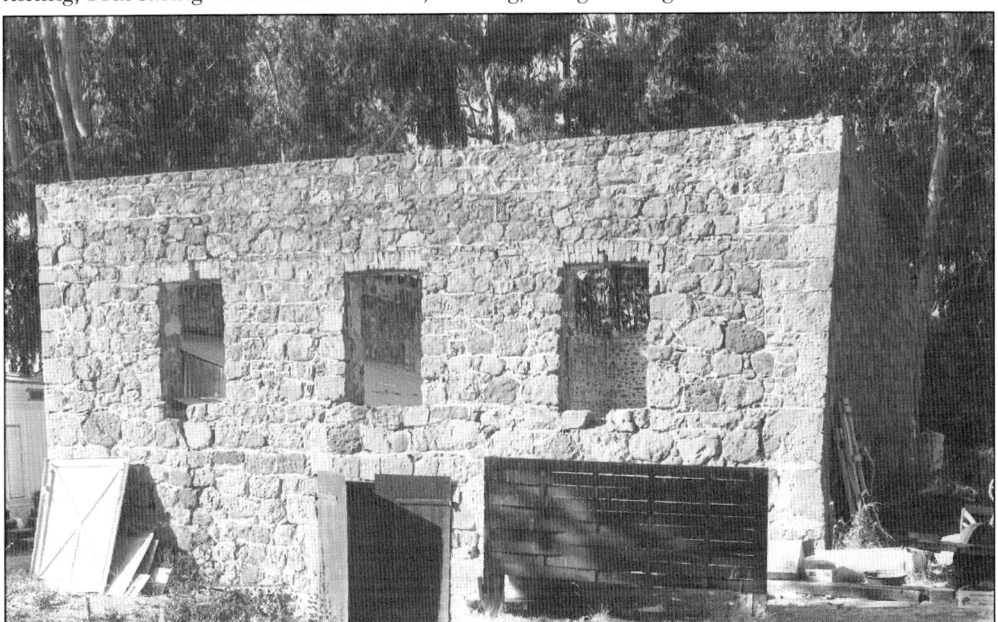

Clement Colombet planted some 60,000 grapevines and built a winery for processing his grapes. The California Agricultural Society of San Jose awarded him a premium for his clarity in 1856. This was the first award given by the society for a California wine. This photograph shows the remains of the Colombet wine cellar, which still survives today.

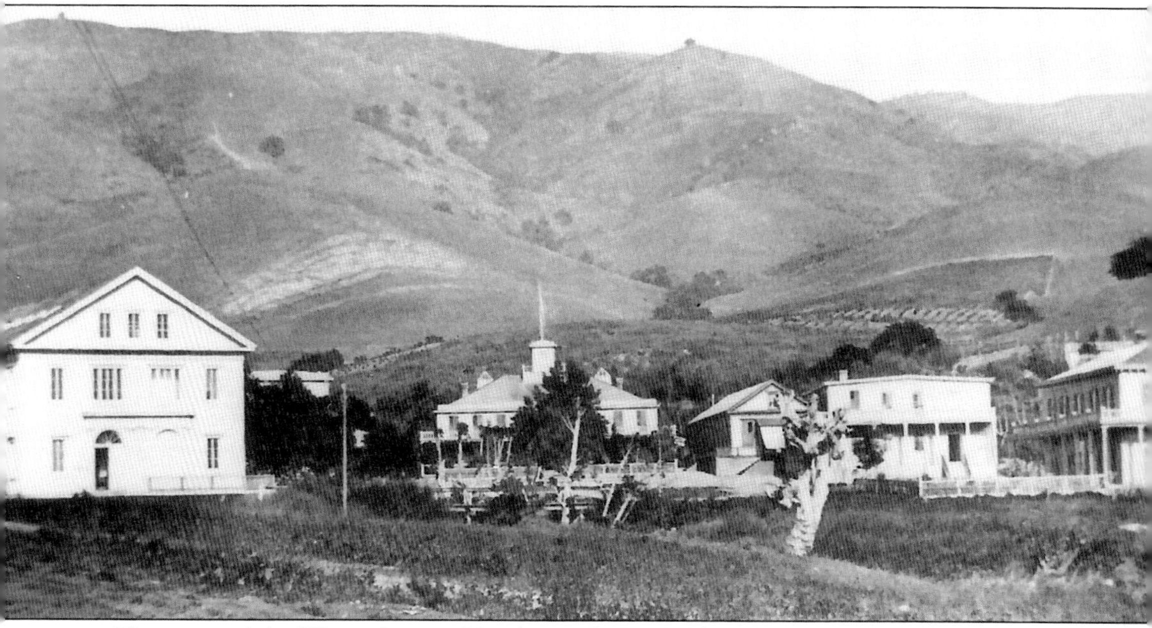

This view of the Warm Springs Hotel complex was taken from the northwest in 1867. The hospital building on the left still had its original roof, which was later replaced with mansards and was further remodeled some time around 1870. The administration building is in the middle of the photograph, just in front of the fountain. Agua Caliente Creek runs to the right of the hospital building.

# *Three*

# Landings, Wine Country, and Settlement

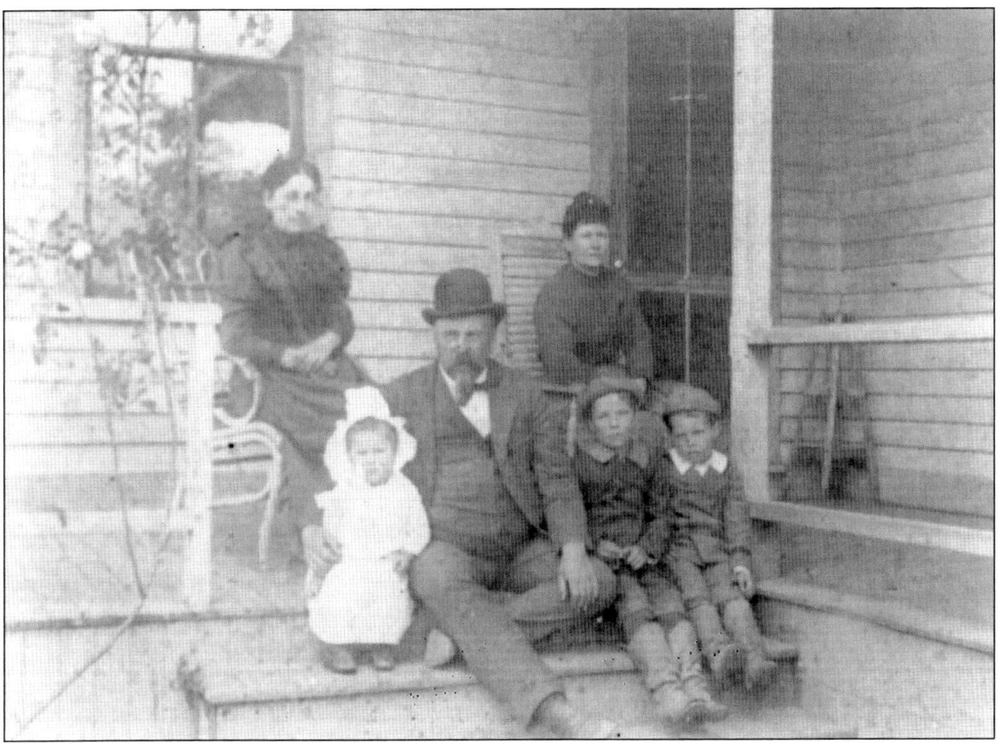

The John Lyman Beard family is seen here by their Warm Springs home about 1890. Beard graduated from the University of California, where he was appointed to the board of regents. He married Elizabeth Hawley in 1880, and they raised their family in Warm Springs and in Alviso. Beard also served in the California state senate from 1894 to 1898.

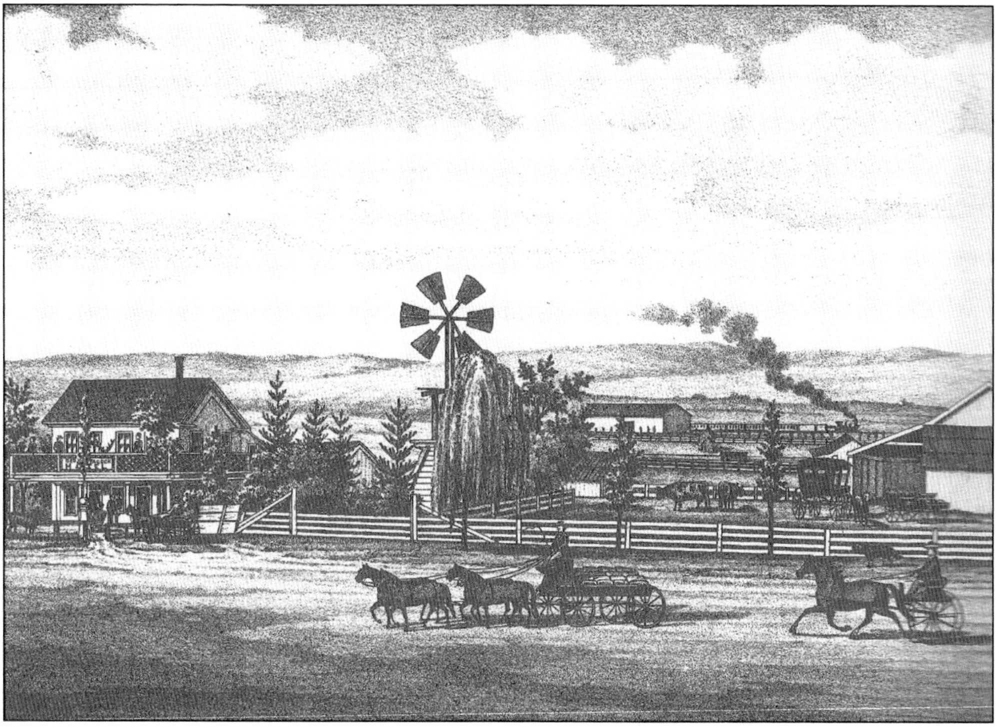

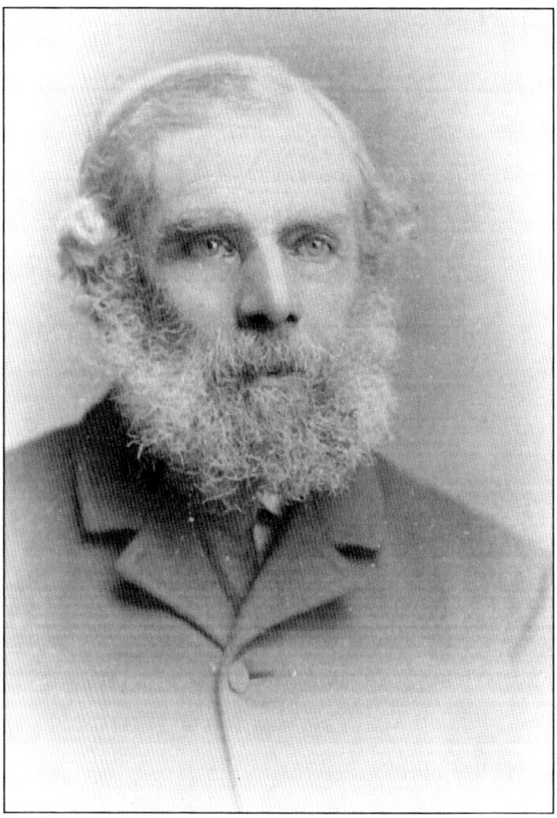

George Peacock came to the area in 1852. The lithograph above shows the building he had constructed in 1861, which served as his residence and the only hotel and store in Harrisburg, as Warm Springs was first known. When Peacock became the first postmaster in 1865, the building also served as the post office. Many social parties, dances, and dinners were held in the second floor of Peacock's Hall. (TW.)

James Sinclair and Calvin Valpey, two sea captains, became partners and operated a trading schooner that went from Union City to San Francisco with grain and returned with supplies for miners. Sinclair, seen here, arrived in California in 1850; Valpey came from Maine a year later. Both men and their families owned property and lived in the new settlement of Harrisburg. Valpey helped establish pioneer landings and built warehouses at Dixon Landing. (MS.)

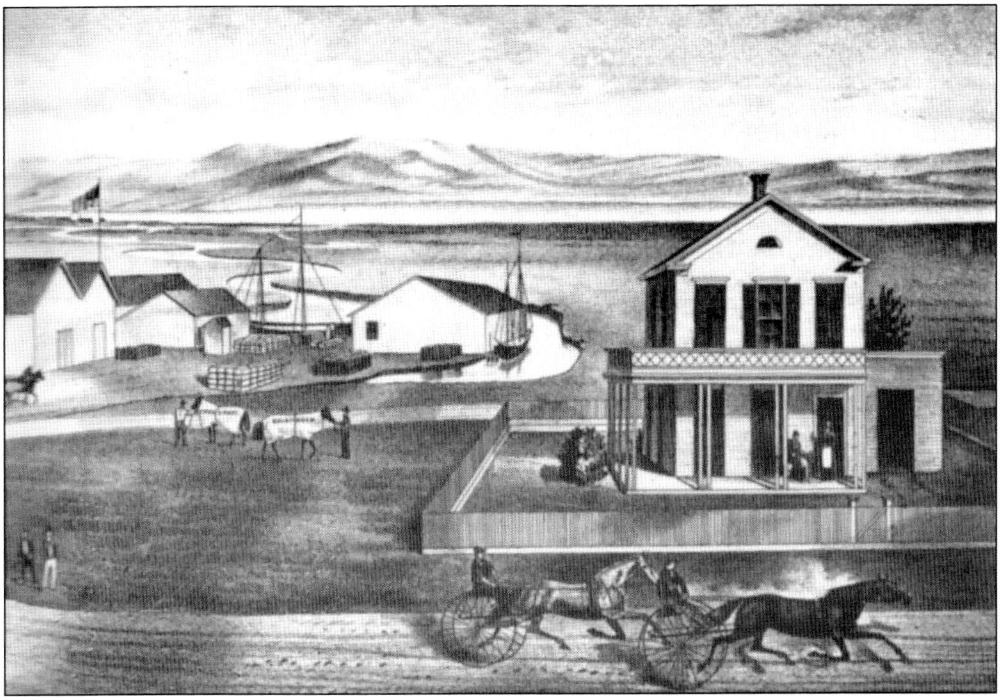

This lithograph, from *The Official and Historical Atlas Map of Alameda County, California*, shows the farm of Joshua Chadbourne, including his home, a racetrack, warehouses, hay and grain brokerages, and schooners. The earthquake of 1868 destroyed most of his warehouses, but he and his partners replaced the ruined buildings. He sold a right-of-way through his property to the Central Pacific Railroad so it could build its line. (TW.)

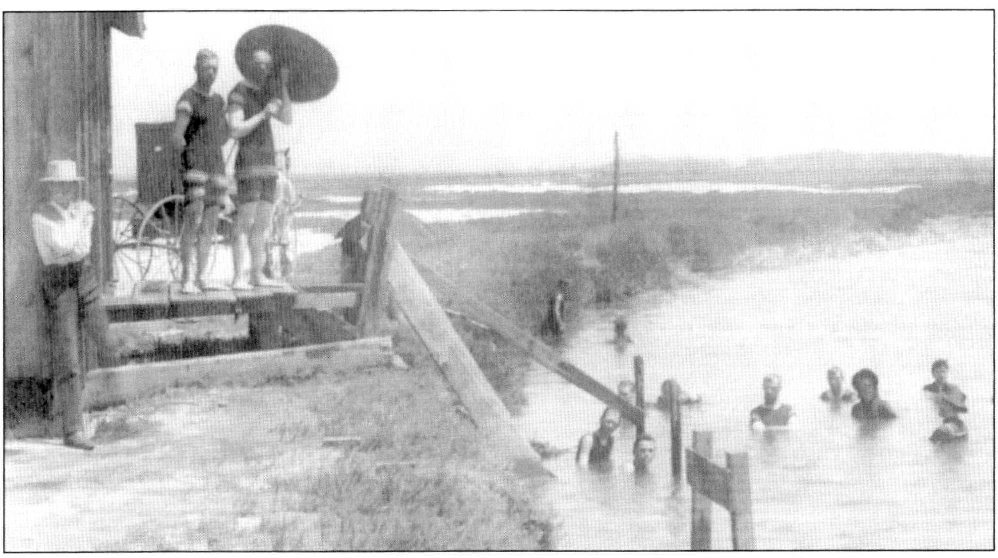

This group of pioneers took time off to swim at Dixon Landing in 1885. Mathew Dixon came to Harrisburg about 1860 before establishing a farm and building a landing in 1868 near the Santa Clara County line, where he could load the crops and hay from his farm on small schooners. In 1872, Dixon was one of the organizers of the Washington College of Science and Industry in Irvington. He was elected to serve in the California State Assembly in 1875 and 1877.

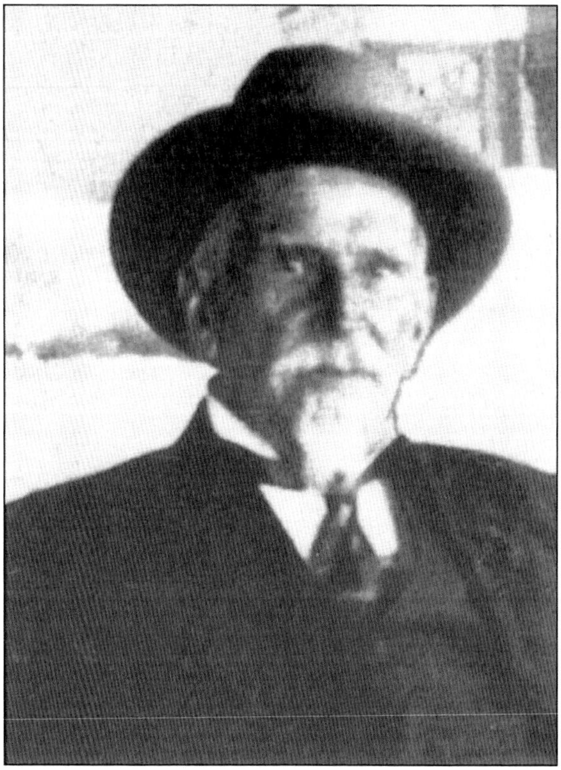

Thomas Millard and his brother, Steven, moved to Warm Springs and farmed part of the Hathaway land south of Agua Caliente Creek. They raised grain and stored it on a platform at Warm Springs Landing until it could be barged to San Francisco. Pictured at left is Steven Millard from the book *Reflections*, compiled and edited by Philip Holmes and Dolores Rose.

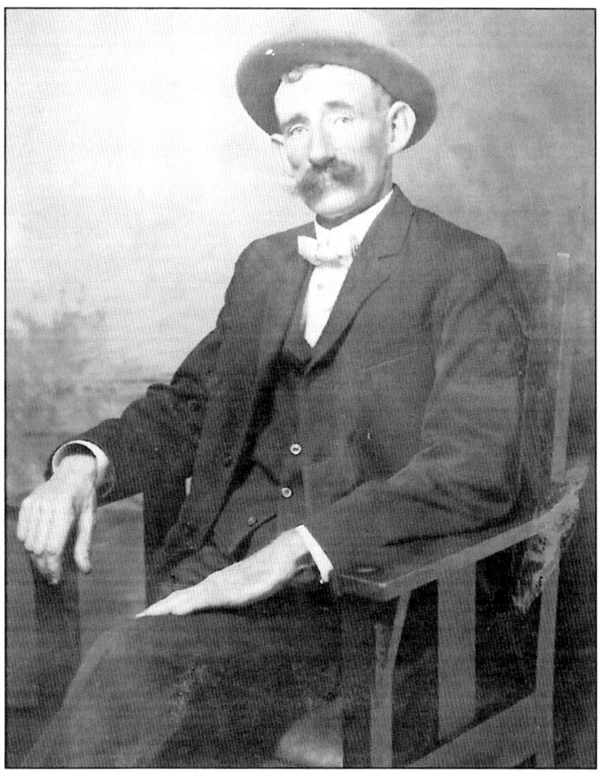

Redding is an important name in Warm Springs history. W. Redding leased the Warm Springs Hotel in 1859 and advertised under the name W. Redding and Co. He was also an agent for Wells Fargo and Company in 1867. John D. and Tom Redding were listed as farmers in 1894 and had a 136-acre farm off of Warm Springs Landing Road. Tom Redding is seen here in his Sunday best. (HA.)

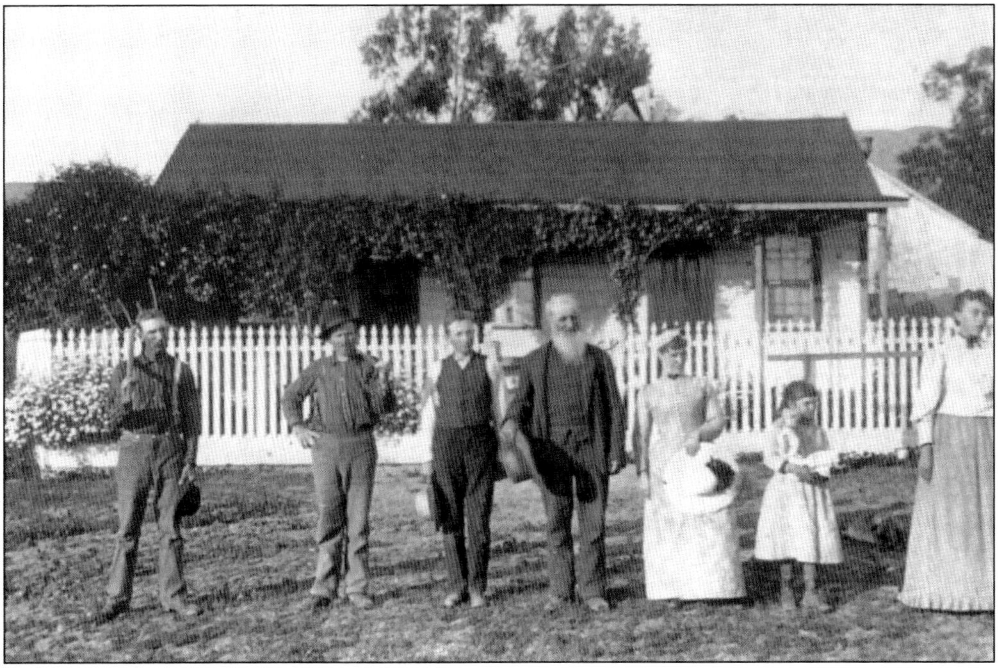

James Leitch came to Warm Springs from Scotland in 1862 and bought 105 acres of land that rose gradually up to the hills. He married his first wife, Christina, in Scotland, and they had two children, James and Katherine. After Christina died, James and his second wife, Isabella, had another daughter, Margaret. James became a trustee of the Warm Springs School District in 1888. His son, James Alexander Leitch, married Georgia Abel and had a son, James Orville Leitch, who was the last to bear the family name. James Orville also became a school trustee. Leitch School was named in honor of the Leitch family. Above, the Leitch family poses in front of their home. They are, from left to right, two unidentified, Jim, James, Isabella, Margaret, and Katherine Leitch. A portion of the Leitch farm is seen below with some livestock. Joe F. and Anna Vargas purchased the farm in 1910. (Both, SVM.)

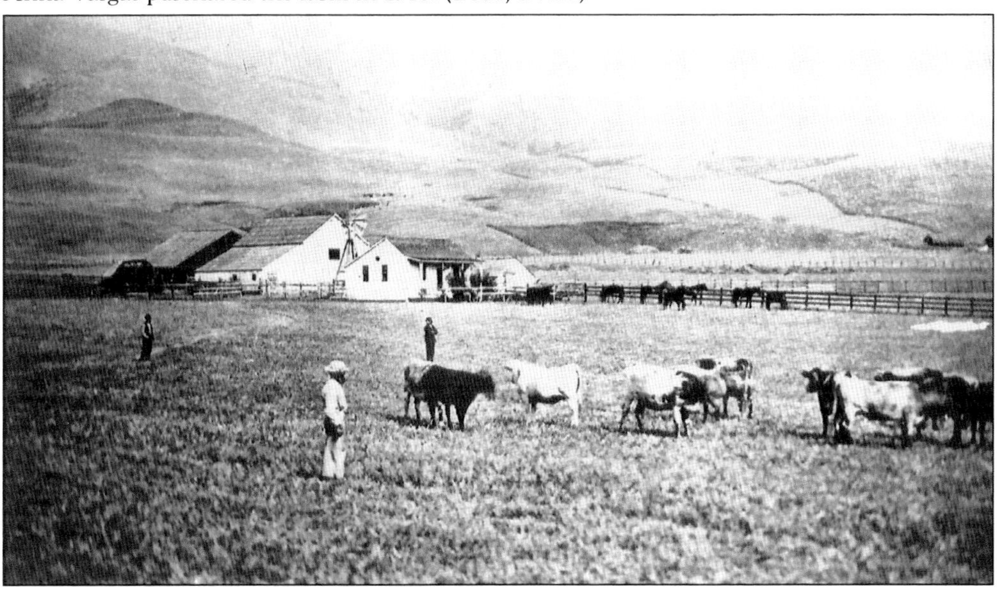

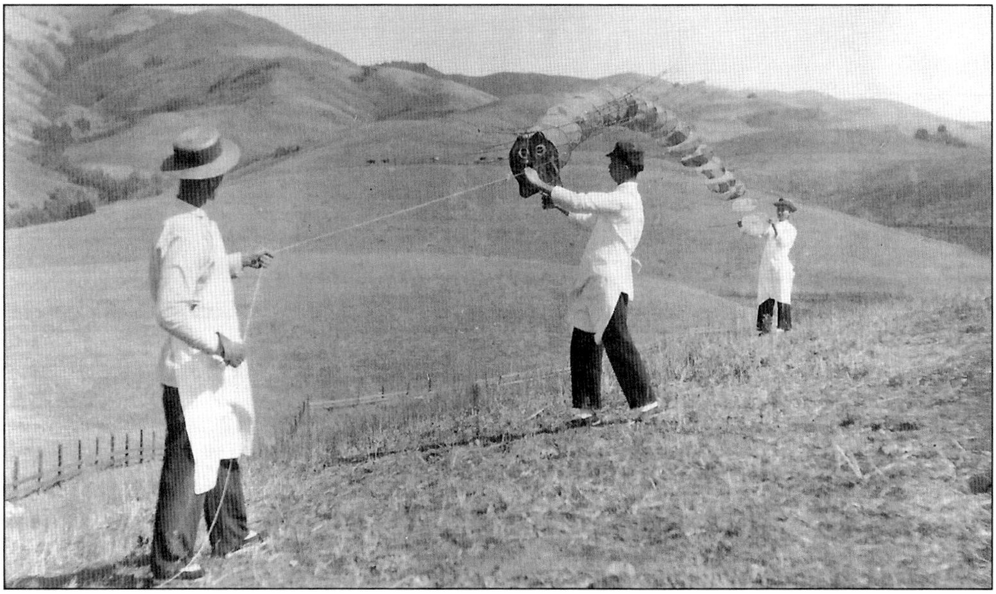

These Chinese immigrants fly kites near the Stanford ranch in the 1890s. "Chinese agricultural laborers came to California in the 1850s because of repression in China and the short supply of laborers in gold-starved California. By the 1870s, Chinese immigrants began to dominate agricultural work in many rural areas of California, especially after the completion of the Transcontinental Railroad in 1869," noted *Santos Barn Relocation–Shinn Historical Park*, by Page & Turnbull, Inc. (Courtesy Robert B. Fisher Collection.)

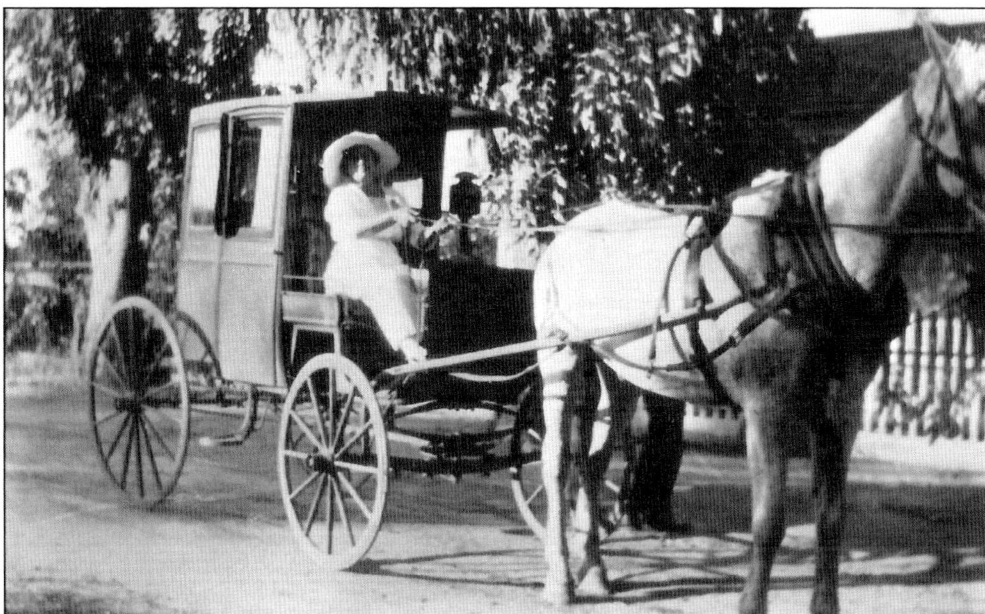

The Rockaway carriage originated around the 1830s in New York and was particularly American with its design of the covered area for the driver. This woman, probably a member of the Powers family, is dressed in fine clothes as she drives the superb cab. The Powers family were early settlers of the area.

As told in Eugene T. Sawyers's *History of Santa Clara County, California*, Henry Curtner (right) arrived on the Pacific coast in 1852 with $20. In 1856, he returned to his native Indiana and married Lydia Kendall, and in the fall of 1857, the young couple moved back to California. By 1868, they had moved to Warm Springs, where they lived for the rest of their lives. Their estate was a little less than 2,000 acres, but Henry added to it from time to time until he owned more than 8,000 acres. (Courtesy History San Jose.)

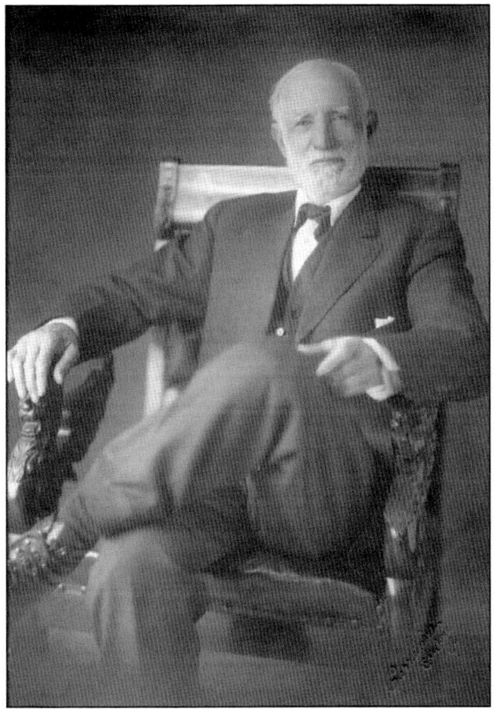

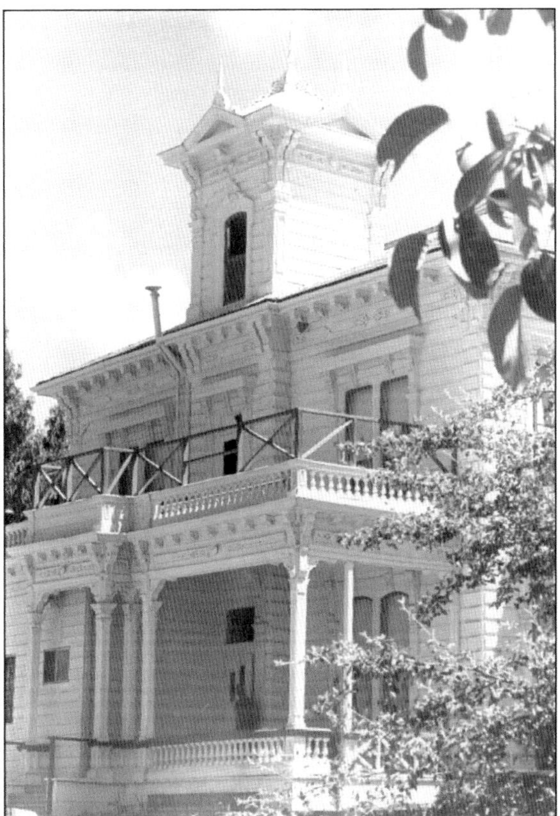

In 1879, Henry Curtner built the 17-room Italianate mansion at left for his family. It was a two-story house built over a basement with a small glassed-in cupola on the third floor overlooking the boats at the landing. Curtner also built a "safe room" with concrete walls. (Photograph by Julianne Howe, courtesy Historical Resources Collection.)

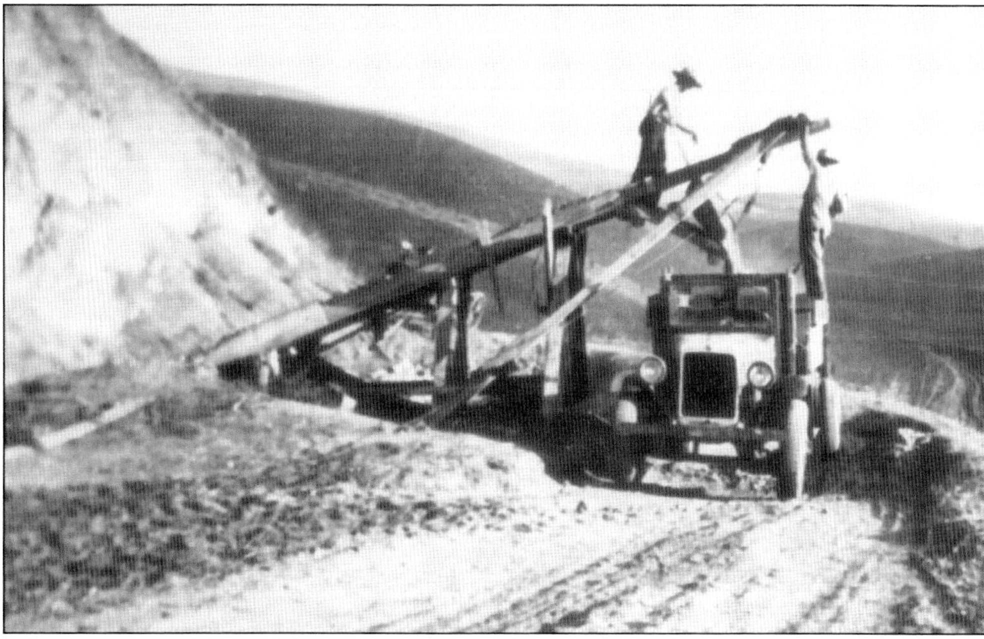

Henry Curtner used gravel from this quarry at the end of Scott Creek Road for miles of roads traversing his property. These men load a truck with a conveyor system around 1920. Roads that were not graveled became very muddy in the rainy season and dusty when it was dry.

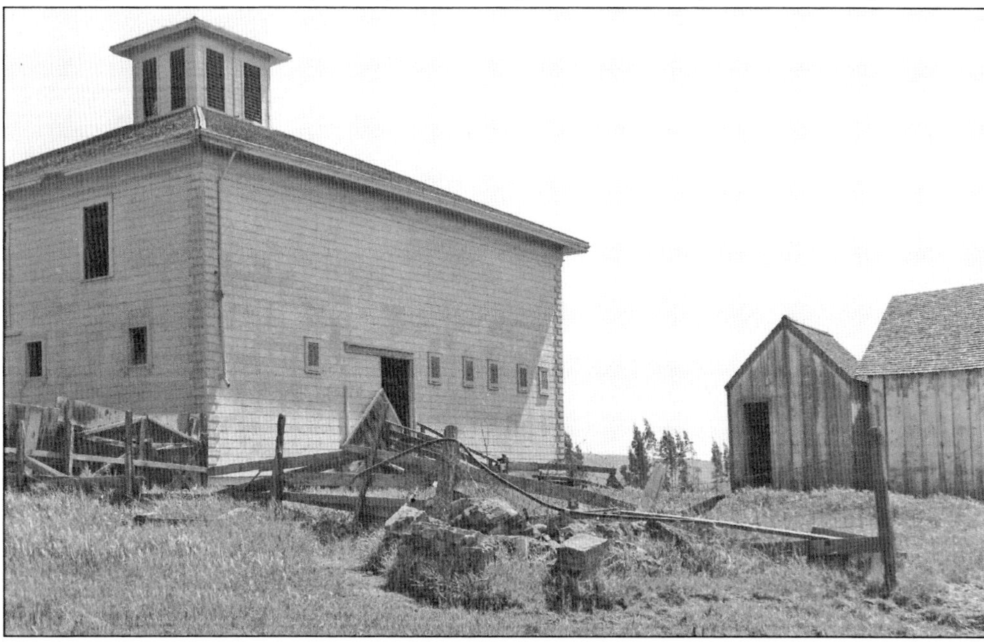

Samuel Rainey is listed in 1889 as a wine grower, along with Josiah Stanford, Henry Curtner, Mathew Dixon, Joseph Mason, Thomas Millard, John Powers, F. Twohig, and C. Weller. The Rainey carriage house was situated among acres of vineyards below Mission Peak northwest of the Stanford Winery. This photograph of the carriage house was taken in 1966 and shows the care taken to construct a lasting and beautiful building. (Photograph by Julianne Howe, courtesy Historical Resources Collection.)

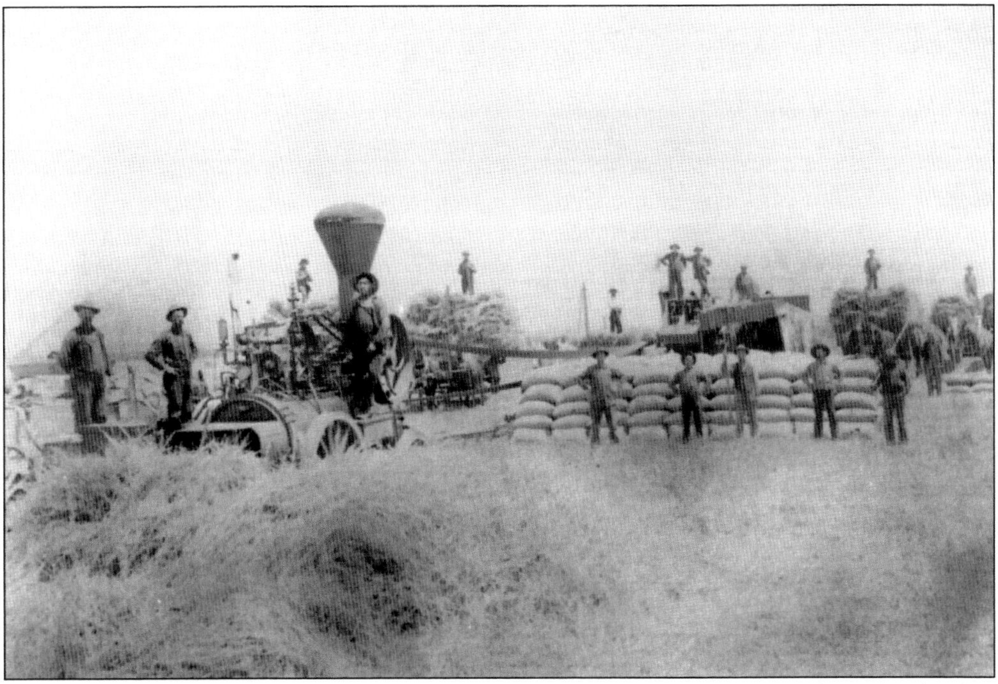

This threshing crew in Warm Springs takes a break from its labor-intensive day. The thresher was driven from the flywheel of a steam traction engine. A giant belt from the flywheel drove a wheel on the thresher that separated the wheat kernels from the stalks. The grain was most likely shipped out from Warm Springs Landing or Dixon Landing on scows or sloops. (SVM.)

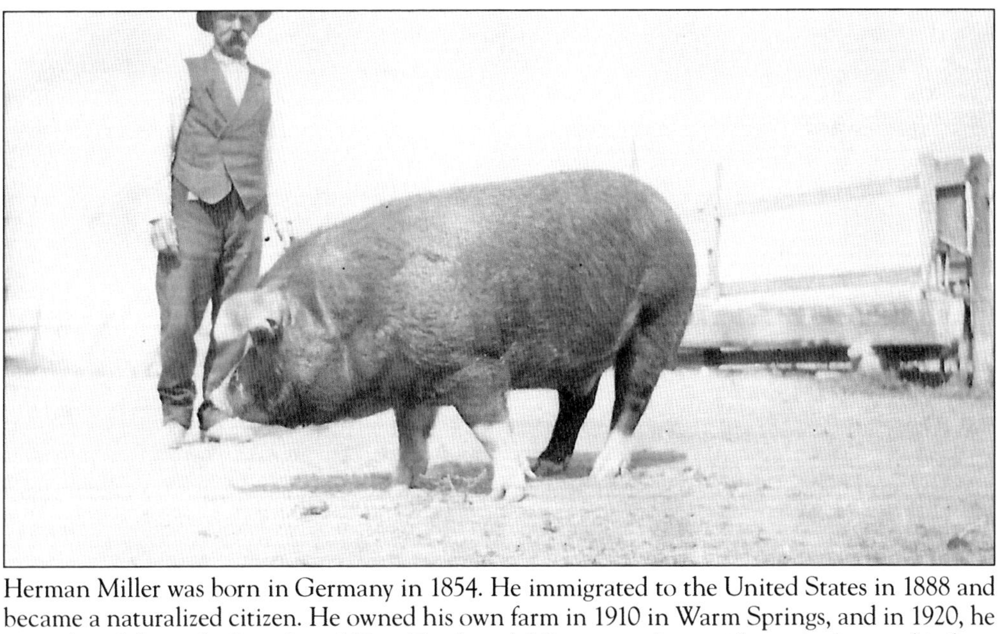

Herman Miller was born in Germany in 1854. He immigrated to the United States in 1888 and became a naturalized citizen. He owned his own farm in 1910 in Warm Springs, and in 1920, he was a farm laborer for Joseph and Kate Trouling. Miller is seen here with a prize hog on his farm around 1915. He died in 1936. (Courtesy Jane Huber.)

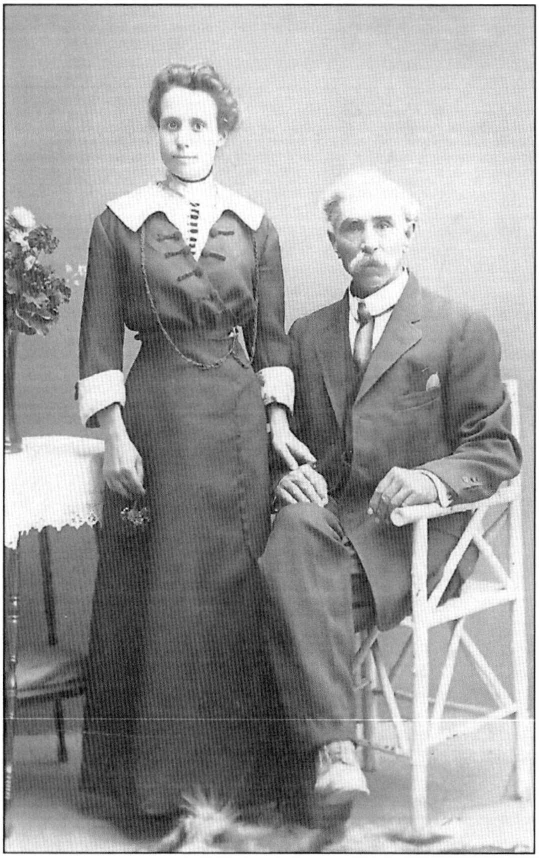

Antonio Caetano Alvernaz (born 1855) and his bride, Maria Espiritu Santo Peixoto Goularte (born 1885) were both from Pico in the Azores and were wed in Niles in 1912. The Alvernazes and their descendants lived on their ranch in Warm Springs until 1956, when the property was sold to the Western Pacific Railroad for the development of the General Motors plant. (HA.)

Onions were a very important cash crop for families and were growing well on the Alvernaz farm in this 1918 photograph. Below, from left to right are Yoniko Kita, Antonio Alvernaz, Maria Alvernaz (holding her daughter Mae), and Elsuko Kita. (HA.)

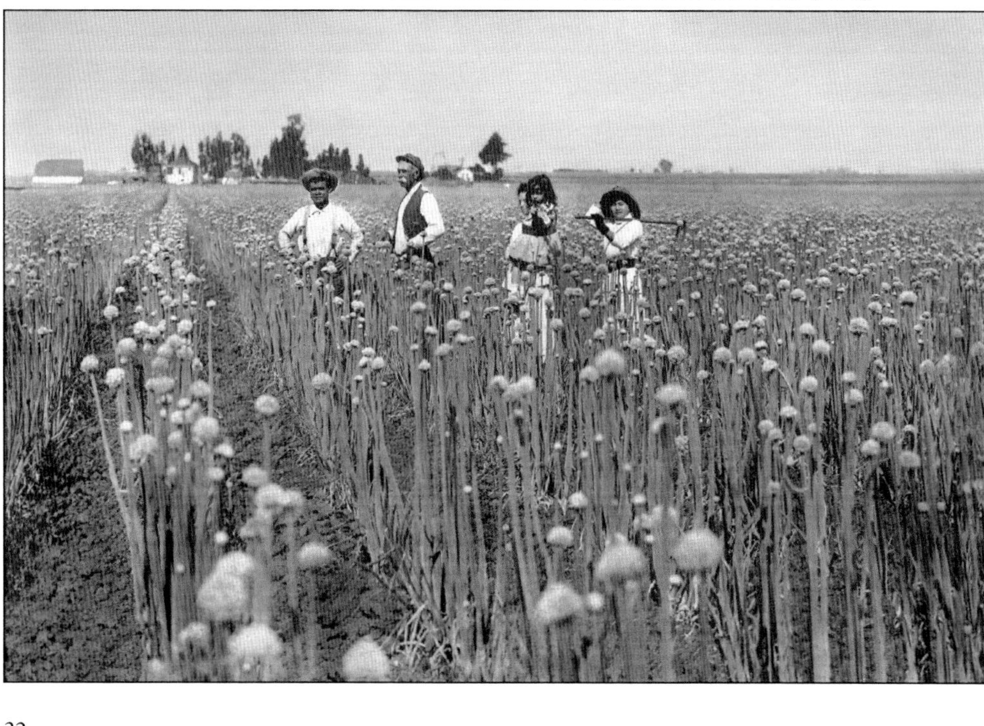

At right, three Japanese children pose on the Alvernaz ranch in the 1920s. They were most likely part of the Kita family, who farmed the land. The photograph below was taken at the funeral of Japanese farmer Mr. Nakamura, which was held on the Alvernaz ranch. There are only two Caucasians in the photograph, Maria Alvernaz and her daughter Eleanor. After Antonio Alvernaz died, his wife, Maria, sharecropped the property out to Japanese farmers for the raising of fruits and vegetables. Although Japanese people were barred from owning land in the United States, Maria courageously fought this discrimination and agreed to hold the land in her name until the children of the Japanese immigrants reached the age of maturity. Lionel Goularte remembers that the Japanese community had a celebration every May at Warm Springs Landing. Families came with tents and tarps and celebrated with food and conversation for the entire day. (Both, HA.)

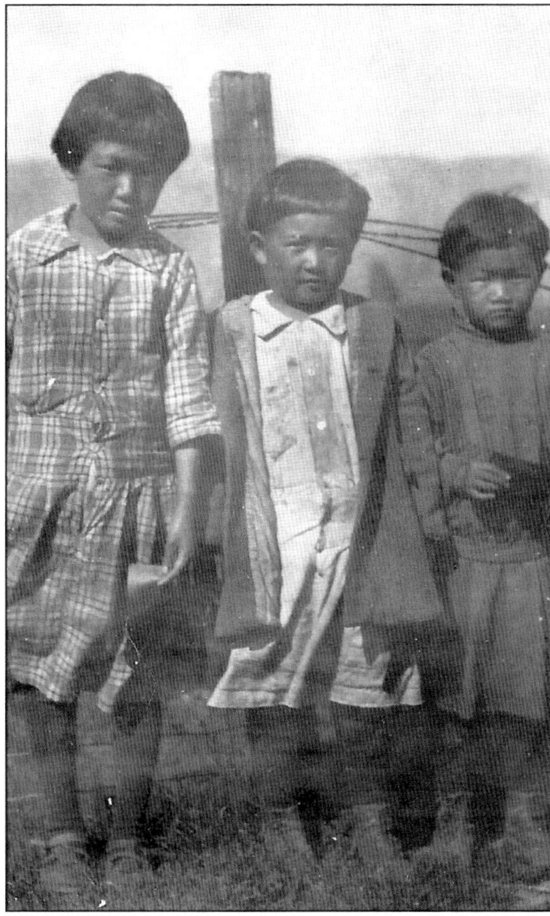

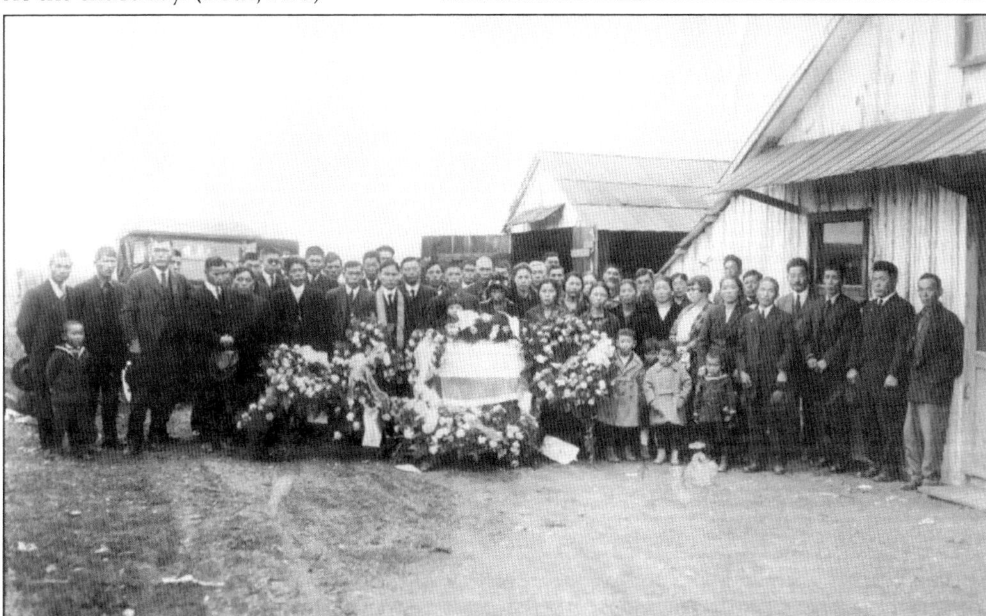

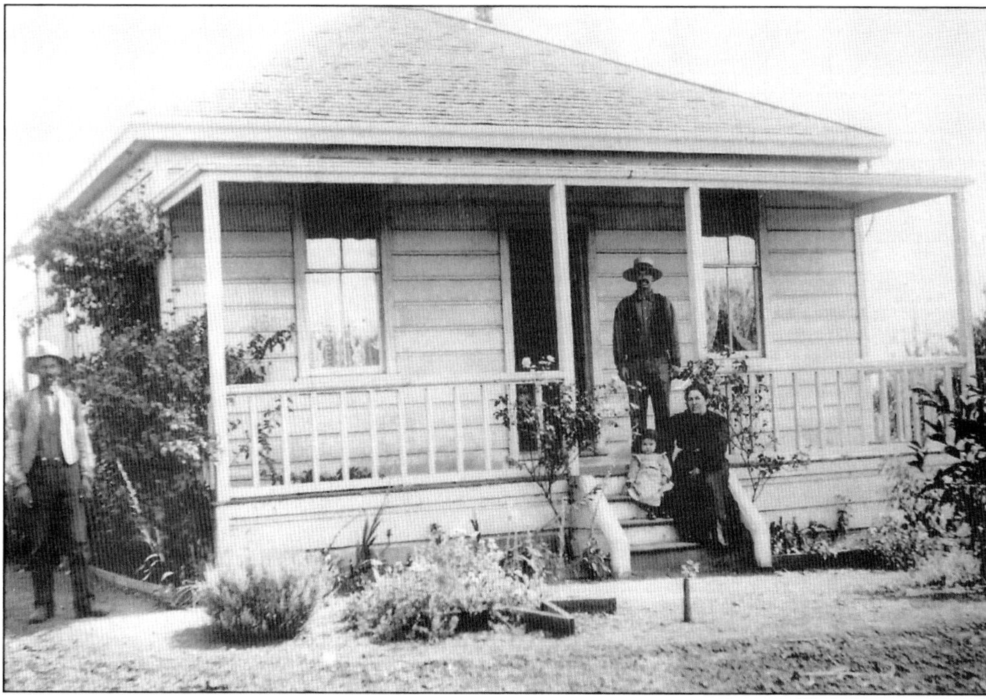

The home of Antone and Louise "Lizzie" Oliver is seen here in 1903. The couple is on the porch with one of their children, probably Mary. Their son, Paul, was a barber in Newark for many years. The farmhouse was typical of the times, with herbs growing in the front yard. (SVM.)

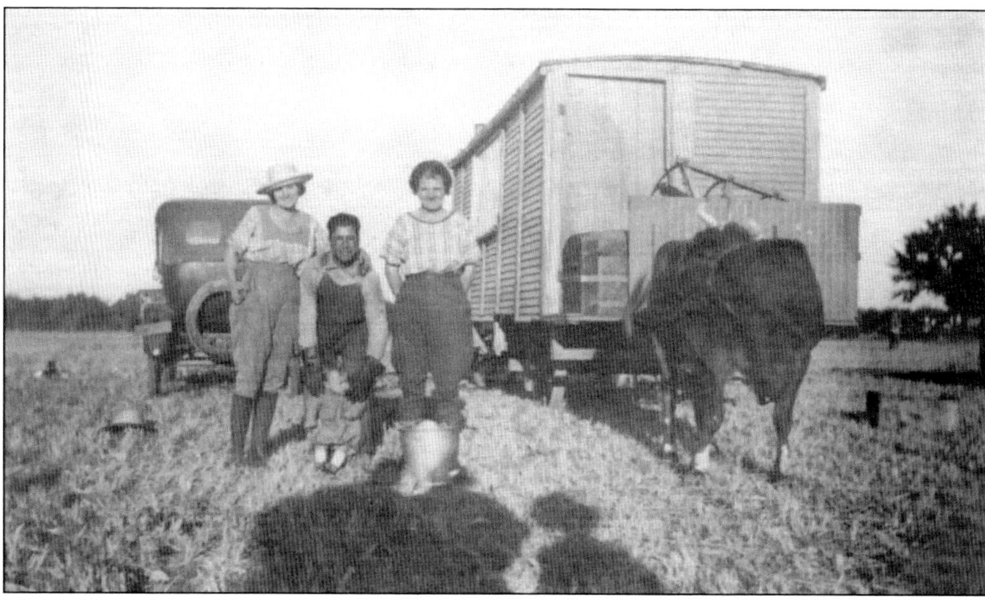

Manuel Ramos owned the only hay press in Warm Springs. Rosie (left) and Manuel (center) Ramos and an unidentified child and woman stand in front of the cook wagon in a hayfield around 1925. Hay crews needed good substantial food when they worked from sunrise to sunset. The cook prepared three meals a day and snacks twice a day. It was hard work cooking out of the wagon on a woodstove. (Courtesy Darren and Sandra Young.)

Joe Francisco Vargas and Anna Lourenco Vargas, from Faial and Flores, respectively, in the Azores, are seen here with their family around 1910. Joe worked for Henry Curtner and lived in the area called Chinatown. Joe and Anna had 10 children, all of whom are seen here except Florence. The family included, from left to right, (first row) Rosie, Joe Sr., baby Manuel, Adeline, and Anna; (second row) Annie, Mary, Alvino, Joe Jr., Minnie, and Tony. Most of the family lived their entire lives in Warm Springs. (SVM.)

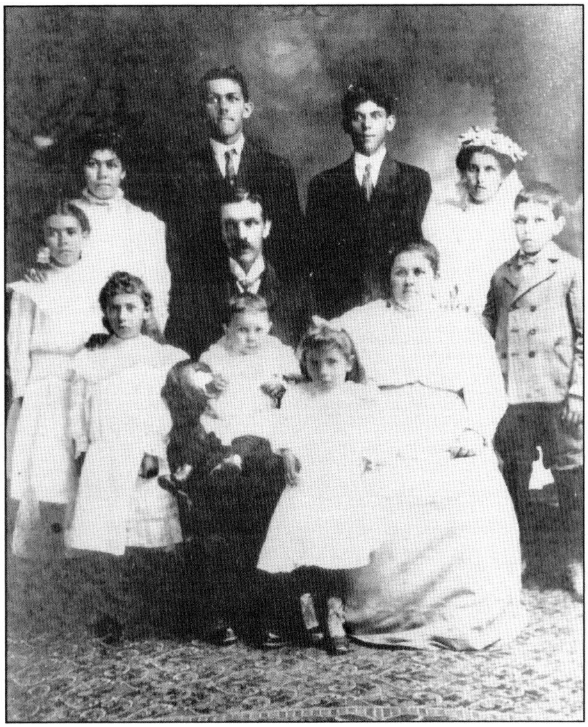

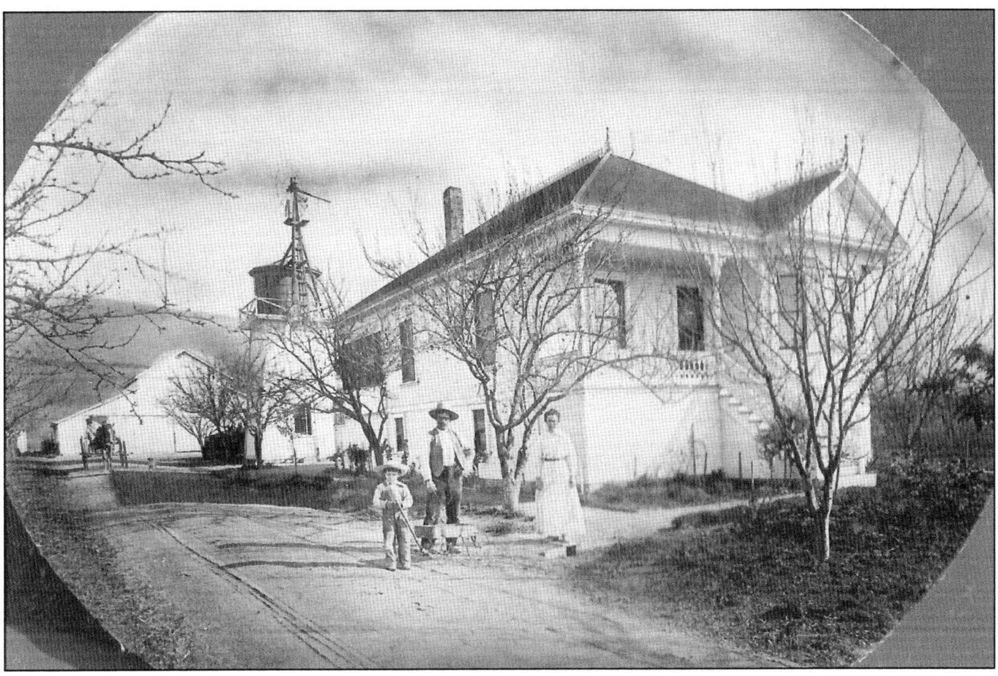

Antone Manuel Silva, his wife, Louisa, and their son, Douglas, posed for this porcelain photograph on the Silva farm with the house, tank house, and barn behind them. The Silvas, also from the Azores, purchased 12.45 acres for a fruit farm in 1905. The Silva apricot orchard, today only 2.67 acres, is the last remaining farm from this era in Warm Springs. Their grandson, Bob Silva, continues to farm the property. (Photograph by Ted Klein.)

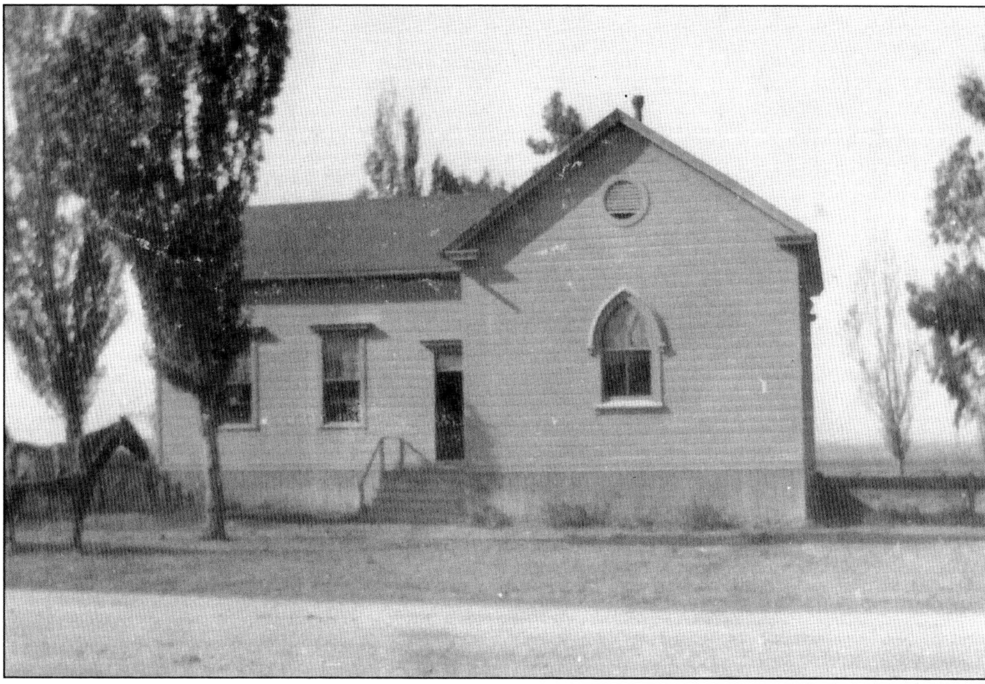

Warm Springs School, first called the Higuera School, opened in a shed in 1863. The first teacher was Lizzie Valpey, who had 13 students. In 1864, this small schoolhouse was built across the road. The name was changed to Warm Spring School in 1866—the "s" was added later. (PH.)

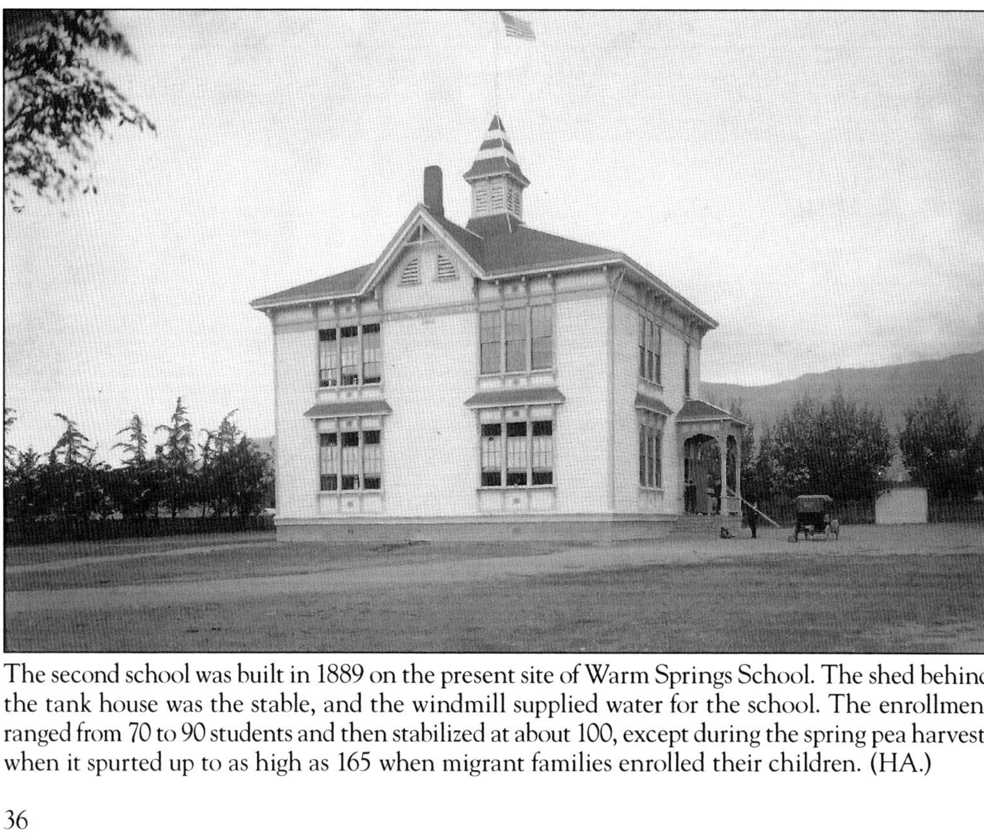

The second school was built in 1889 on the present site of Warm Springs School. The shed behind the tank house was the stable, and the windmill supplied water for the school. The enrollment ranged from 70 to 90 students and then stabilized at about 100, except during the spring pea harvest, when it spurted up to as high as 165 when migrant families enrolled their children. (HA.)

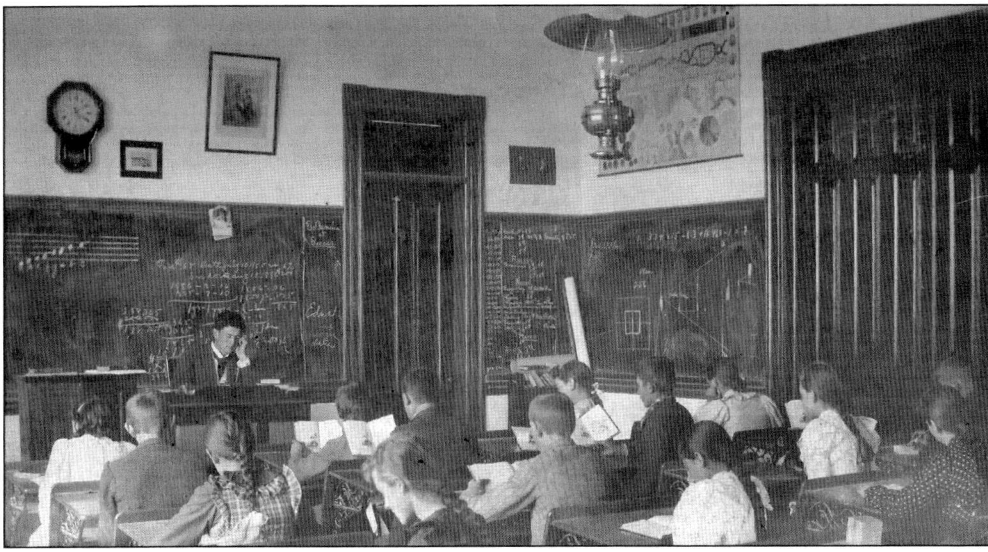

A Warm Springs School classroom is seen here in 1900. At the time, one teacher would teach students in several grades and a variety of subjects, including mathematics, music, history, geometry, grammar, geography, reading, and spelling. Math problems, the daily schedule, and music scales are displayed on the blackboard. The name of a student who had to stay in at recess is also listed. The classroom had tall doors and a gaslight.

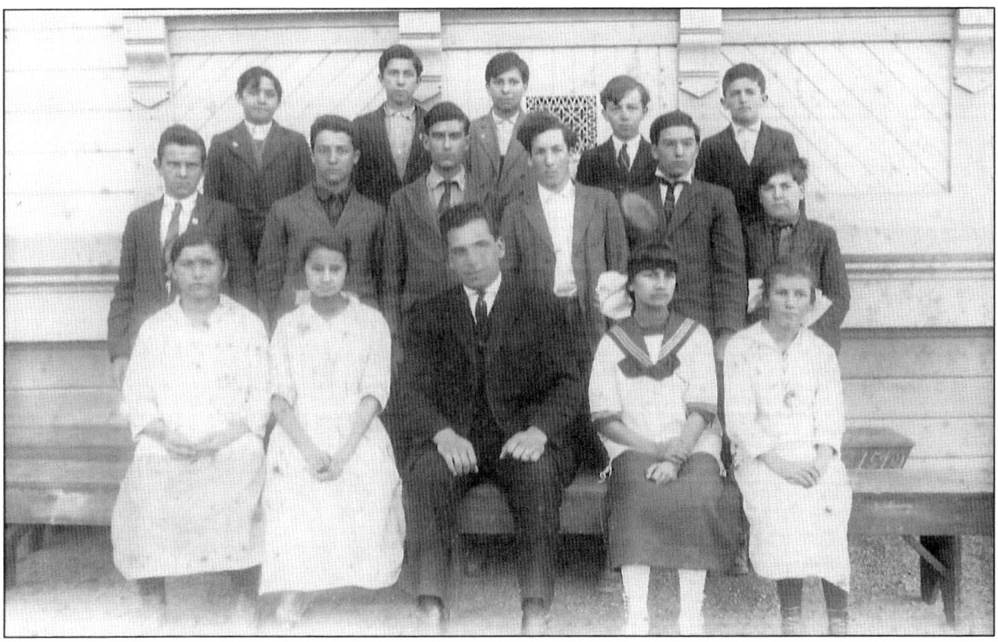

The class of 1911 poses in front of the second Warm Springs School with principal and teacher Francis Joseph Lazarus, who taught there for 11 years, from 1909 to 1920. Lazarus was an active member of the UPEC Council No. 67 of Warm Springs, a Portuguese fraternal organization. From left to right are, (first row) Mary Martin, Mildred Andrade, Frank Lazarus, Lena Goularte, and Rose Vargas; (second row) Joe Silveira or Joe Rose, Tony Lawrence, Manuel Briar, Edwin Sarmento, Ernest Silva (?), and Joe Silva (?); (third row) two unidentified, Arthur Goularte, Bert Dutra, and unidentified. (HA.)

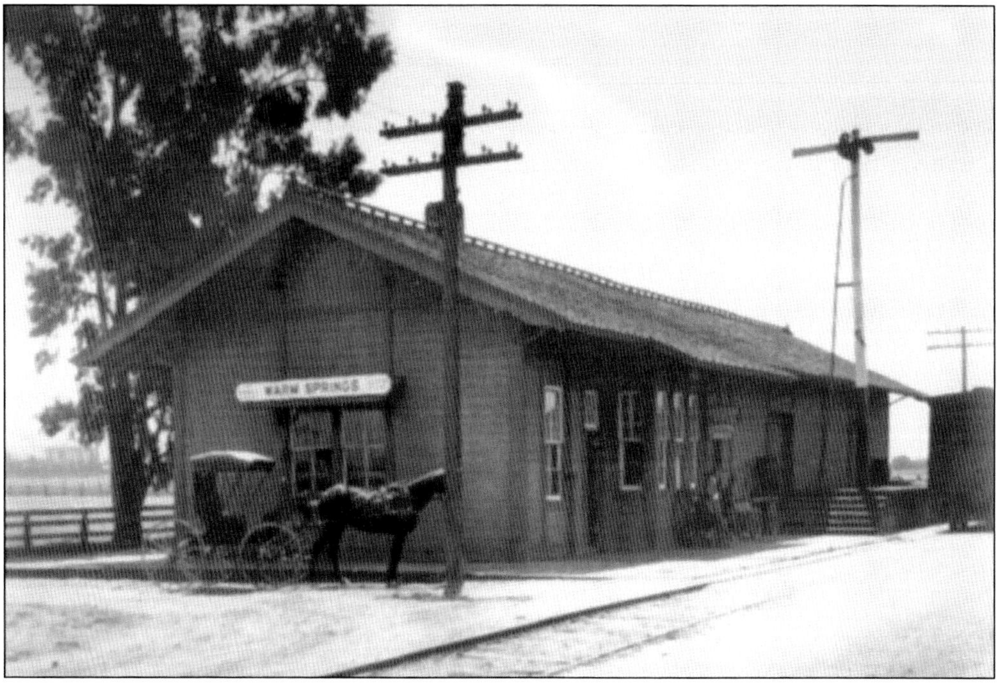


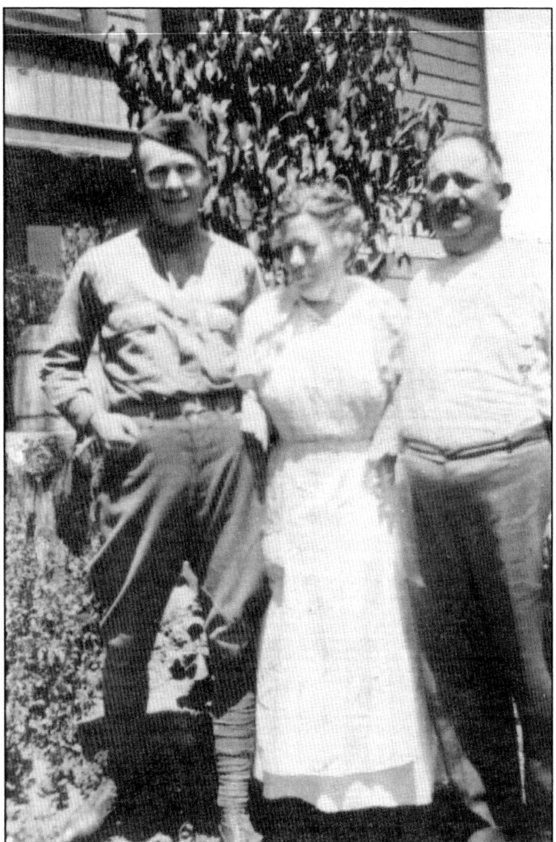

The Western Pacific Railroad came through the Warm Springs area west of the village of Harrisburg (later Warm Springs). Warehouses were erected but no depot was built at first. This one-story combination passenger and freight structure was built with electric lights around 1912. Notice the lone horse and buggy waiting beside the station and the school in the background. (Courtesy Bay Area Electric Railway Association.)

Henry Allard was a native of France who came to Mission San Jose in 1891. By 1902, he moved to Warm Springs and married Annie Stachler, a widow with two children. They had a daughter, Florence. The Allards are seen here with Annie's son (far left) in 1918. They ran a general store across the road from the Warm Springs Store, which was operated by Jacob Steinmetz and his family. (Courtesy Jane Huber.)

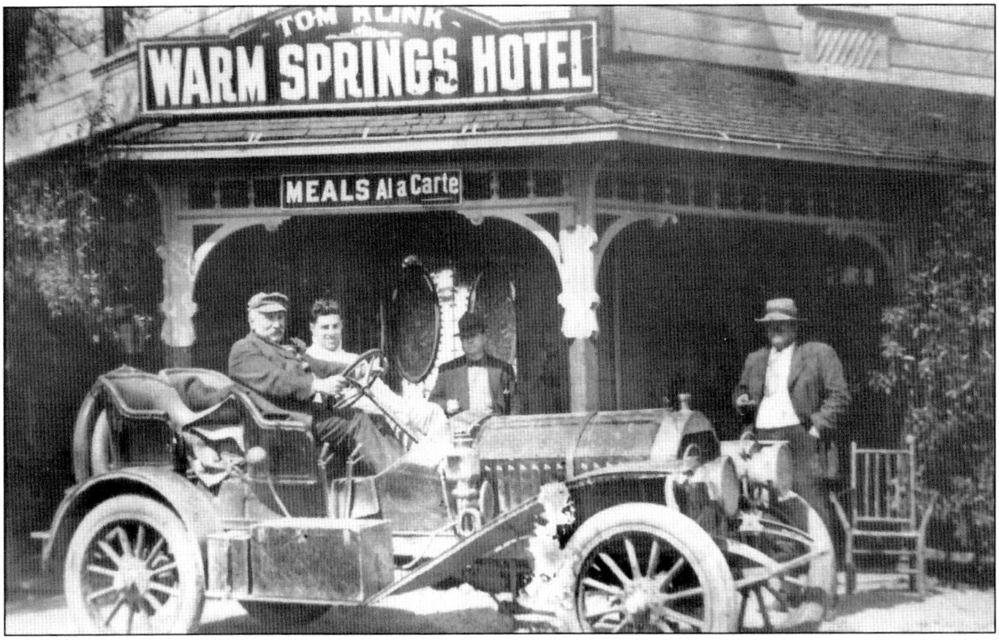


There were several hotels called Warm Springs through the years. James Murray owned the Harrisburg Hotel, which later became known as the Rural Hotel. This photograph shows the Warm Springs Hotel in 1907, when it was owned by Tom Klink, seen here driving his car. (PH.)

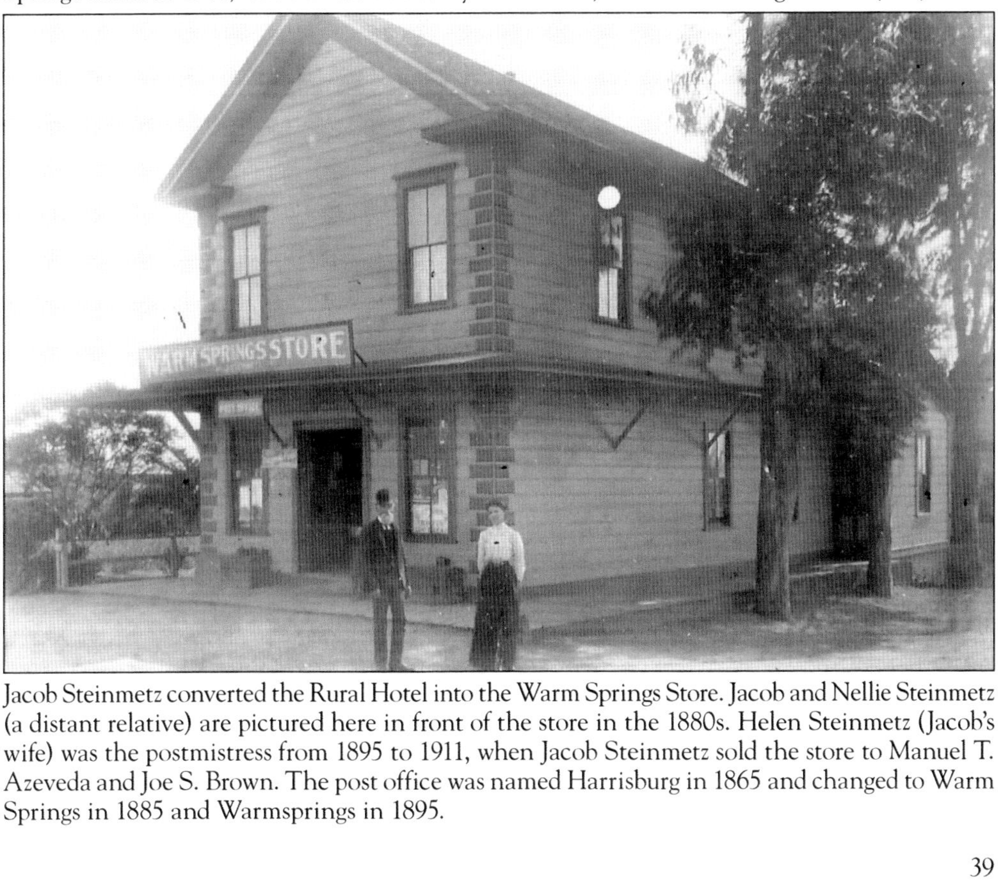


Jacob Steinmetz converted the Rural Hotel into the Warm Springs Store. Jacob and Nellie Steinmetz (a distant relative) are pictured here in front of the store in the 1880s. Helen Steinmetz (Jacob's wife) was the postmistress from 1895 to 1911, when Jacob Steinmetz sold the store to Manuel T. Azeveda and Joe S. Brown. The post office was named Harrisburg in 1865 and changed to Warm Springs in 1885 and Warmsprings in 1895.

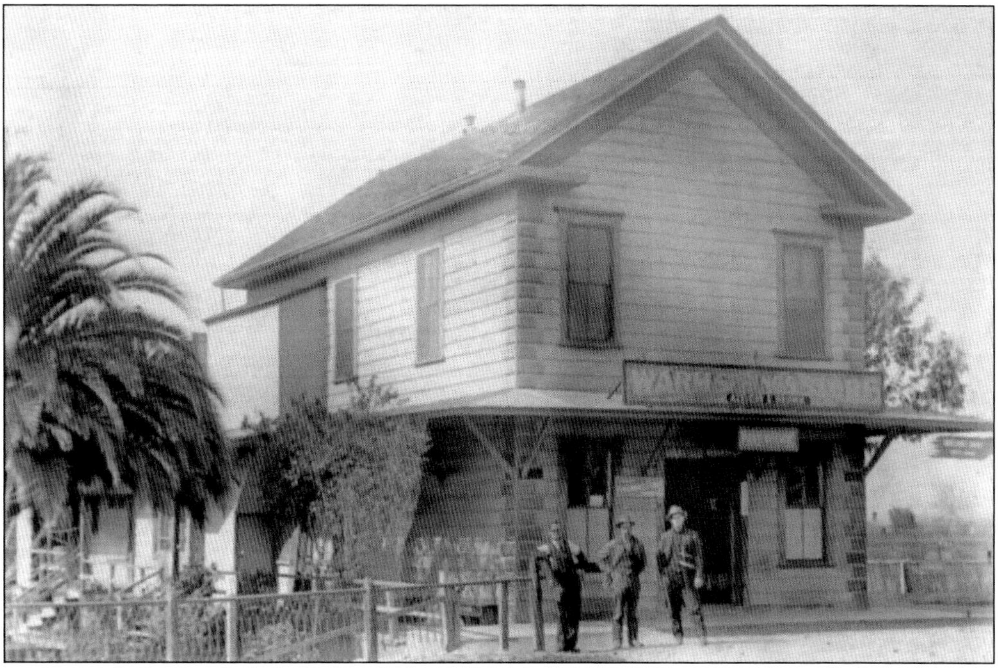

Joe S. Brown (left), Manuel T. Azeveda (center), and an unidentified person are seen here in front of the Warm Springs Store in 1912, a year after Brown and Azaveda bought it. Brown served as postmaster from 1912 until his death in 1957. His wife, Rosie Brown, was postmistress from 1959 to 1969. In 1960, the Warm Springs postmark was discontinued when it was consolidated into the Fremont post office. (Courtesy Mollie Sinclair and Evelyn Brown Rose.)

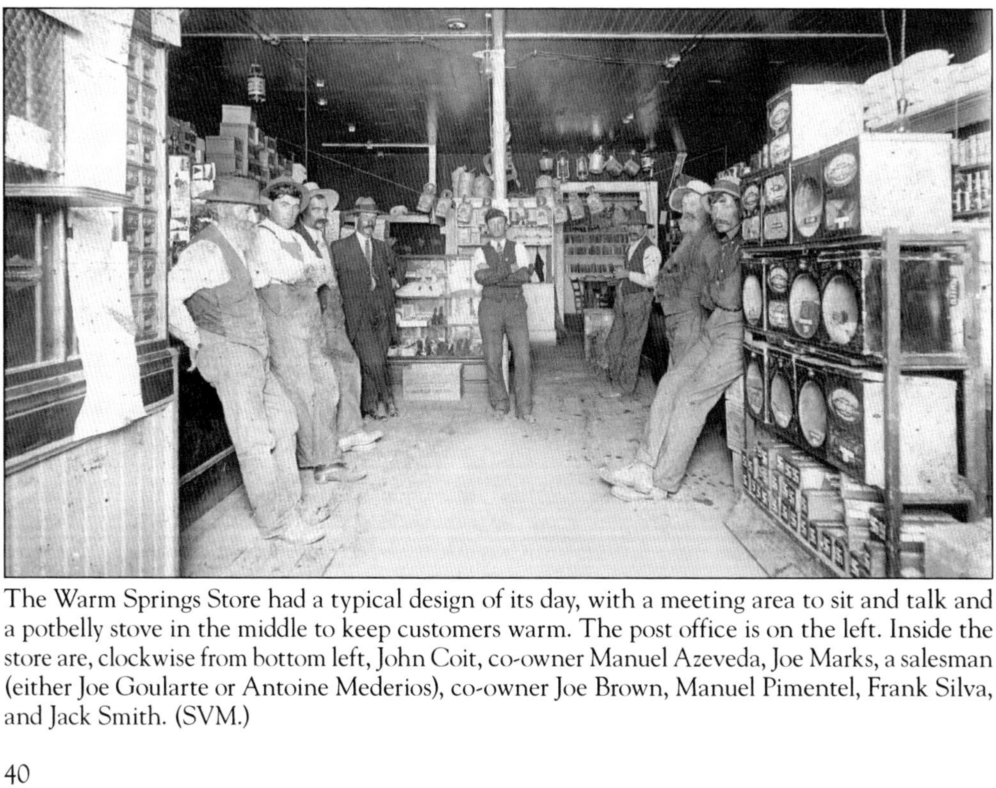

The Warm Springs Store had a typical design of its day, with a meeting area to sit and talk and a potbelly stove in the middle to keep customers warm. The post office is on the left. Inside the store are, clockwise from bottom left, John Coit, co-owner Manuel Azeveda, Joe Marks, a salesman (either Joe Goularte or Antoine Mederios), co-owner Joe Brown, Manuel Pimentel, Frank Silva, and Jack Smith. (SVM.)

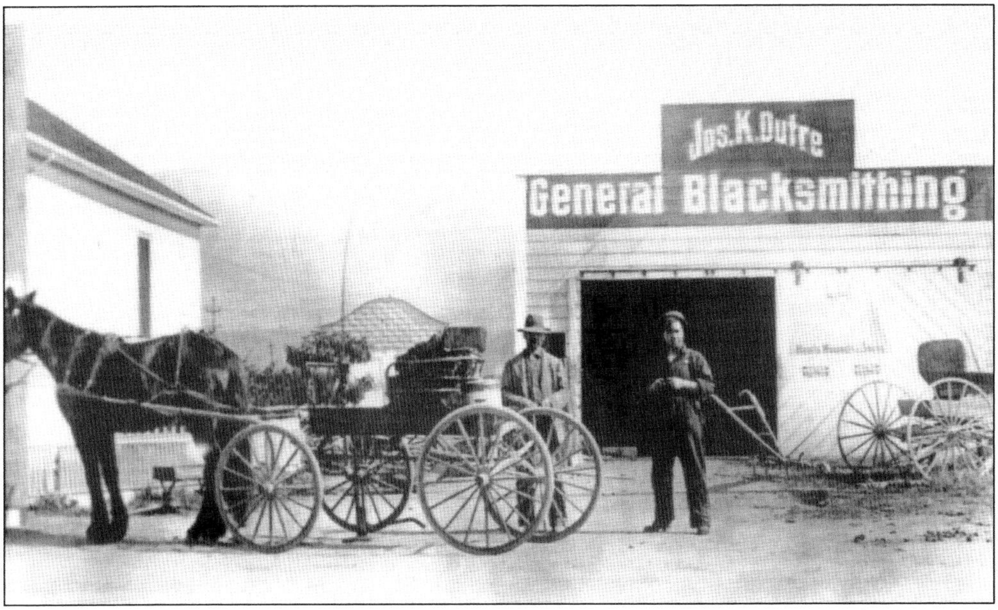


Joseph K. Dutre stands in front of his blacksmith shop around 1910. The man by the four-wheel buggy is Mr. Duarte. Behind Joseph, to the right, is a cultivator and another buggy. Four blacksmiths worked in Warm Springs through the years: George Beaty, S. Pierson, Dutre, and Edwin Winsor. The sign on the shop door reads "Heals Wounds and Sores." (SVM.)

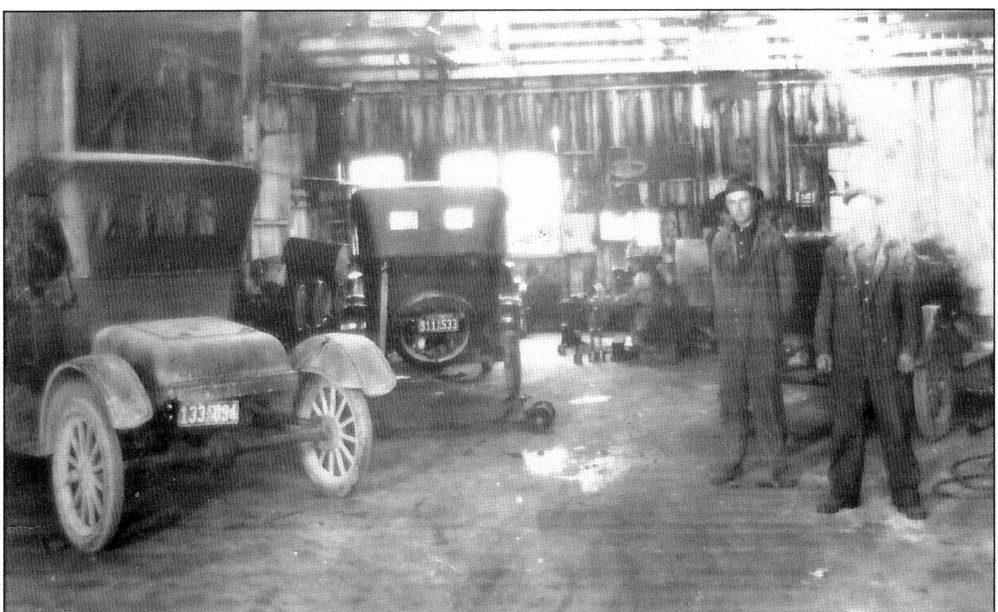

Joseph K. Dutre was a blacksmith who had fixed his 60 horsepower Hudson from a wreck to a racing car. He converted his blacksmith shop into the Liberty Garage when automobiles became popular. These two cars are being repaired in the Liberty Garage in 1924.

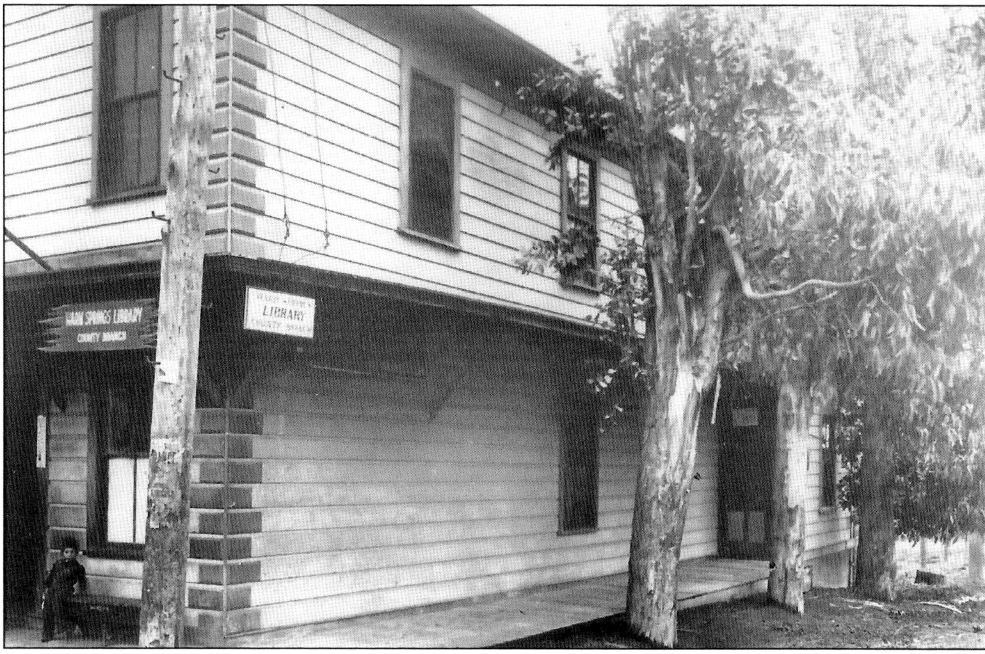

Joe Brown and Manuel Azeveda established the Warm Springs Library in February 1912 within the Warm Springs Store. Joe Brown and then his wife, Rosie, were librarians until 1949, followed by Virginia Steinmetz (1949–1950), Lillian Rodrigues (1950–1955), and Rose Resend (1955–1960). In 1960, the library was closed, and a bookmobile began service in front of the same location. The library is seen here about 1920.

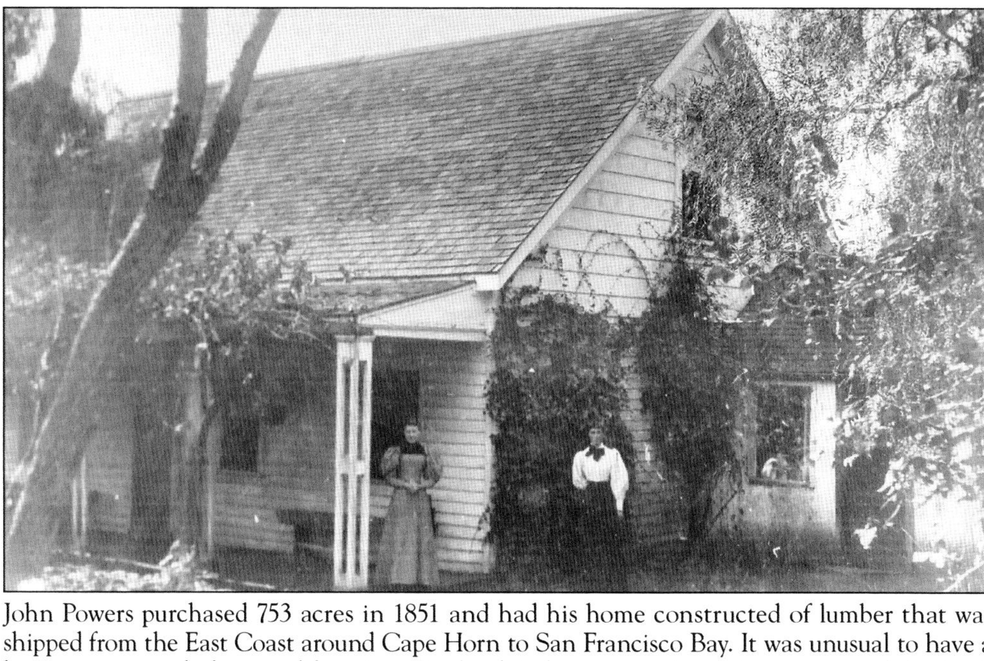

John Powers purchased 753 acres in 1851 and had his home constructed of lumber that was shipped from the East Coast around Cape Horn to San Francisco Bay. It was unusual to have a house constructed of material from New England. In later years, Prune Avenue crossed this land. Powers's neighbors included John Beard, Higuera descendants, and Origin Mowry, and across the Mission Road was the Stanford Ranch. Pictured are two women in front of the Powers home.

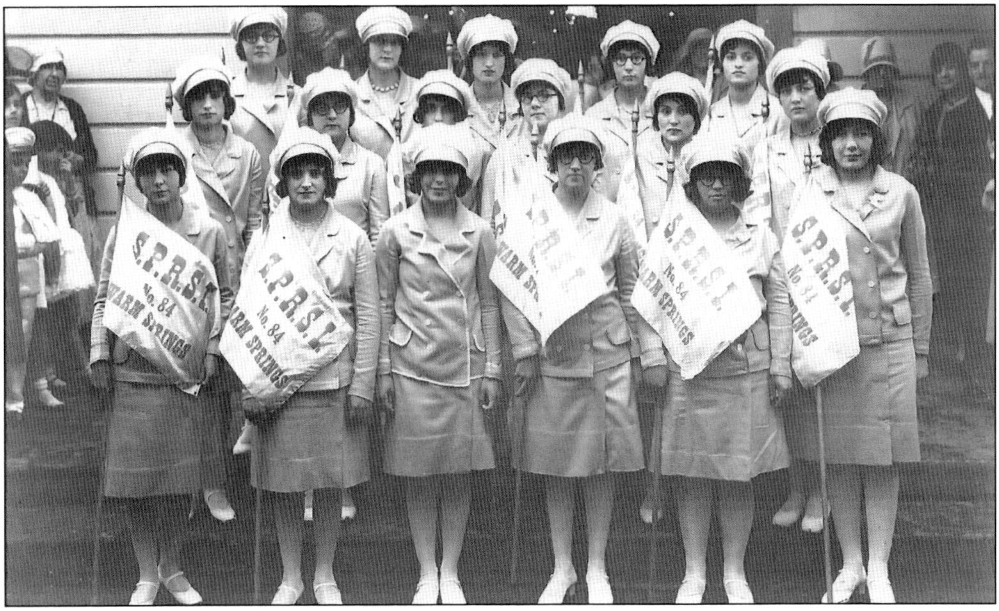


Sociedade Portuguesa Rainha Santa Isabel (SPRSI) No. 84, a Portuguese organization, was organized in 1910. The 1929 drill team included, from left to right, (first row) Carrie Silva Lawrence, Annie Lawrence Leal, Emma Garcia Smith, Rosie Vargas Brown, Annie Francis Vargas, and Helen Perry; (second row) Ida Lawrence Oliver, Alice Lawrence Rose, Edna Silva Castro, Adeline Vargas Swartz, Mary Sarmento Enos, and unidentified; (third row) Florence Vargas Brazil Stonecypher, Mary Briar Andrade, Madeline Lawrence Smith, Louisa Oliver, and Rosalind Enos Souza. (SVM.)

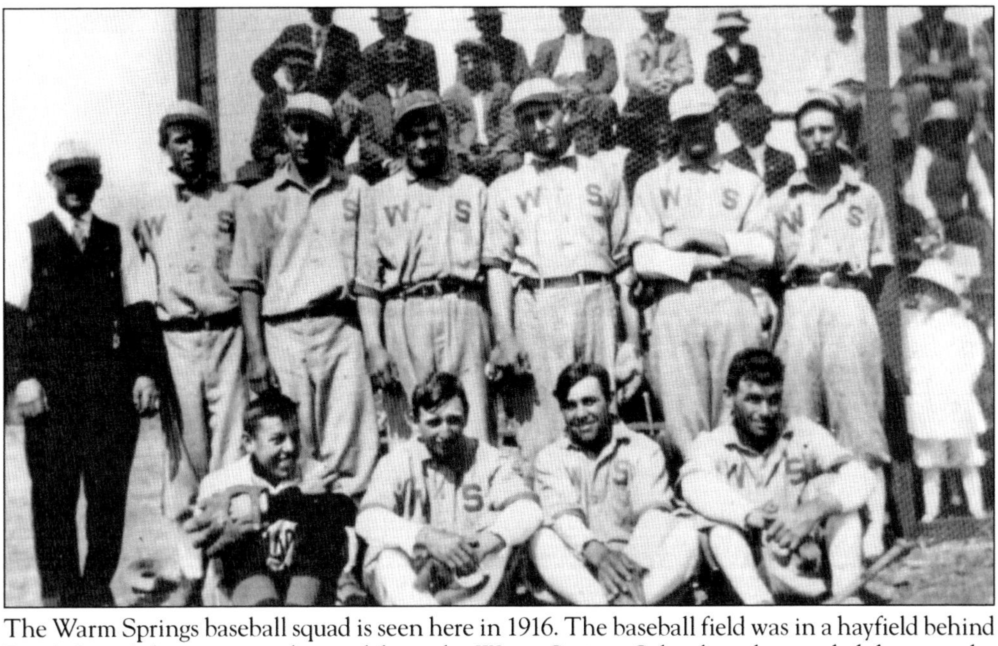

The Warm Springs baseball squad is seen here in 1916. The baseball field was in a hayfield behind Frank Serpa's barn, across the road from the Warm Springs School, and extended down to the railroad tracks. The team, which won the championship of the Santa Clara Valley League that year, included (first row) Ted Silveira (third from left); (second row) manager Joe S. Brown (far left), Joe Marks (fourth from left), and Joe Briar (far right). (SVM.)

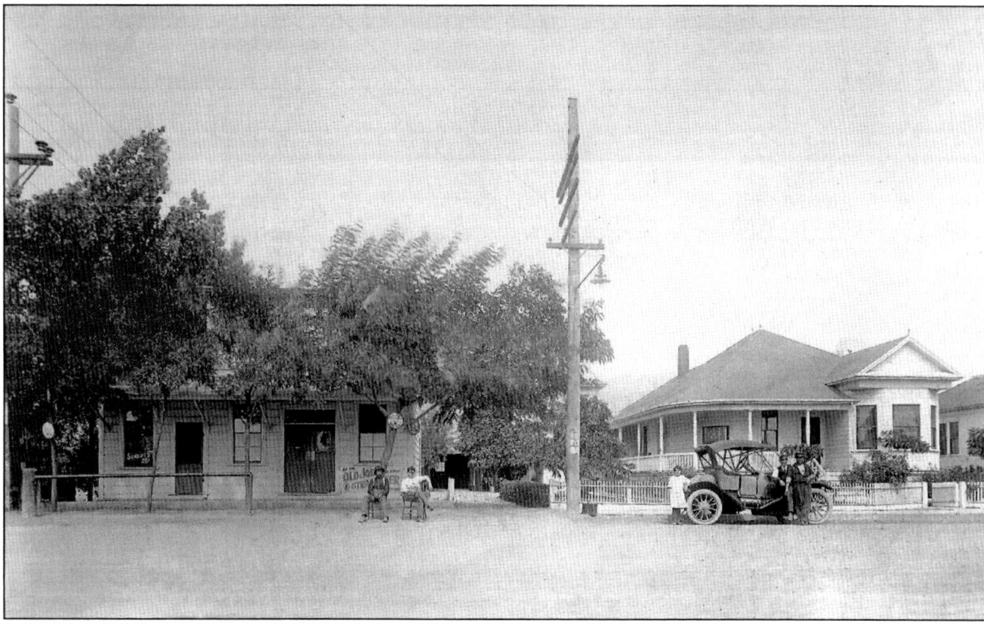

This is a rarely photographed area of Warm Springs, across the street from the Warm Springs Store. Two men sit in front of a bar that advertises Old Joe's Steam Beer. There is a hitching post for horses and there is an automobile parked in front of the house. By this point, the town has paved roads and electricity. Telephone service first came in 1901, and natural gas was available in 1930. (Courtesy Mollie Sinclair.)

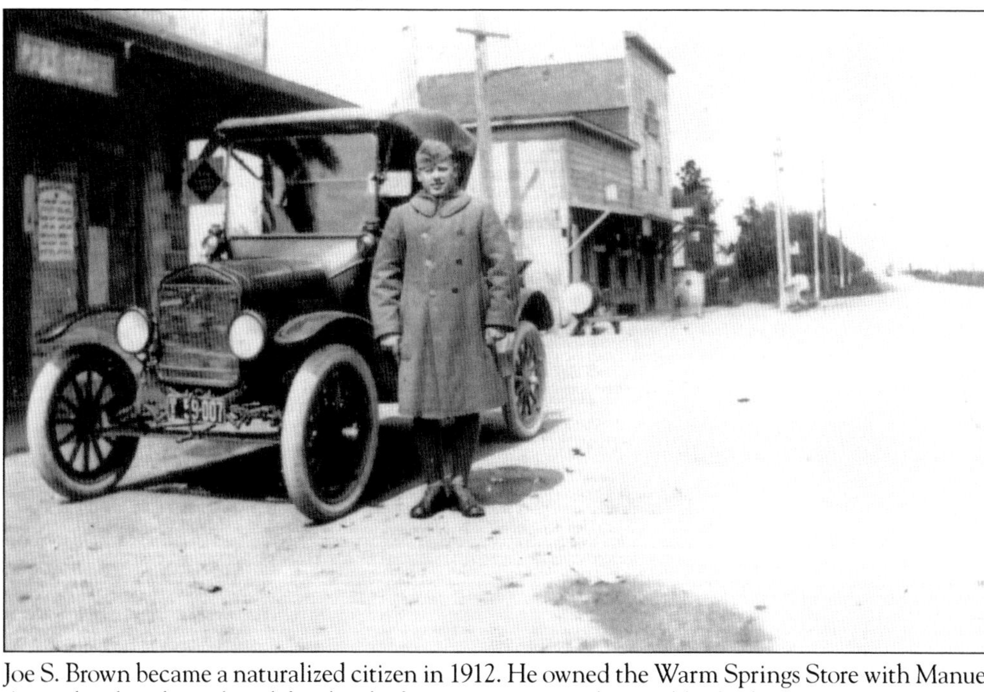

Joe S. Brown became a naturalized citizen in 1912. He owned the Warm Springs Store with Manuel Azeveda when he enlisted for the draft in 1918. He was honorably discharged as a corporal in 1919 after having served in France during World War I. He is seen here in his uniform in front of his store in 1918. (SVM.)

# *Four*

# LELAND STANFORD LEGACY

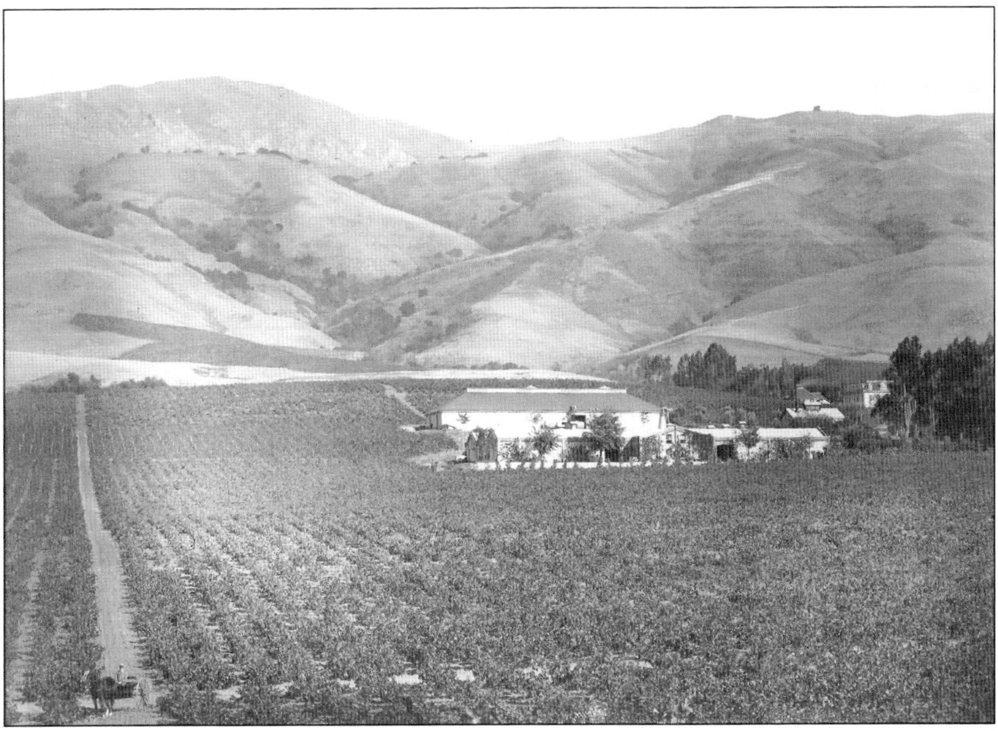

Leland Stanford bought the Warm Springs Hotel complex in 1869 after an earthquake had changed the springs. Stanford planned to enlarge the vineyards and raise Thoroughbred horses. The lake from the resort time was filled in and converted to a horse track. Josiah Stanford, Leland's older brother, and Josiah Winslow Stanford, his nephew, took over management of the ranch. They planted grape vines and enlarged the winery. There were two large wine cellars on the ranch, one with a capacity of 400,000 gallons and the other able to hold 500,000 gallons. Louis Juichard, the vintner, was a native of Switzerland, and all the machinery at the winery was of the newest patents.

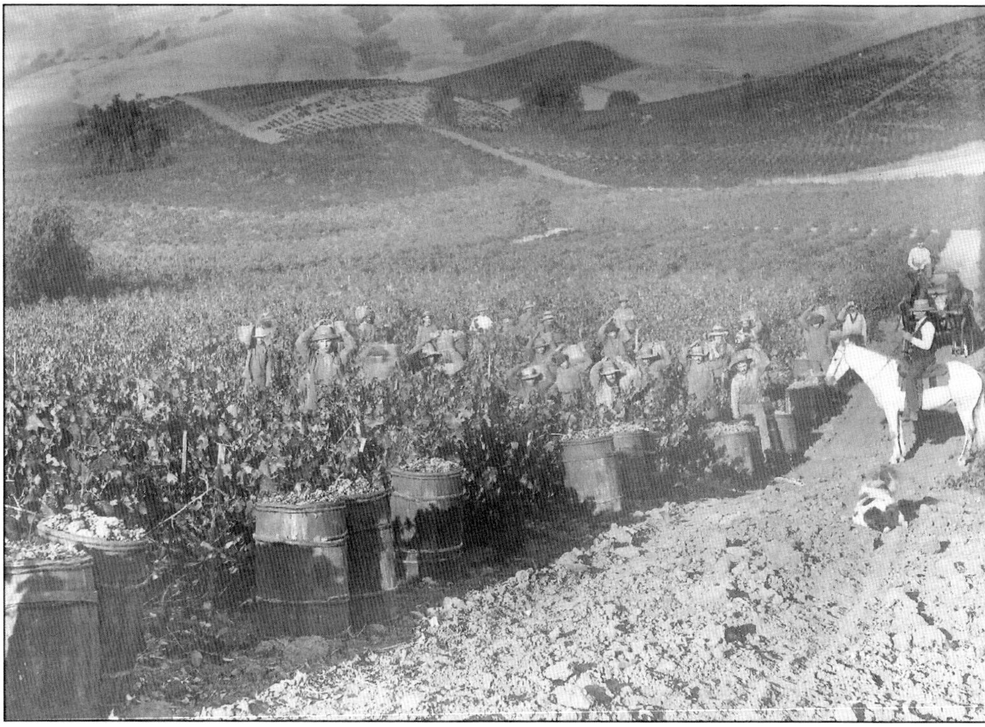

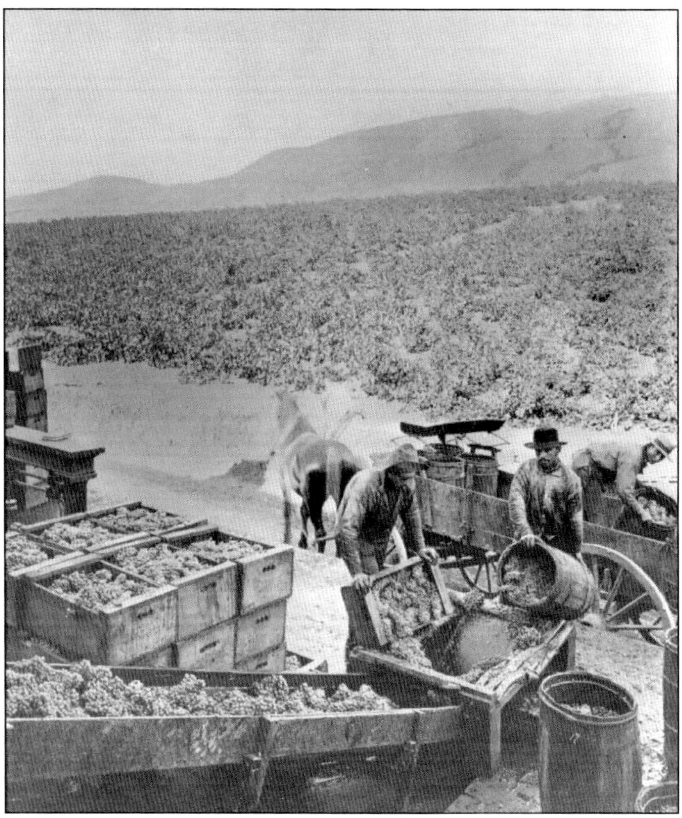

Wine production was hard work, and it employed many workers. These workers pick grapes and put them in barrels, which will be transported by cart through the Stanford vineyard to the winery for processing. The man on the white horse is the foreman, Cass Rorabach. The vineyard above lies to the south of the production buildings.

Workers unload the just-picked grapes from boxes and barrels onto a conveyor belt, which will load them into wagons to be transported to the crushers. This loading area seems to be close to the main roadway, which became Mission Boulevard.

This 1879 bottle of Riesling from the Warm Springs Vineyard is in the Museum of Local History. Most of the wine was shipped to eastern cities in bulk, so very little was marketed locally, making this bottle a rare artifact. (MLH.)

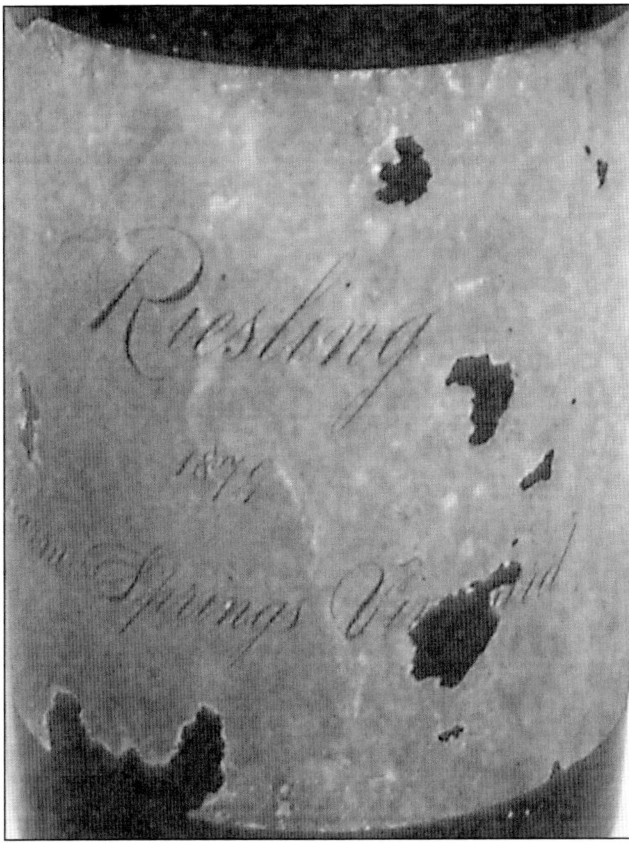


The man below at the right stands in the fermenting house. The two men on the left, by the fermenting vat, appear to be sweeping the floor. The equipment in the center of the photograph appears to be a grape crusher. Louis Juichard, the wine master, kept everything very clean in and around the cellar; the walls were whitewashed and the concrete floor had ample drains.

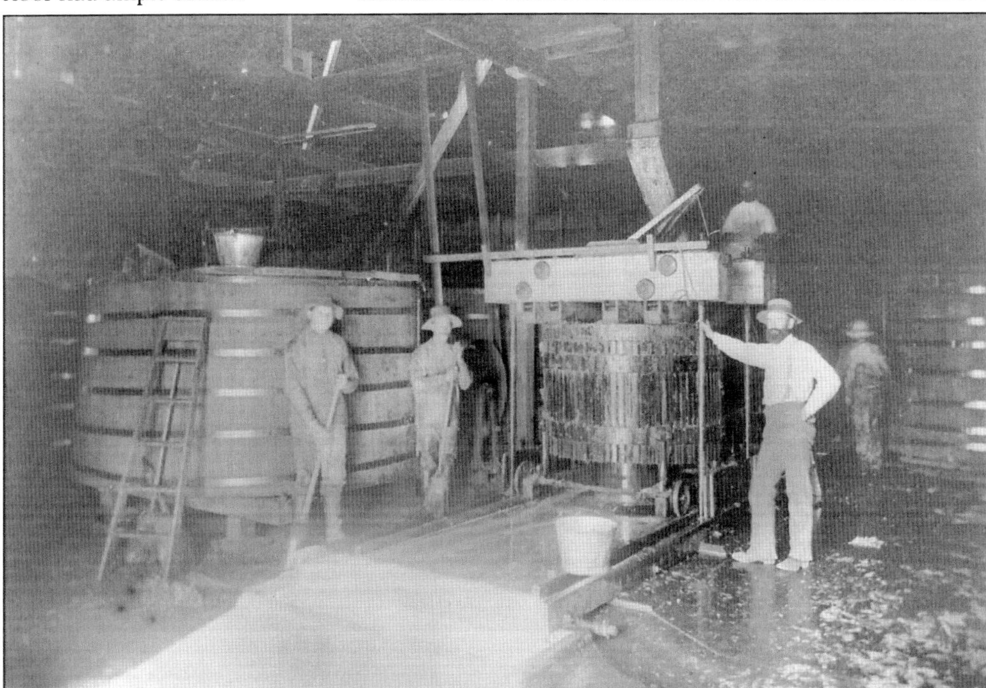

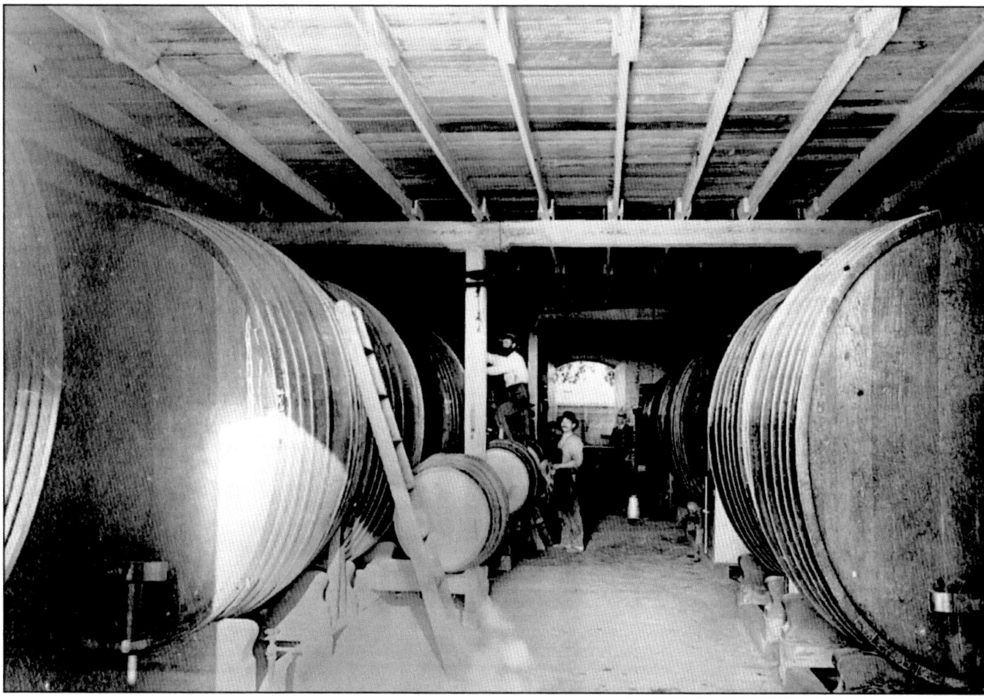

After the wine was fermented, it was transferred to the aging vat.

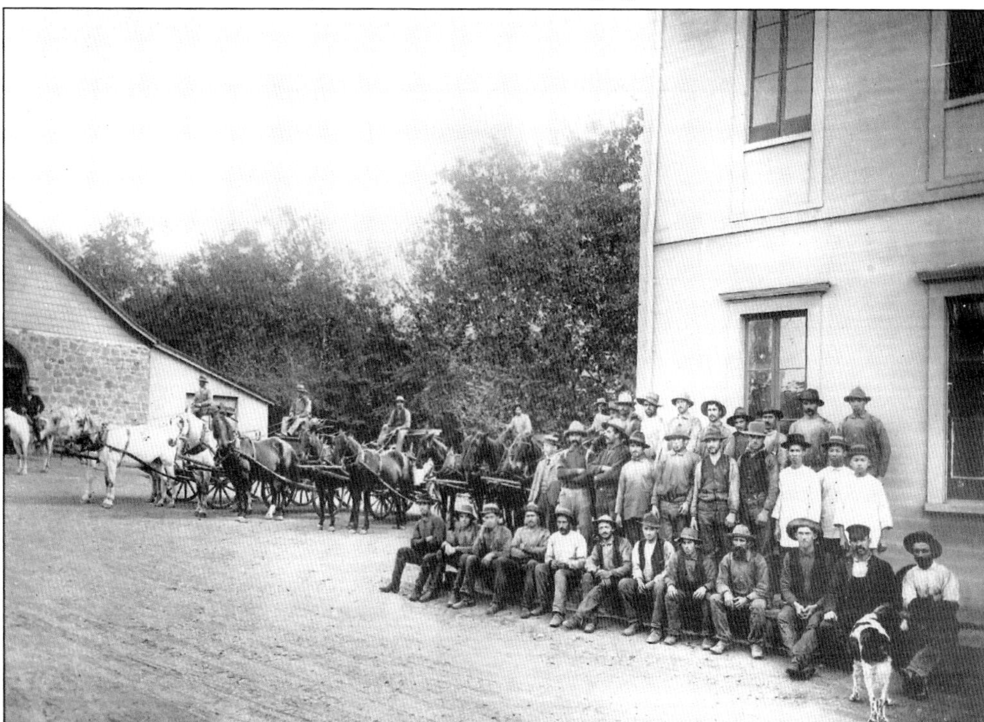

These Stanford winery workers pose in front of Clement Colombet's original hotel building, which served as their bunkhouse. There are three Chinese workers in the photograph.

Josiah Stanford remodeled the central hotel building from Colombet's Warm Springs Resort into the family residence. People continued to come, not realizing the resort was closed, and he allowed people to bathe on the property until 1874. Seen here on the porch of the family residence are, from left to right, Helen Alice Herrick, Josiah Winslow Stanford's second wife; Agnes Taylor, Stanford's half-sister from his father's first wife, Elvina Griffin Taylor; and Josiah Winslow Stanford.

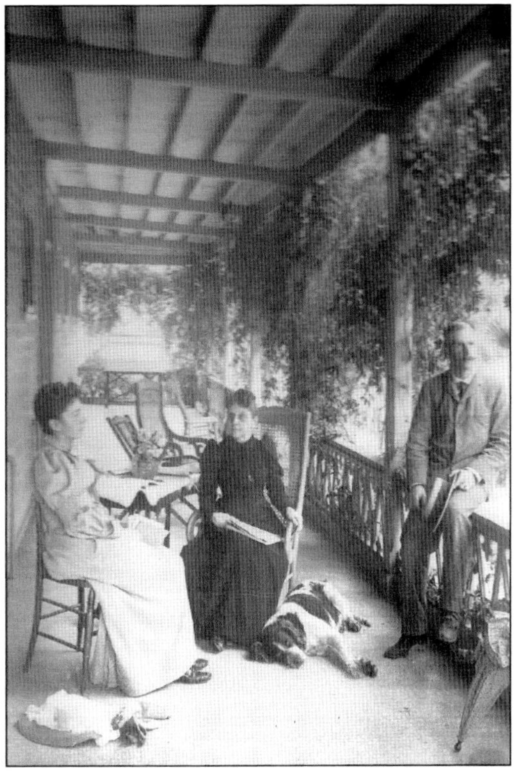

Josiah Winslow Stanford developed elaborately landscaped gardens around the main house (below). He built an extensive system of paths lined with hedgerows, flowers, and fruit trees and also planted a variety of palm and olive trees. Some of the palms were grown from pits planted by his grandmother. Other exotic trees included black locust, white mulberry, and elms. He also planted olive trees on Stanford Avenue at this time.

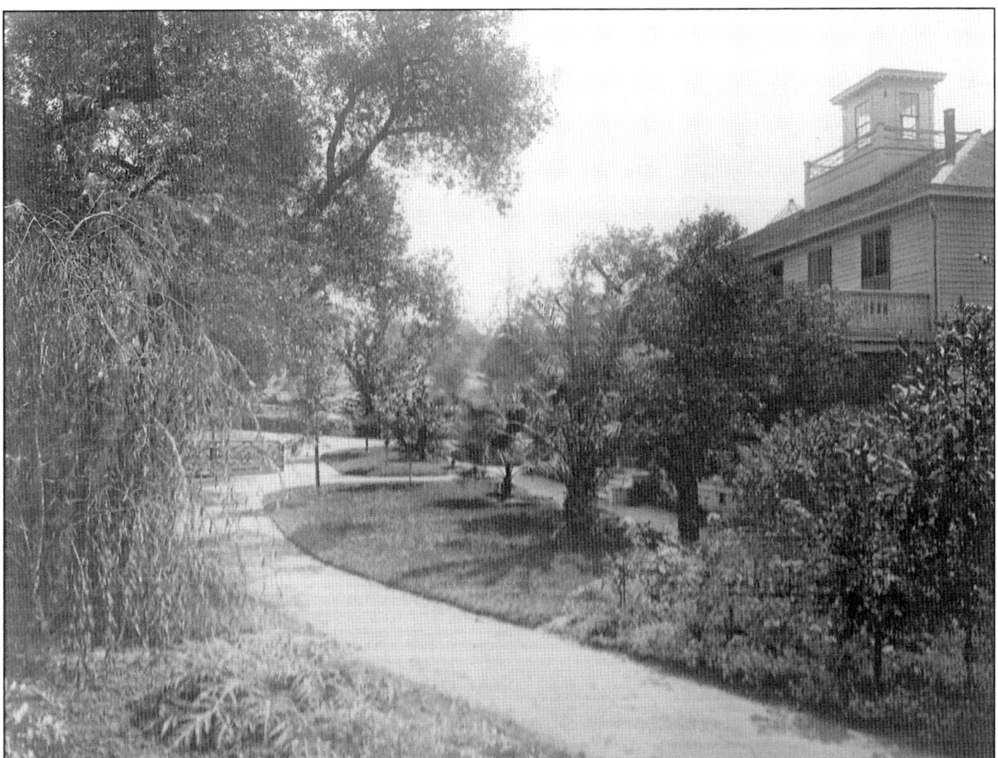

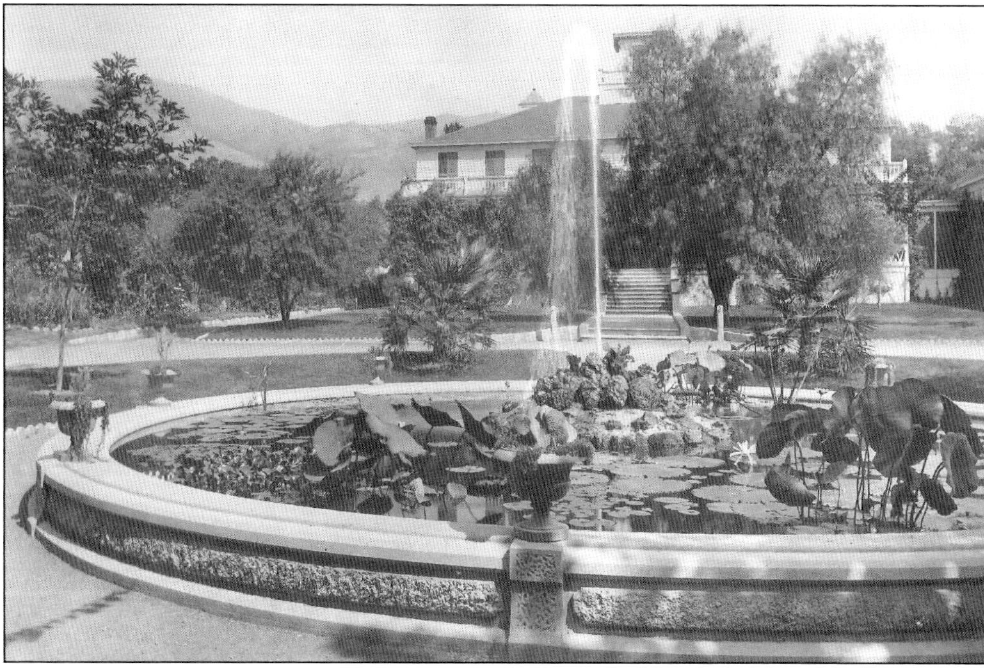

This circular fountain adorned the entrance to the main residence and was made of red brick topped with cement. It was used as the logo on the resort's menus and advertisements. The circular fountain was more than 29 feet in diameter with a six-foot-wide concrete walkway around the perimeter. Josiah Winslow Stanford covered one of the springs, excavated a small reservoir, and placed young alligators from Florida in the reservoir.

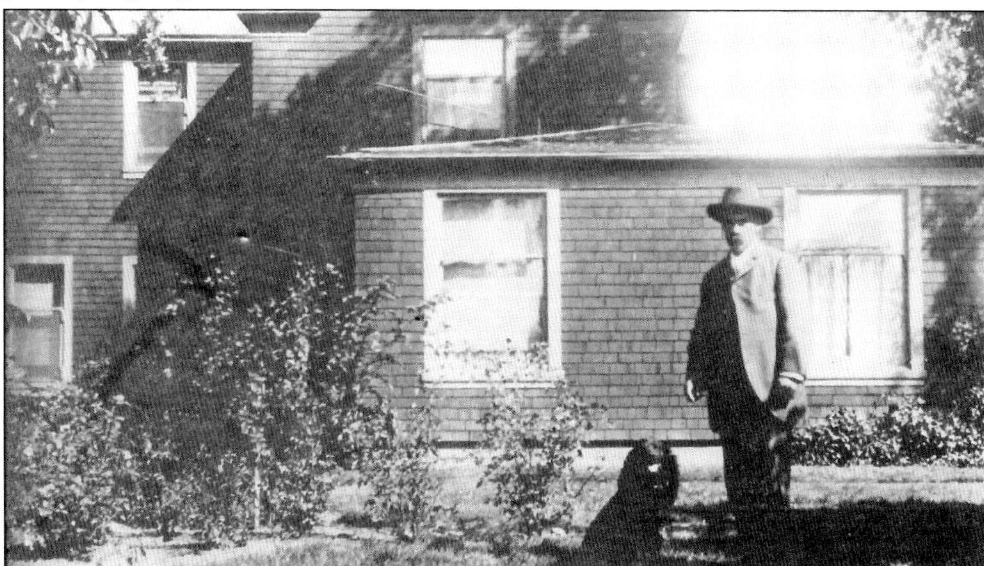

Josiah Winslow Stanford owned and operated an 1899 Winton. He was an excellent mechanic and performed the necessary maintenance and repairs himself. He was probably the first man in Washington Township to own an automobile and sometimes motored to Oakland, where he lived in his later years. Pictured around 1914 is Josiah W. Stanford with his dog in front of a home on the Stanford ranch in Warm Springs.

# *Five*

# Ghost Town in the Bay

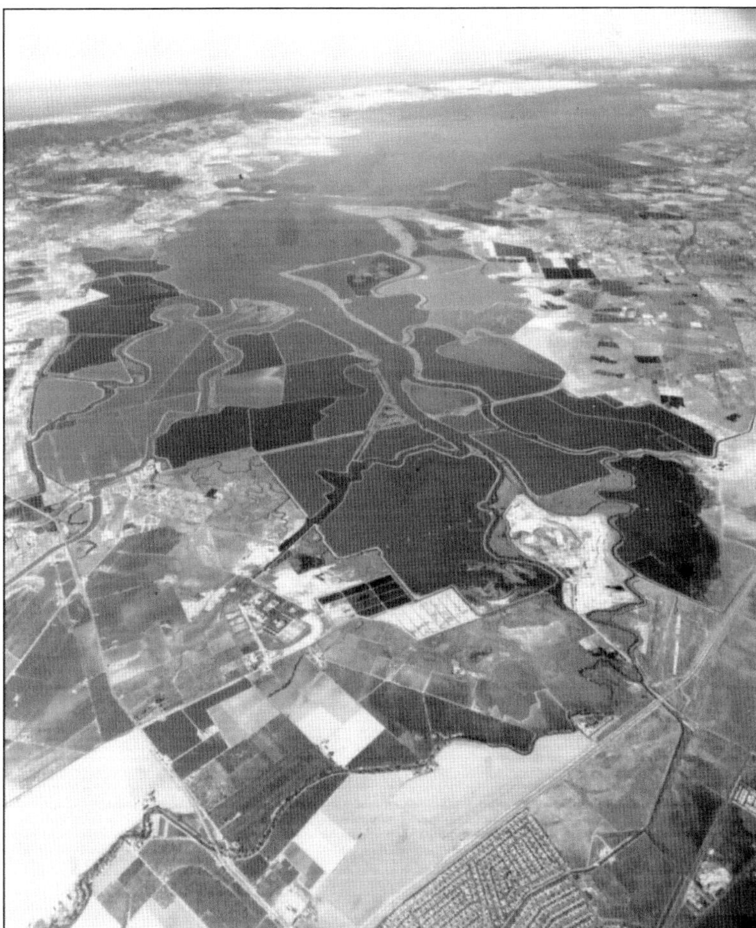

Warm Springs Slough and Coyote Slough were navigable waterways on the southern edge of Alameda County with a flat, marshy island stretched between them. The South Pacific Coast Railroad purchased the Santa Clara Valley Railroad, which held rights to the island. The town of Drawbridge was at the south end of San Francisco Bay looking west. This aerial photograph was taken when the salt ponds were in operation in the 1960s. (DE.)

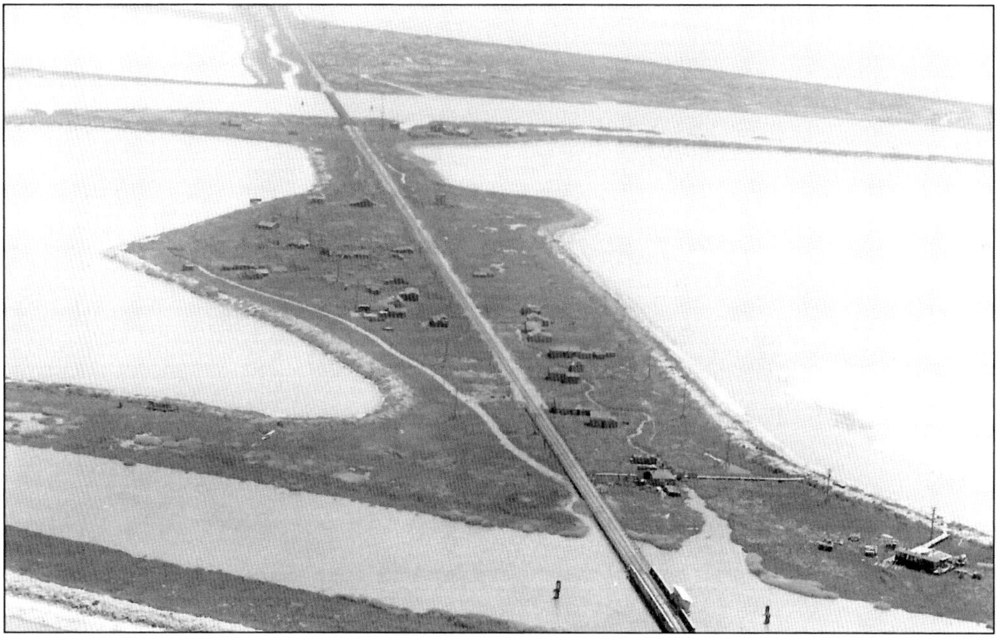

Chinese laborers laid narrow-gauge railroad tracks south from Newark to Warm Springs Slough in 1876. The South Pacific Coast Railroad (SPCRR) bought a 100-foot right-of-way across the island, between the two sloughs. This aerial view of Drawbridge looks south, with Coyote Slough at the far end of town and Mud Slough in the foreground (north). (DE.)

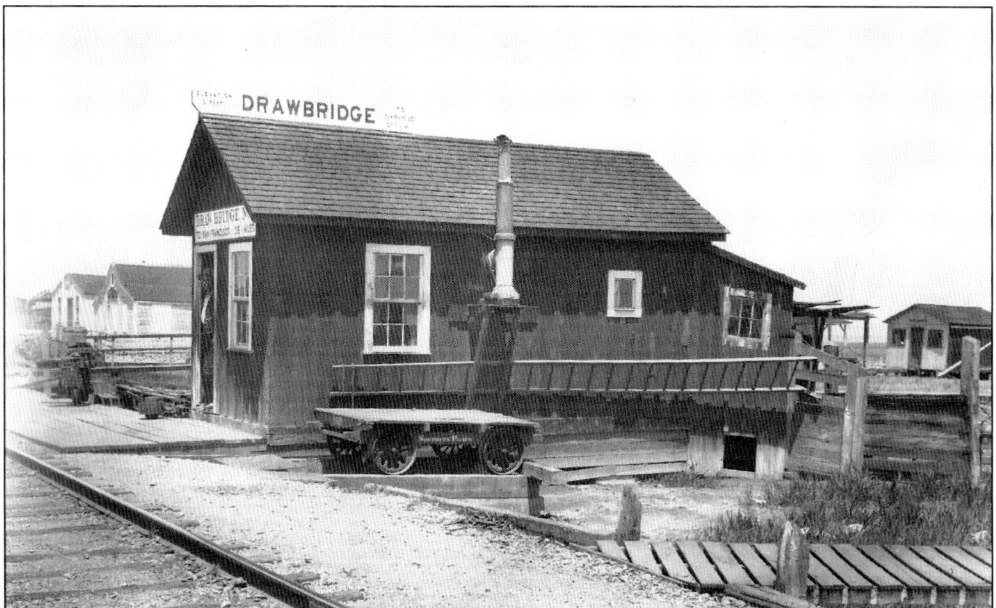


The Drawbridge Depot is seen here in 1912. The first structure in Drawbridge was a two-room cabin the railroad built for the bridge tender, George Mandershied. His job was to open the bridge with a hand crank when a boat blew its whistle for passage. The SPCRR became a tremendous money-maker because of the track. (Courtesy William G. Wullenjohn Sr. Collection, Union Pacific Museum.)

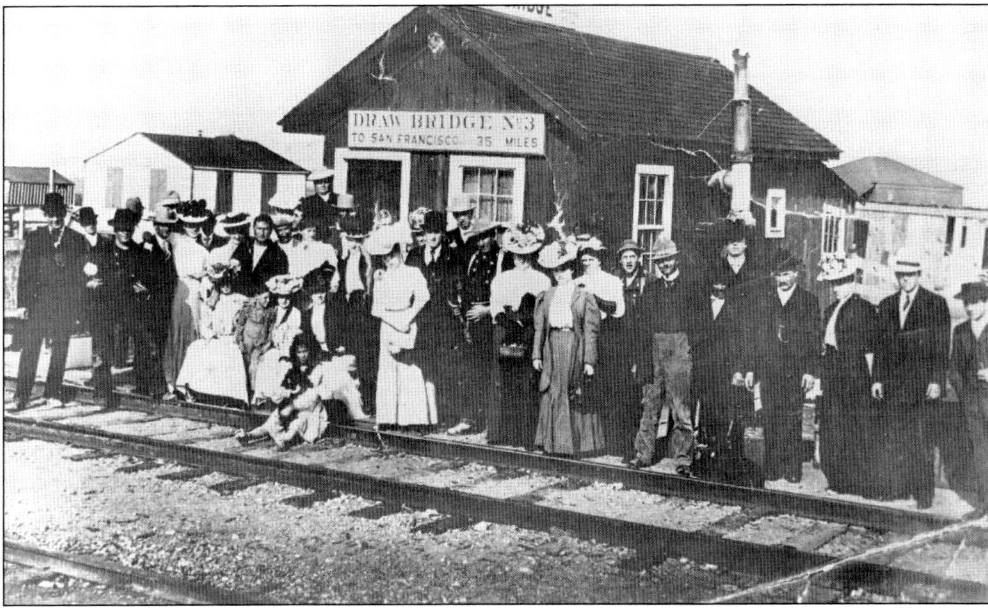


Residents and visitors wait for the train in Drawbridge in 1904. Typically, visitors were middle or upper class, such as doctors, dentists, store owners, and businessmen. (DE.)

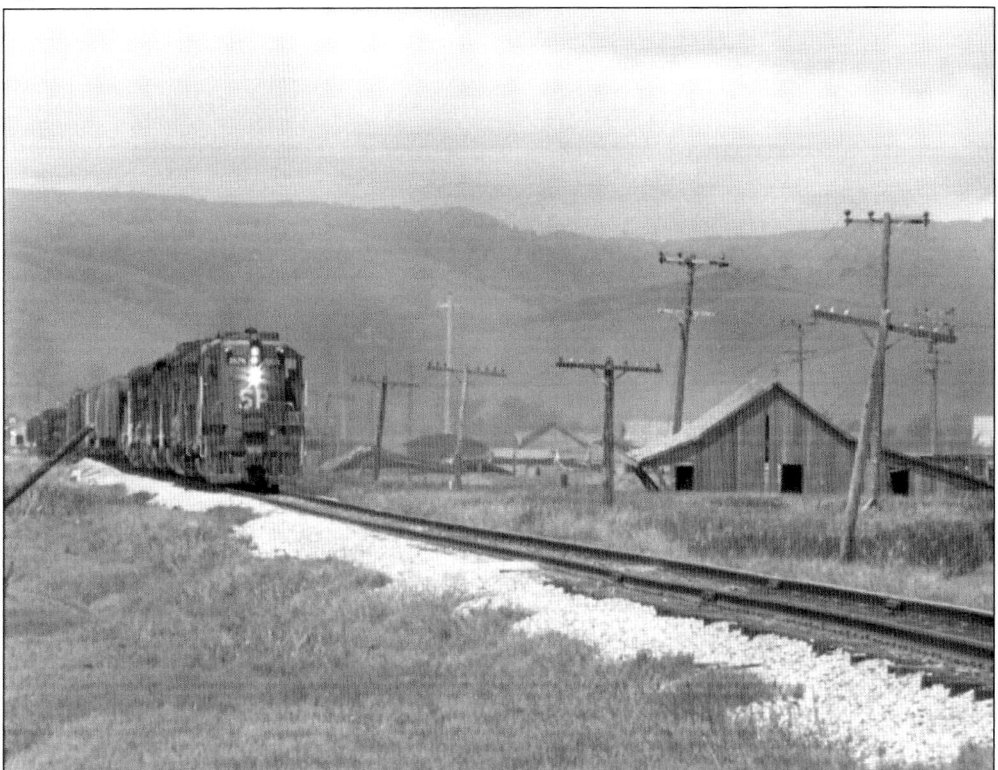

The Pacific Coast Railroad had two trains that stopped on Sundays, No. 3 going south and No. 36 going north. Here, Southern Pacific No. 9155 heads south toward San Jose. When the line was leased to Southern Pacific in 1887, it was the most profitable railroad per mile in California. (DE.)

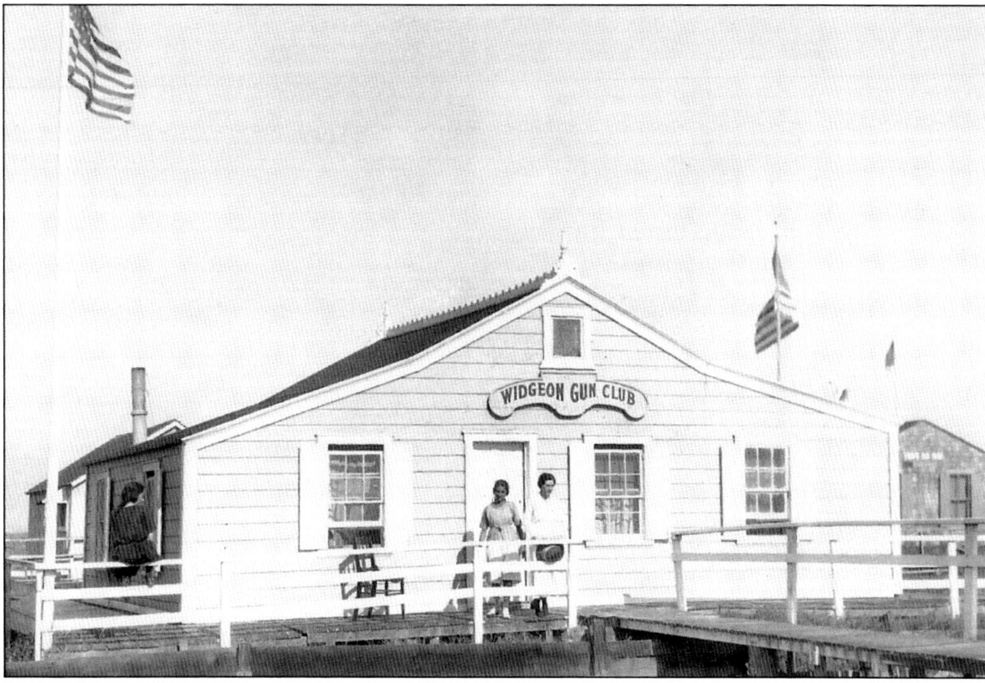


Great flocks of ducks attracted hordes of duck hunters to Drawbridge, so cabins and blinds were built on the island before permanent houses developed. The exciting atmosphere drew up to 2,000 people with their guns, dogs, whiskey, and weekend supplies. The Widgeon Gun Club is seen here after it was remodeled in the 1920s. Some property owners chose humorous names for their gun clubs, such as the Sprig, the Tule, the Lomida, the Clambake, Twilight, Recreation, Sorry, and Don't Worry. (DE.)

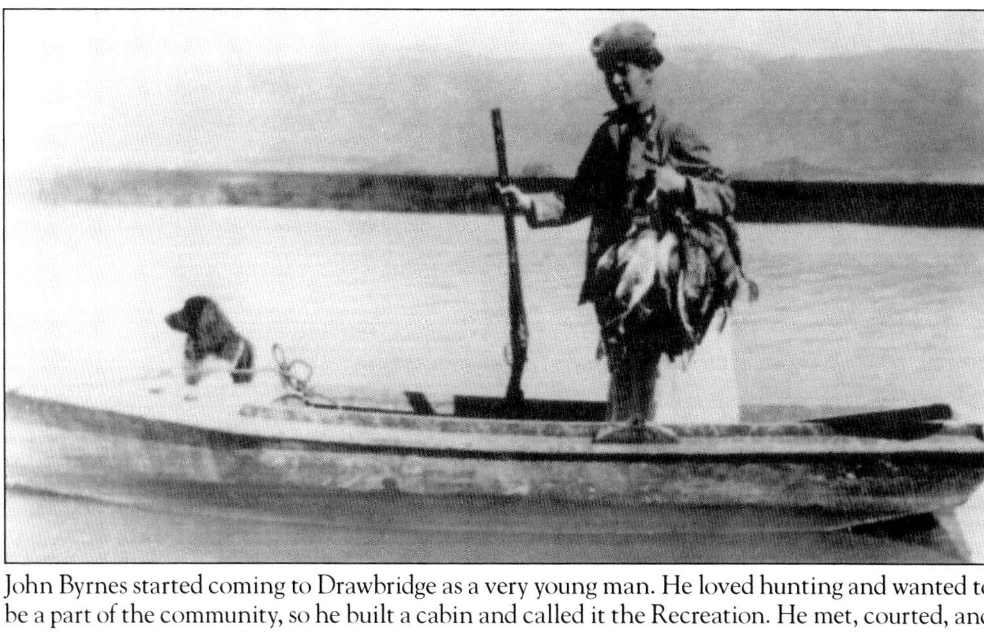

John Byrnes started coming to Drawbridge as a very young man. He loved hunting and wanted to be a part of the community, so he built a cabin and called it the Recreation. He met, courted, and married Ann Deasy and they spent their honeymoon in the cabin and many a day in Drawbridge. Not to be outdone by her husband, Ann, seen here, was a great duck hunter as well. (DE.)

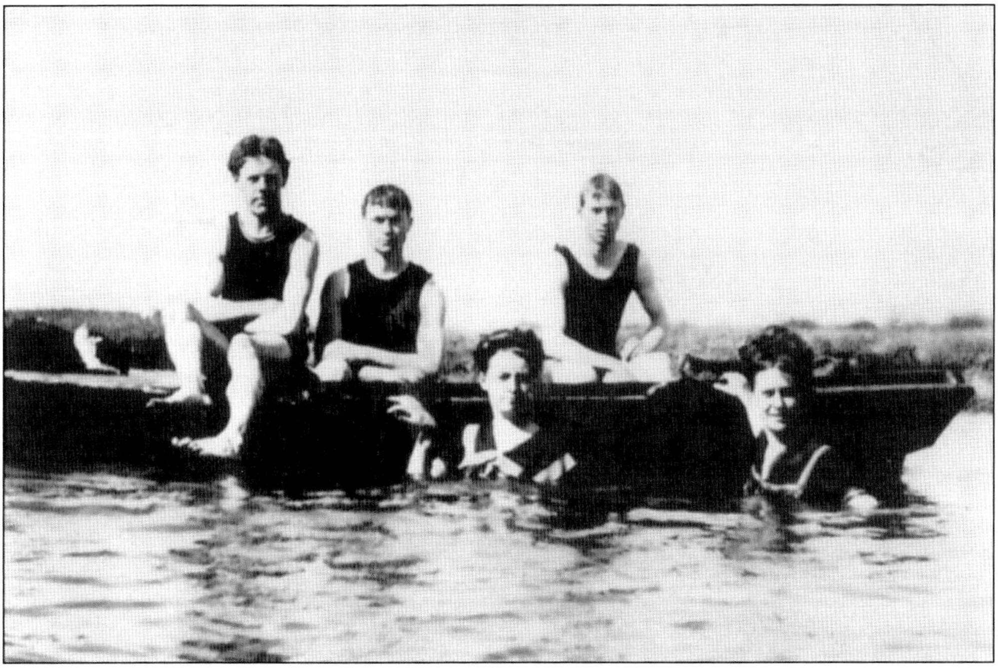

Swimming was a popular pastime in Drawbridge. Here, John (far left) and Ann Byrnes (far right) and their friends show the swimming fashions of the time. In the late 1930s, the marshland area in the south bay began to change, and swimming was no longer possible. (DE.)

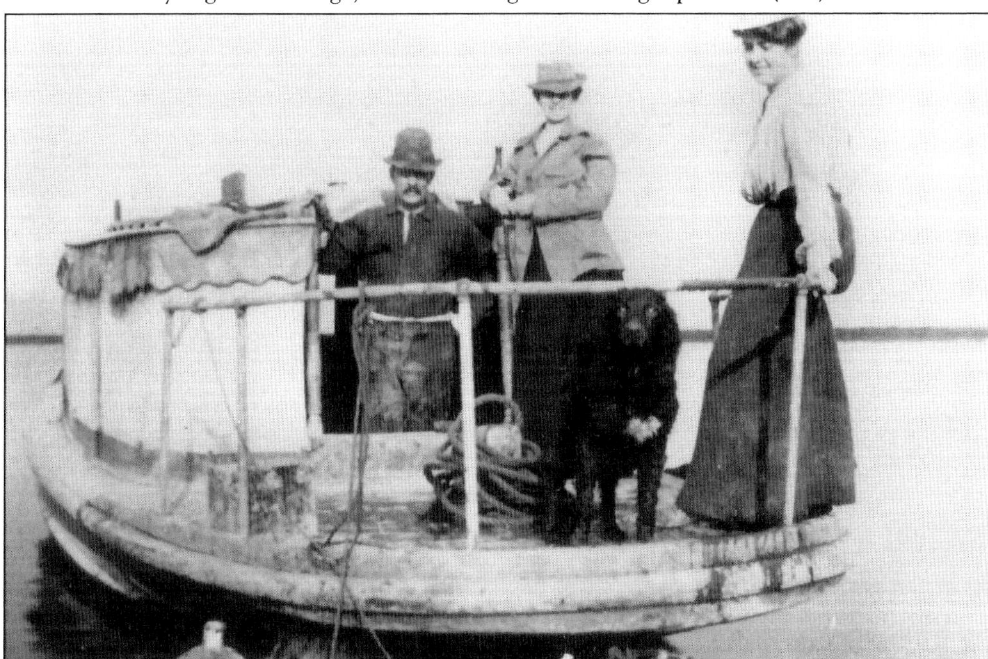

Almost everyone in Drawbridge had a boat, either a motorboat or a scull sailing boat. Residents used the railroad track as the main road to transport themselves and heavy loads around town. Ann Byrnes (far right) is seen here with Mr. and Mrs. Smith on the Smiths' powerboat in the 1920s. (DE.)

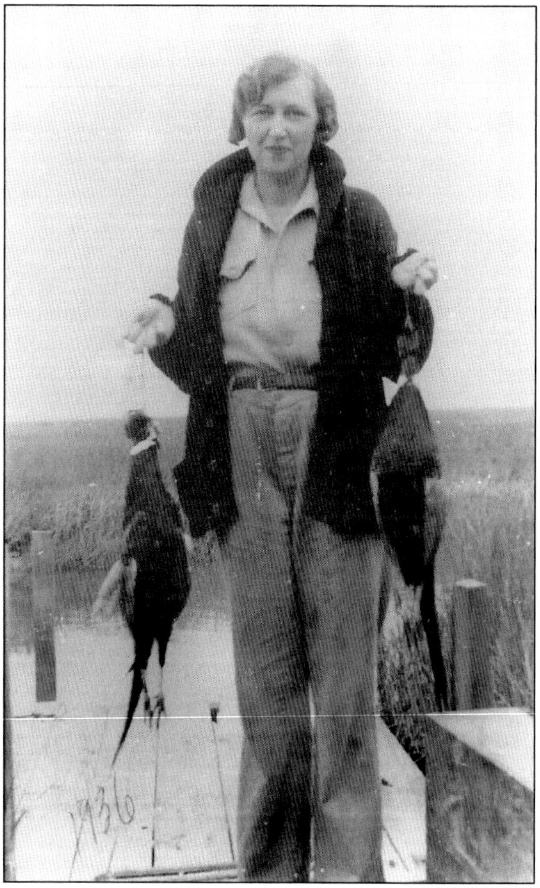


Hunting and fishing continued at Drawbridge through the 1960s. Here, a woman shows off two pheasants she has caught. (DE.)

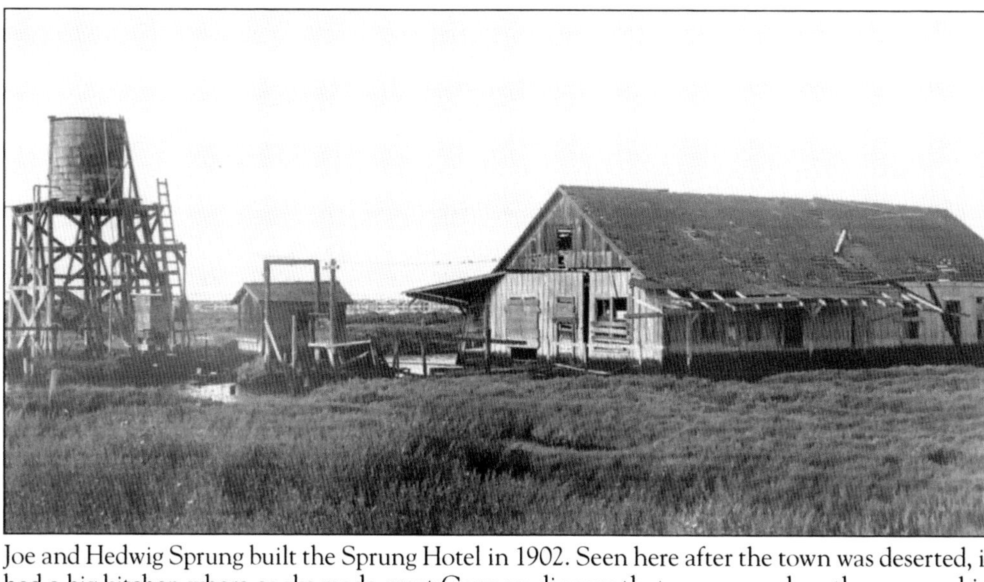

Joe and Hedwig Sprung built the Sprung Hotel in 1902. Seen here after the town was deserted, it had a big kitchen where cooks made great German dinners that were served on the screened-in front porch. The hotel was a large, impressive building but had small bedrooms. The water tower on the left was built over the well, which brought water to the hotel. (JH.)

This unidentified boy is ready to dive into the cool waters. By 1926, Drawbridge was a town with 90 cabins and five passenger trains a day. Electricity was brought to the island in 1933, and there were soon 80 subscriptions. The children of Drawbridge went to school in Alviso by train, boat, bicycle, or just by walking along the tracks. (DE.)

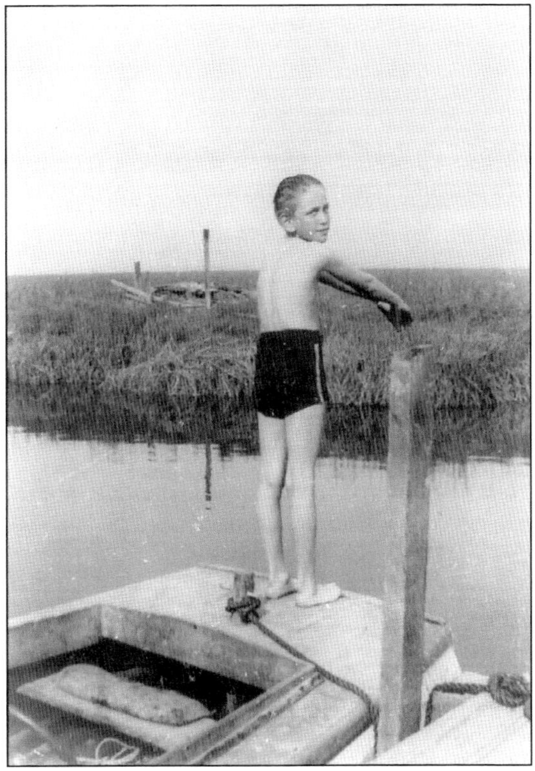

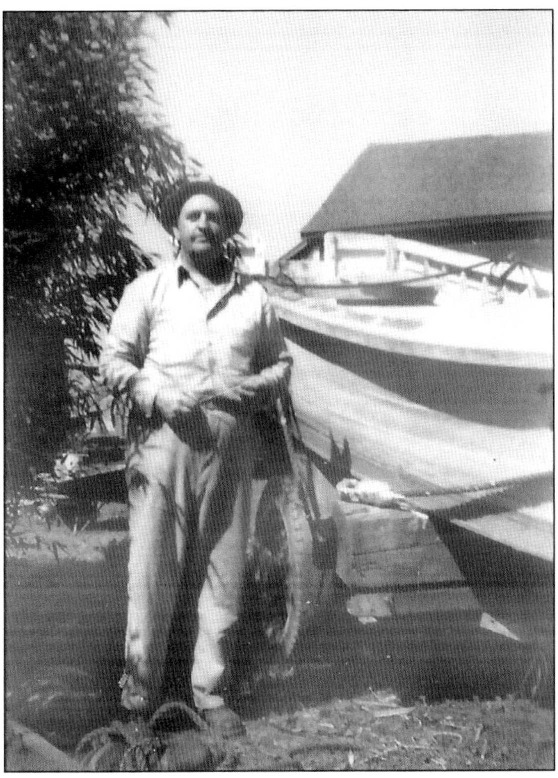

In this 1945 photograph, Lawrence O. Bunting Sr. stands beside his boat, which was built in 1938 by Drawbridge resident Bill Simpson. The boat was made of oak and constructed with no nails—only screws. (Courtesy B.J. Bunting.)

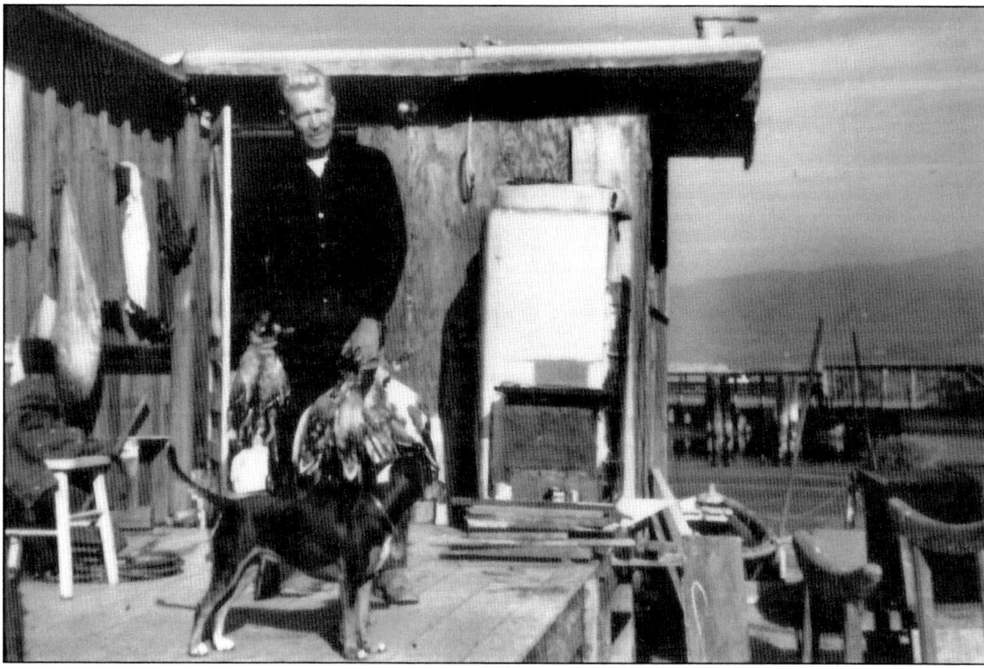

Water shortage, pollution, and the expansion of the Arden Salt Company changed the area. The tides, which kept the waterways clean and open, were closed out, and after a time, trains no longer stopped on a regular basis. In 1970, the railroad station was torn down. By 1976, there were only 25 houses and one taxed resident, Charlie Luce, who is seen here in front of his cabin with his dog, Quincy, and two hands full of ducks. Luce left Station Island in 1979 after he sold his property to the US Fish and Wildlife Service. (DE.)

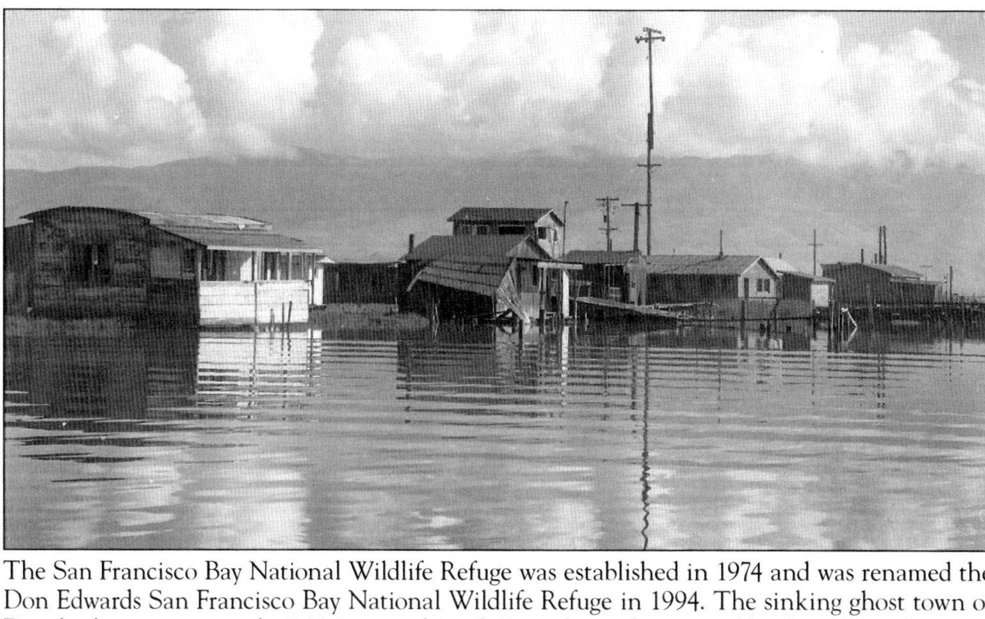

The San Francisco Bay National Wildlife Refuge was established in 1974 and was renamed the Don Edwards San Francisco Bay National Wildlife Refuge in 1994. The sinking ghost town of Drawbridge now sits amidst 9,000 acres of South Bay salt ponds acquired by the refuge. The town survived for 103 years, from 1876 to 1979, and trains still pass through the area where the pickle weed and marsh grasses now thrive. (JH.)

# Six

# OUR FERTILE FARMLAND

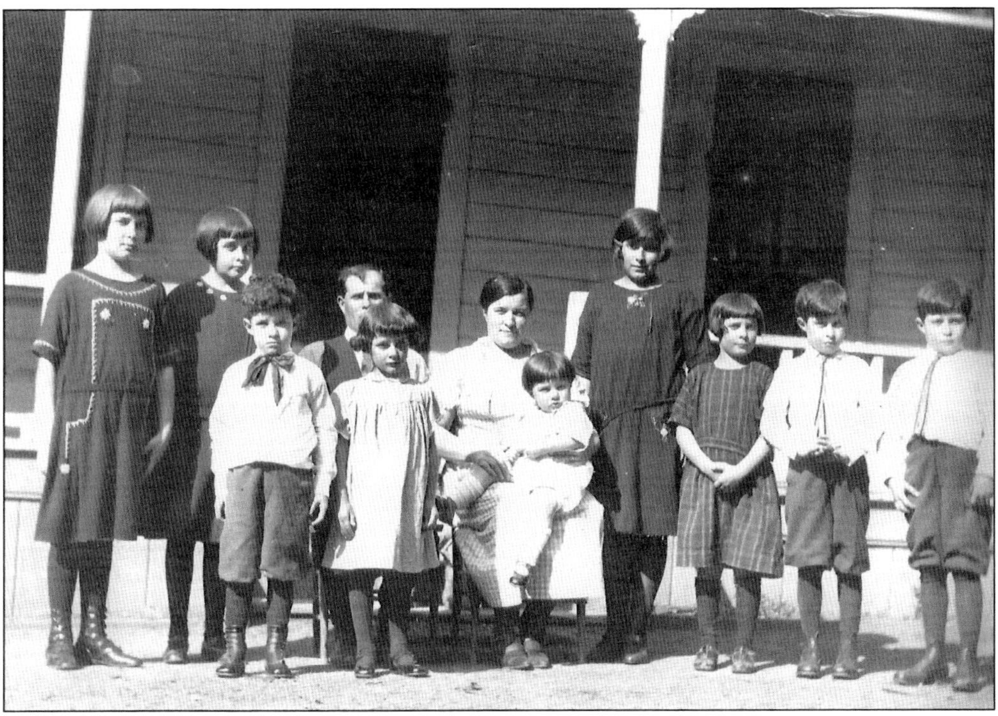

Joaquin "Jack" and Adelaide Goularte, from Pico and Faial, respectively, in the Azores, moved to Warm Springs in 1913. Jack worked as a foreman for Henry Curtner and later for Curtner's son, Arthur. The Goulartes raised a family of 15 children here. In 1927, Arthur Curtner sold the Silva property to Goularte. As it was very good soil, Jack planted orchards of prunes, apricots, and walnuts on most of the 50 acres, leaving room for a large vegetable garden and pasture land for the animals, including horses and a few cows. The Goularte family posed for this photograph in 1924 in front of their home, the former Curtner home. From left to right, they are Eleanor, Dorothy, Leland, Leona, Jack, Adelaide (holding baby Joe), Belmida, Esther, Jack, and George in 1924. (SVM.)

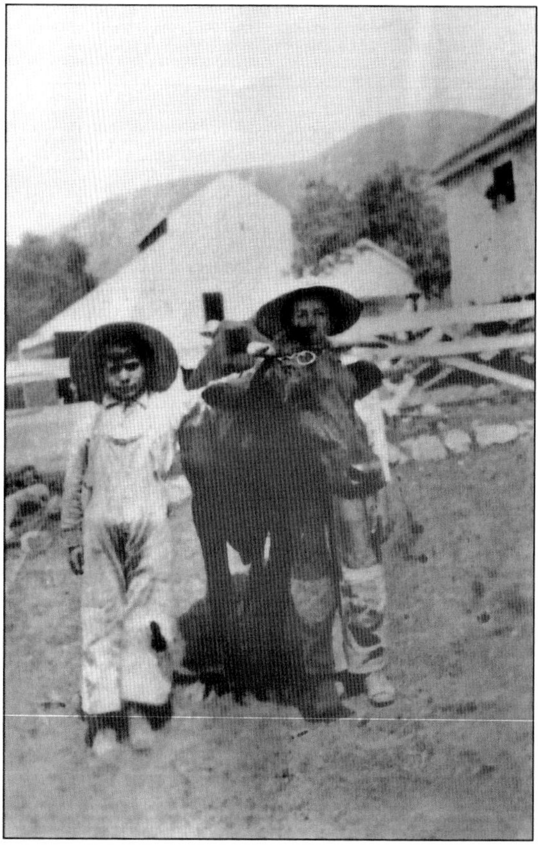

Manuel F. Silva operated a dairy on the Higuera Adobe property. The property was owned by the Curtner family at the time, and was near the "high road" to San Jose, just east of what is now Mission Boulevard. The Silva children are seen here with a calf on the family dairy about 1910, with the hay barn and other dairy buildings in the background.

The Goulartes used their workhorses (below) to prepare the pastures for hay and other food crops. The white horse was named Bess. The remnants of the Silva family milk-processing building are to the left of the horses, and the slaughterhouse is behind them to the right.

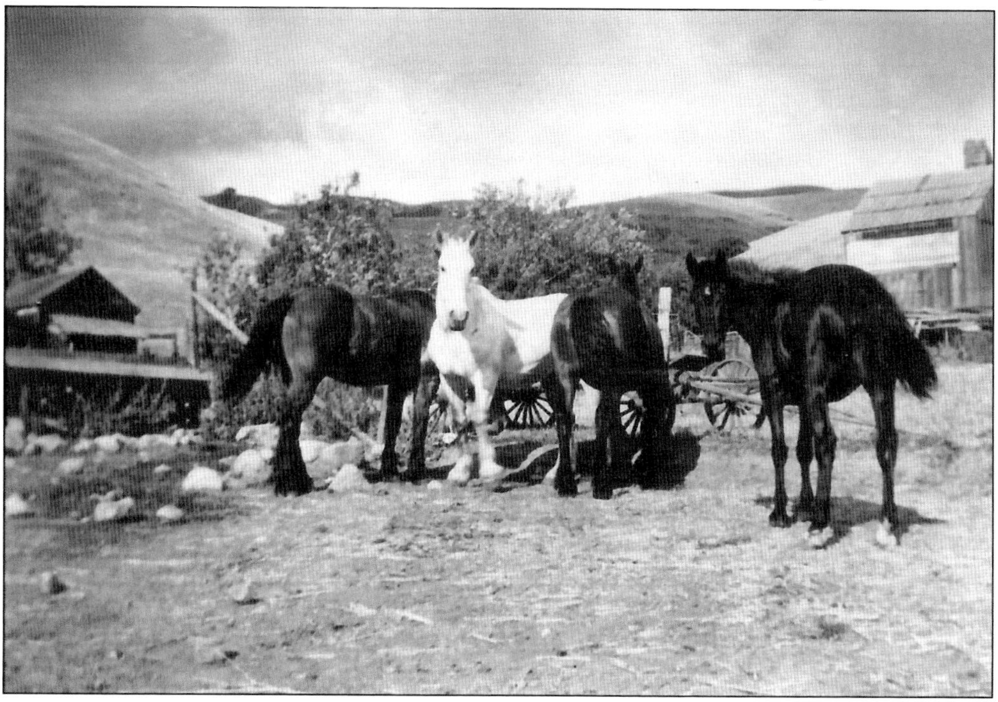

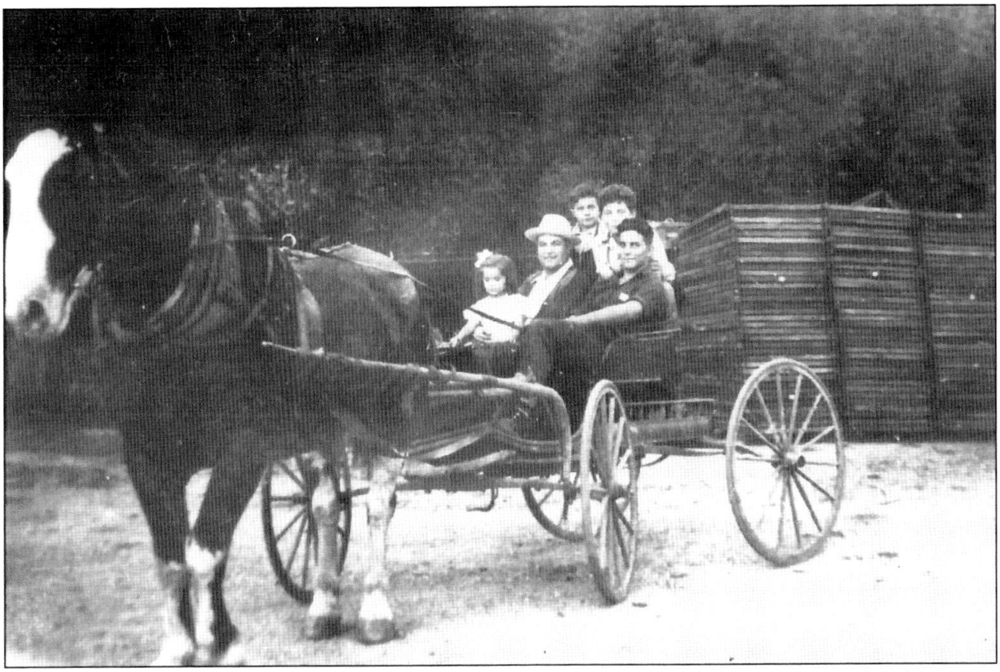

Goularte family members are seen here in a buggy on their property off of Curtner Road in the 1940s. They are, from left to right, Diane and Manuel Caldera and Arthur, Dan, and Tony Goularte.

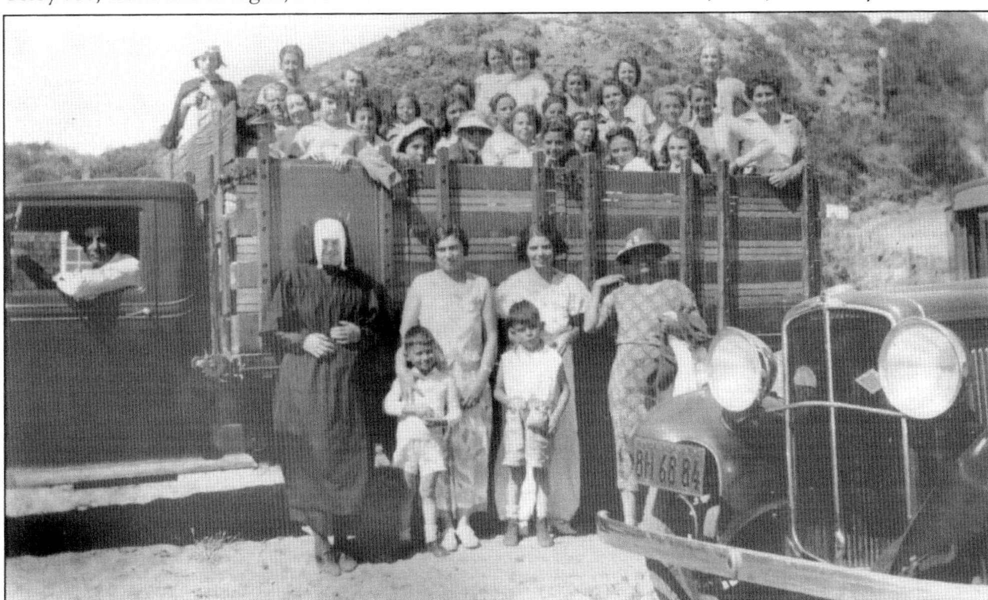


The Sisters of the Holy Names of Jesus and Mary purchased the Stanford Ranch from Lawrence A. Kelley in 1927. They conducted summer camps for girls there from 1933 to 1935 to defray property expenses. Here, Joe Maciel drives campers to Half Moon Bay. Next to the unidentified Sister in front are, from left to right, Leonard Perry; his mother, Ida; Manuel Maciel; his sister Anita; and their mother, Annie Maciel. In the back of the truck above the arm hanging down on the left is Evelyn Rose. To the right of her, wearing the white hat, is Isabel Maciel. The Maciel and Perry families were caretakers on the property. (SVM.)

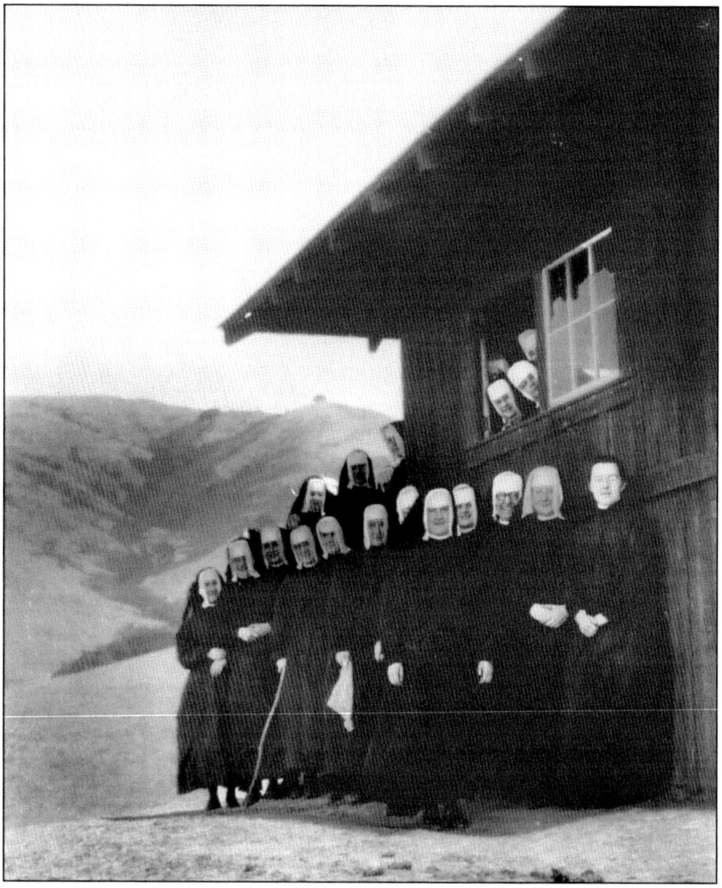

The ranch was reserved as a vacation center for Sisters based in California from 1936 to 1938. Practically every Sister was allowed to spend two weeks during her vacation at the ranch, which helped fill spiritual and physical needs. About 60 Sisters could be accommodated at one time. This hiking group of Sisters is seen here with the Mission hills in the background around 1940. (Archives of the Sisters of the Holy Names of Jesus and Mary, US–Ontario Province.)

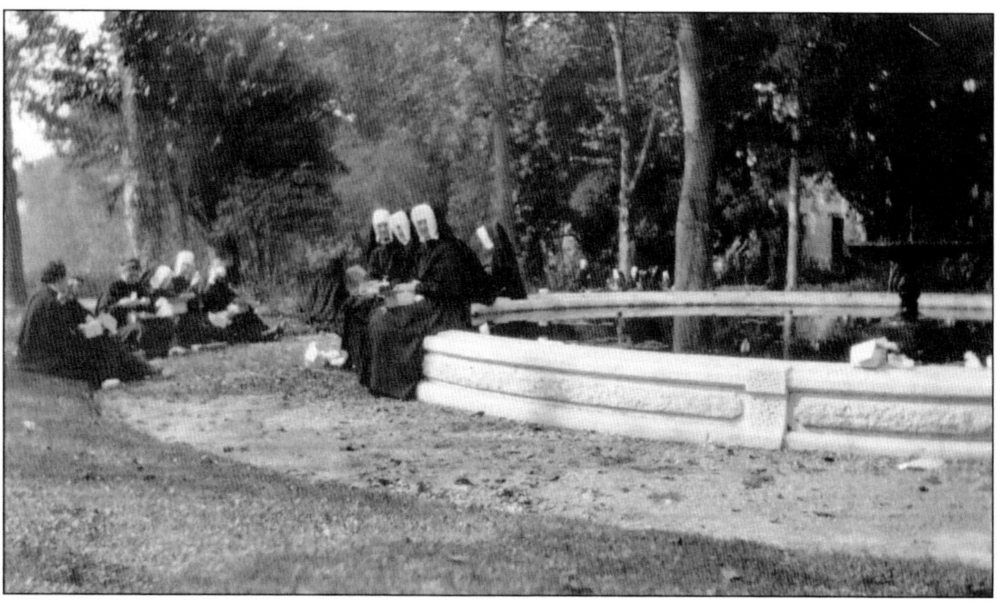

Here, the Sisters have a picnic lunch at the famous fountain at the Warm Springs Ranch around 1940. (Archives of the Sisters of the Holy Names of Jesus and Mary, US–Ontario Province.)

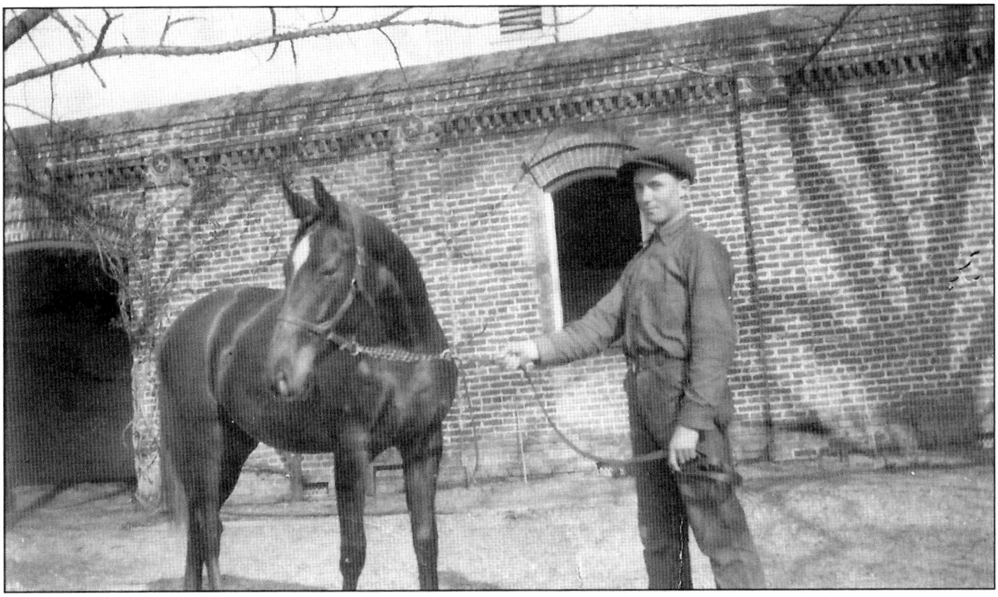

Above, Joe Briar holds the reins of a horse in front of the old Stanford winery building. Briar was a member of the Warm Springs baseball team in 1916 and was described as the Joe DiMaggio of the team; he could hit a baseball out of sight. (HA.)

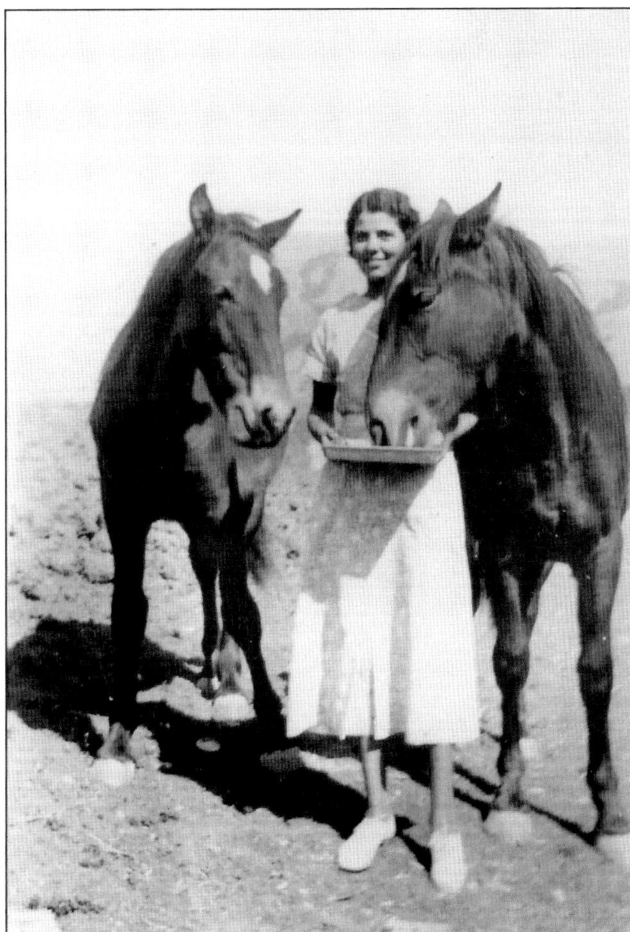

Anita Maciel, the daughter of Joe E. and Annie Maciel, feeds the family horses on the former Stanford Ranch in 1935, when it was owned by the Sisters of the Holy Names. Anita lived her entire life in Warm Springs and married Tony DeValle in 1937. They had one son, Gregory. (SVM.)

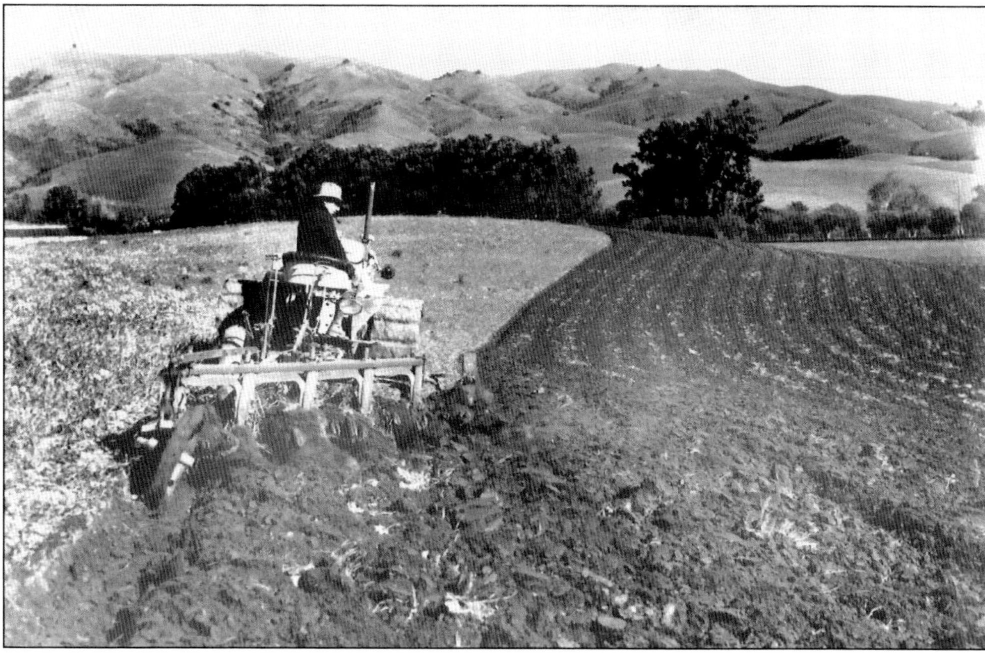

Joe Maciel came to the United States from Faial, in the Azores, in 1913. He worked for four consecutive owners of the ranch property: the Stanfords, the Kelleys, the Sisters of the Holy Names, and the Goossens. Here, he plows land around 1940. Maciel partnered with his brothers-in-law Joe and Tony Vargas to sharecrop the land from 1928 to 1940. (SVM.)

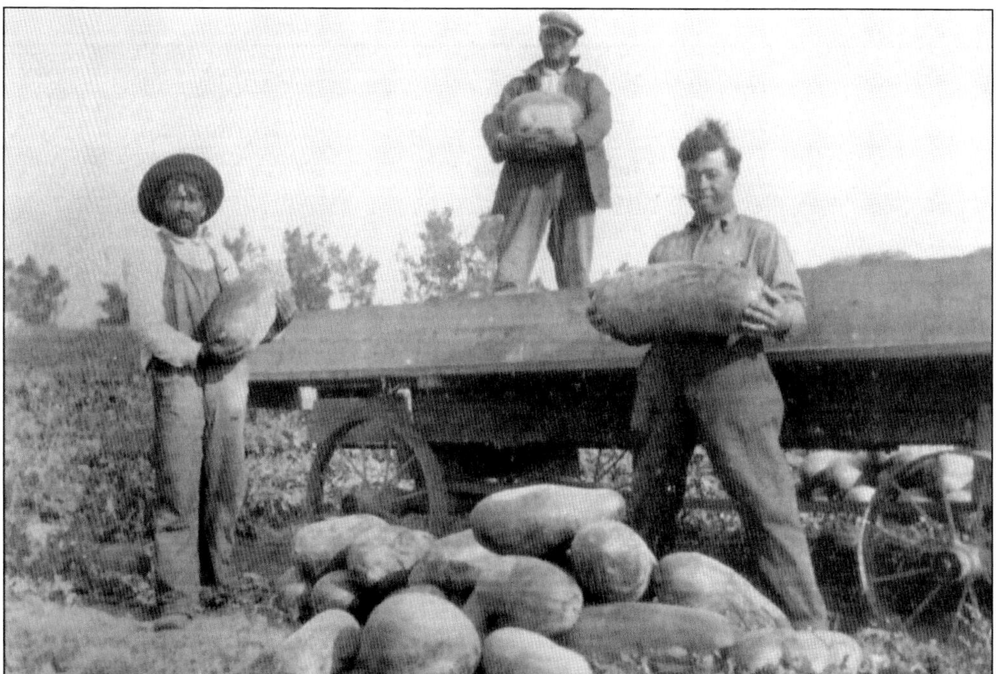

Joseph K. Dutre (right) holds a giant watermelon grown in Warm Springs as they are loaded on the wagon to be shipped to San Francisco and other markets. (SVM.)

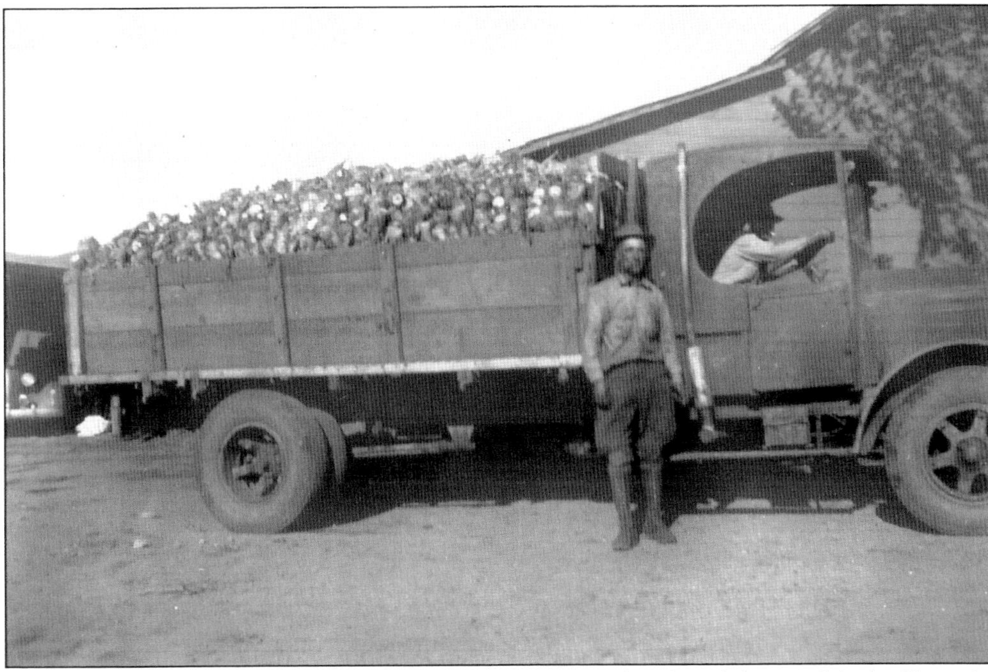

Joe Maciel stands by his crop of sugar beets in 1942 on the ranch. This Kleiber truck had a Chevrolet engine with a selective sliding transmission and solid wheels. When the truck delivered sugar beets to the Holly Sugar Company in Alvarado, it dumped its cargo sideways. (SVM.)

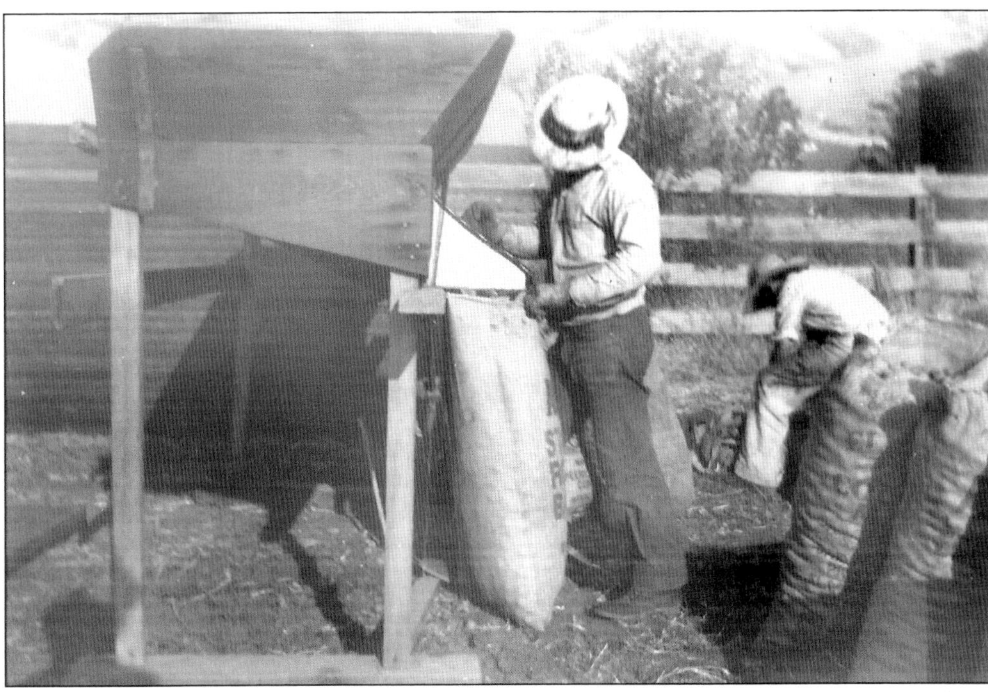

Workers harvest the walnut crop on the ranch for Joe Maciel. Ed Andrade is bagging the walnuts on the left, and Joe's son, Tony Maciel, is sacking the walnuts on the right. (SVM.)

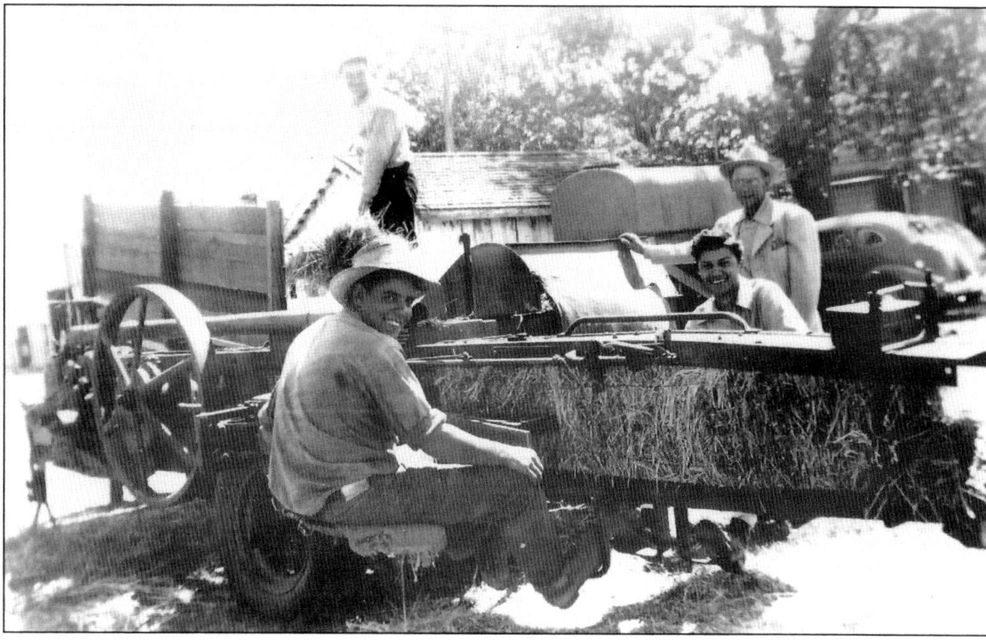

Hay harvesting became much easier for Joe Maciel and his family with the invention of the automated hay press. Here, in 1939, Ernest Vargas (standing up on machine) feeds the hay in while Manuel Maciel (left) and Leonard Perry sit to tie wire. Joe Maciel's brother-in-law Joe Vargas (far right, in hat) watches them work. (SVM.)

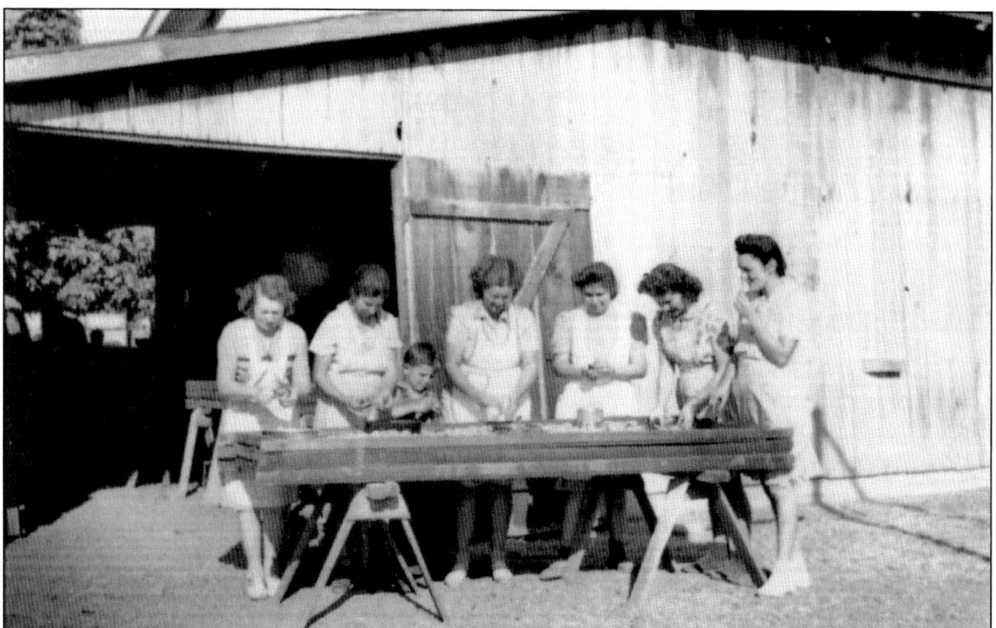

Families and friends worked together to help cut apricots, locally called "cots." Here, in 1942, Rosalind Smith (third from right), Lillian Sarmento Rodrigues (far right), and other unidentified women work in front of the barn of Minnie (Vargas) Sarmento Souza. (SVM.)

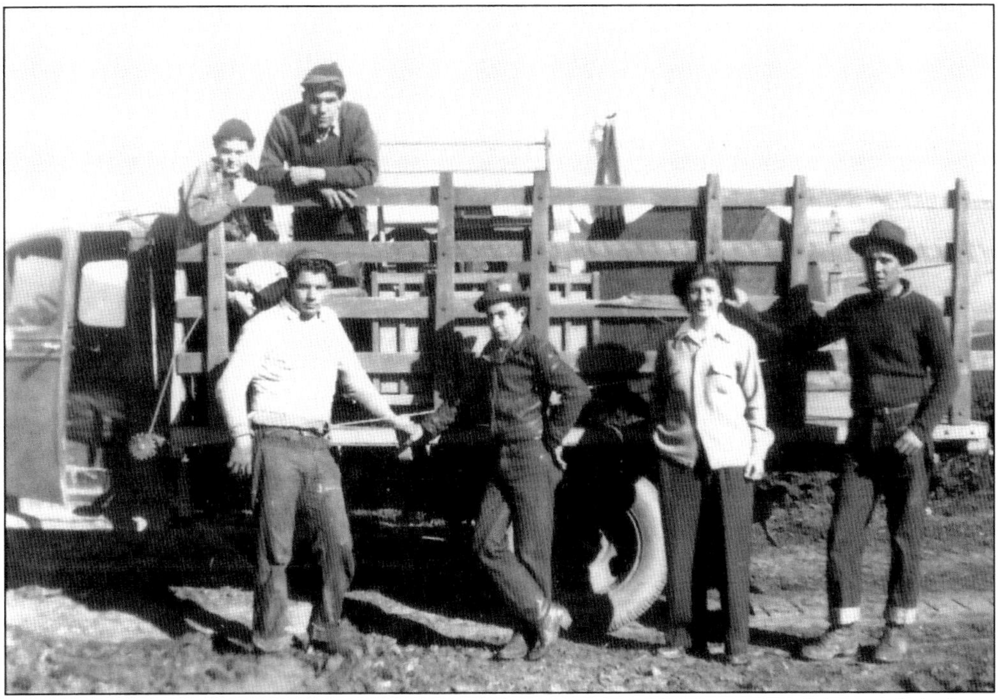

These farmers pose for a photograph in December 1945. Standing on top of the truck bed are Bob (left) and Donald Brazil, and standing on the ground are, from left to right, Manuel Maciel; Joe Souza; Florence Brazil, Bob and Donald's mother; and Tony Maciel. (SVM.)

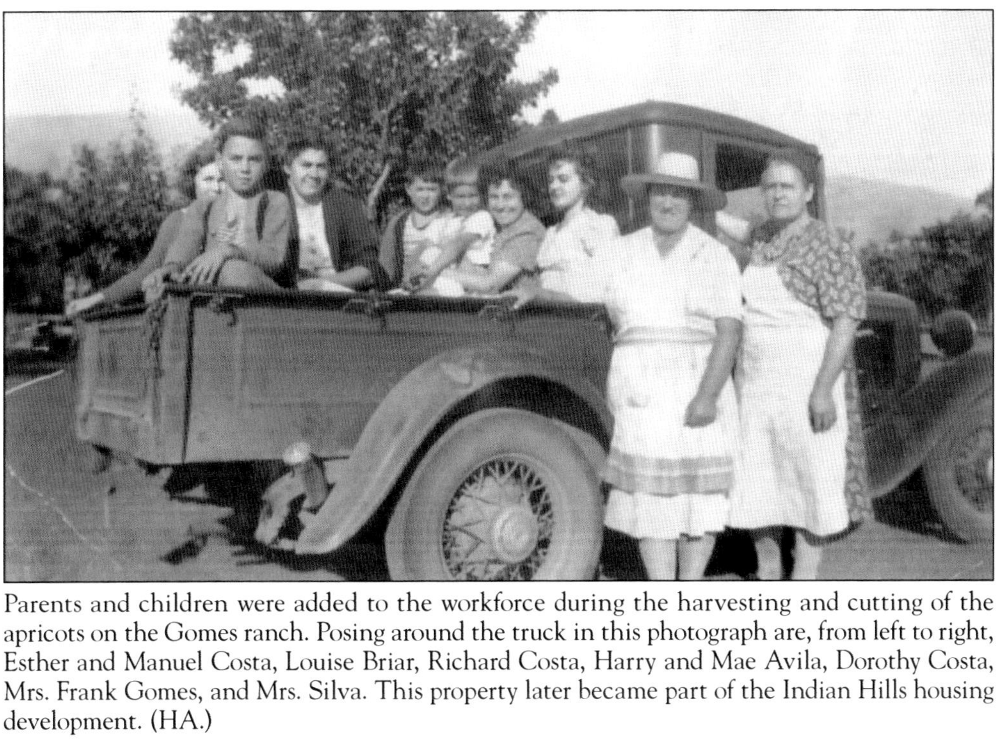

Parents and children were added to the workforce during the harvesting and cutting of the apricots on the Gomes ranch. Posing around the truck in this photograph are, from left to right, Esther and Manuel Costa, Louise Briar, Richard Costa, Harry and Mae Avila, Dorothy Costa, Mrs. Frank Gomes, and Mrs. Silva. This property later became part of the Indian Hills housing development. (HA.)

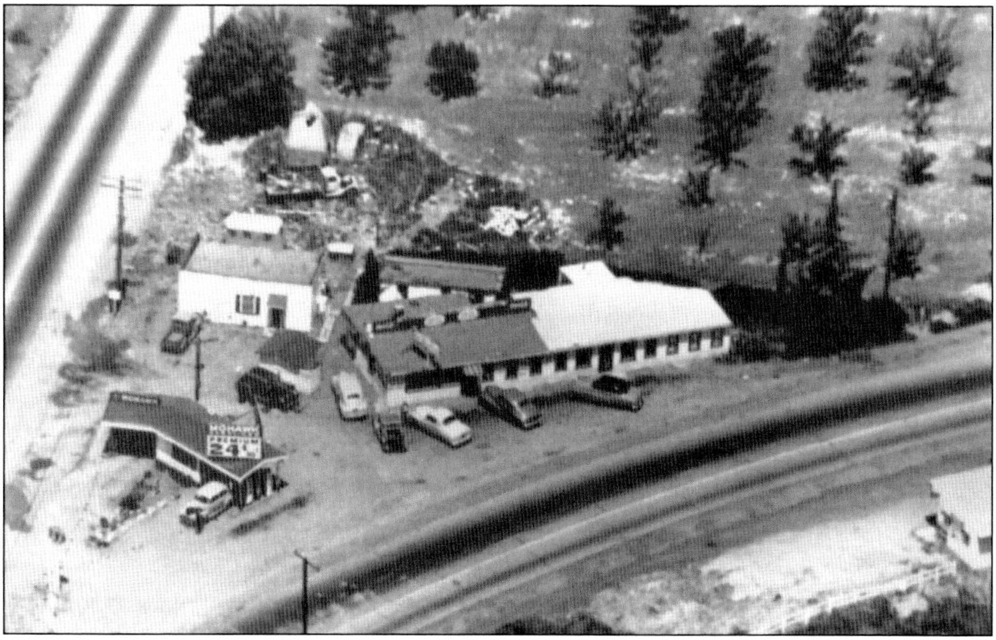

Frank Vargas II and his father, Frank, sharecrop farmed for Henry Curtner until about 1918, when they saved enough money to purchase 28 acres of land bordered by what was called the "Y": Highway 17 toward Irvington, Highway 21 toward Mission San Jose, and Brown Road. They planted apricot and prune orchards and a small vineyard. In the mid-1920s, a speculator from New York approached the Vargas family and offered to build a motel, a gas station, and a restaurant at the Y and lease it back. They agreed, and the Junction Inn complex (above) was built. In 1954, when the road was widened, the Junction Inn was torn down. Below, around 1935, a motorist stopped and asked if he could take a photograph of Frank Vargas II and his son, Frank Vargas III, plowing peas between the prune trees on their property. A few weeks later, the man returned with this photograph. (Both, courtesy Frank Vargas.)

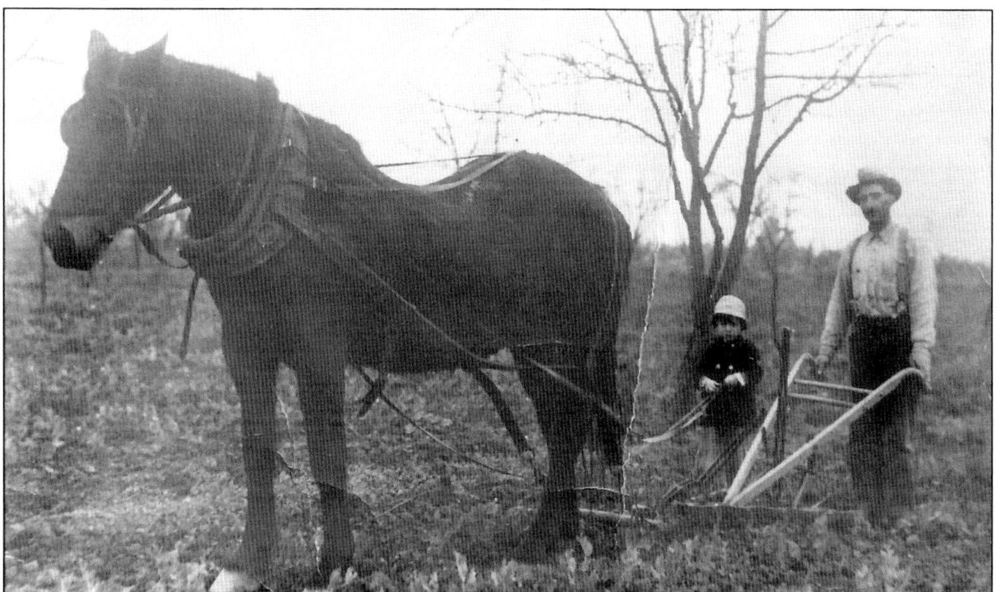

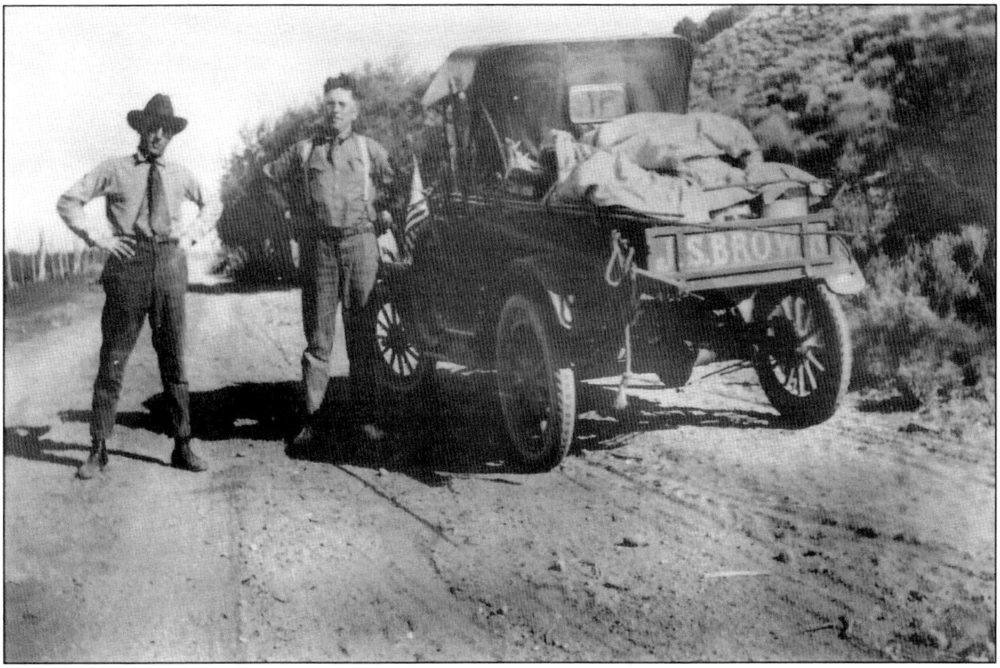

Standing next to Joe S. Brown's delivery truck are local residents Edwin Sarmento (left) and Fred Breitweiser. The truck was sometimes used to deliver groceries and other products to customers. (TK.)

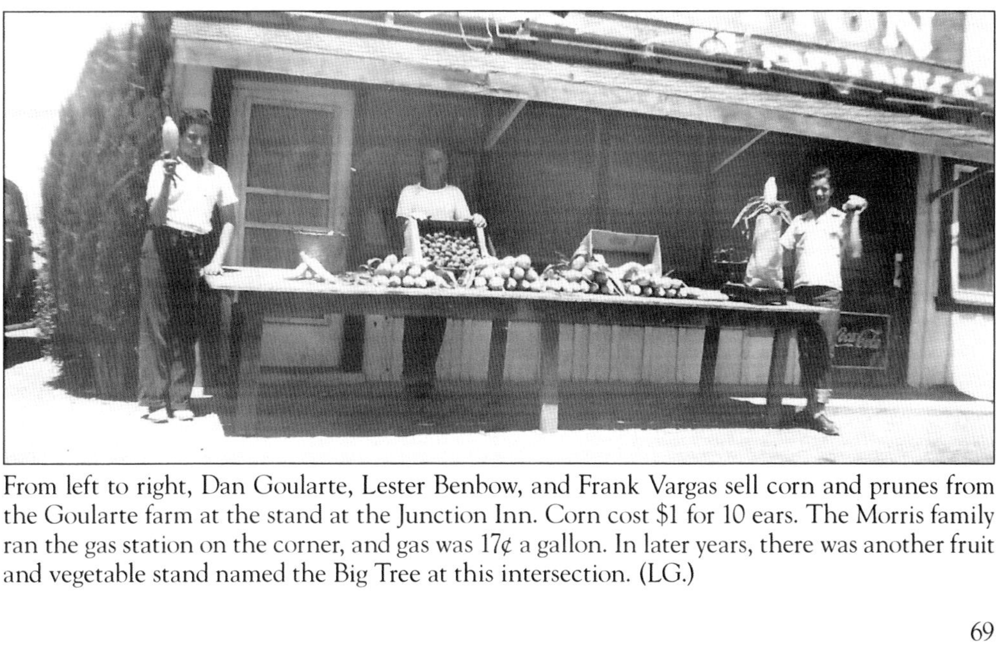


From left to right, Dan Goularte, Lester Benbow, and Frank Vargas sell corn and prunes from the Goularte farm at the stand at the Junction Inn. Corn cost $1 for 10 ears. The Morris family ran the gas station on the corner, and gas was 17¢ a gallon. In later years, there was another fruit and vegetable stand named the Big Tree at this intersection. (LG.)

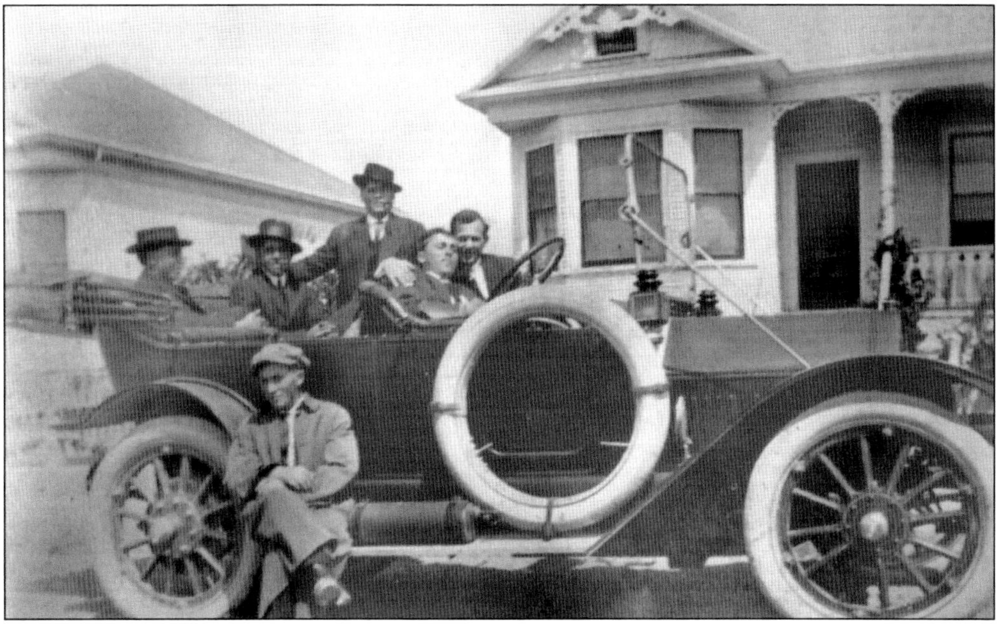

This Great Western 40 touring car, seen here in 1913, belonged to Joe Dutre, the owner of Liberty Garage, who added the doors on the front and the lanterns by the windshield. The headlights were run by gas, and the gas container is on the running board, where Jack Gomes sits. In the car are, from left to right, an unidentified man, Joseph Dutre, Jack Pacheco, Frank Gomes, and Joe S. Brown. (SVM.)

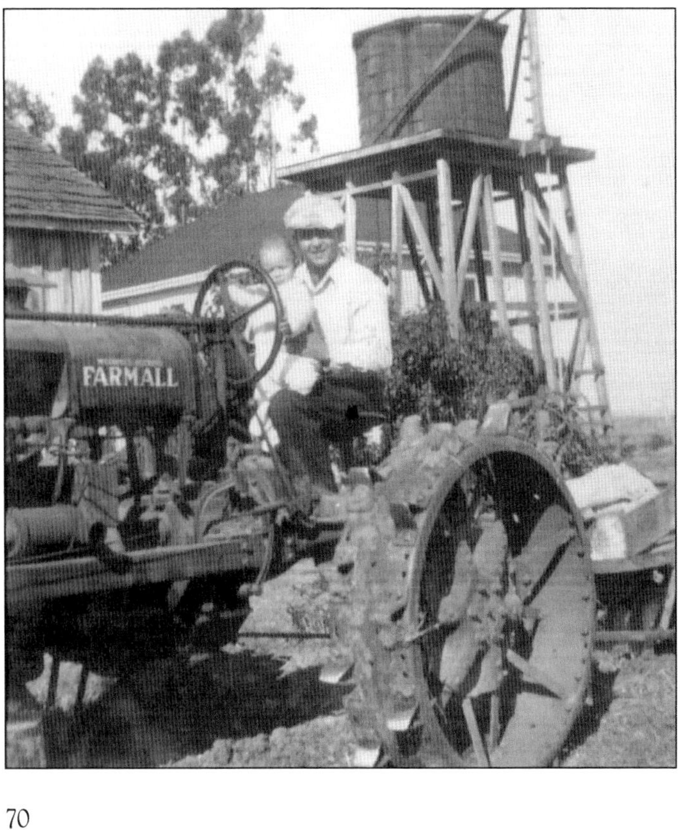


Harry M. Avila and his son, Harry, pose for this photograph on a Farmall tractor on the Alvernaz farm about 1939. In the winter or spring, they would put cleats on the wheels that would be removed in the summer. The tank house is in the background, and the granary is next to it on the left. (HA.)

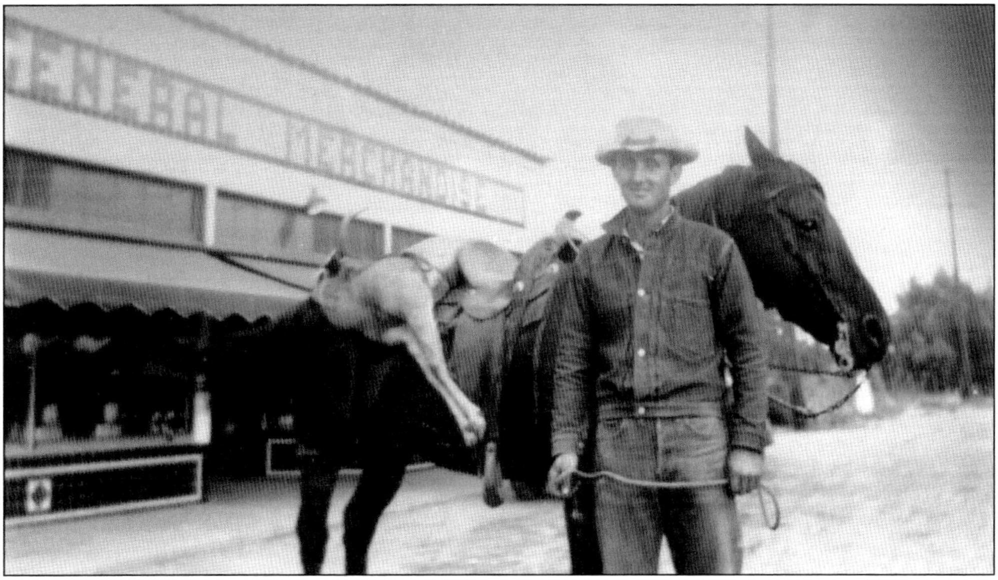

Joe Sarmento poses with his horse and a buck that he shot on a hunting expedition in the Warm Springs hills. He is standing on Main Street in front of the recently remodeled Warm Springs Store about 1935. (SVM.)

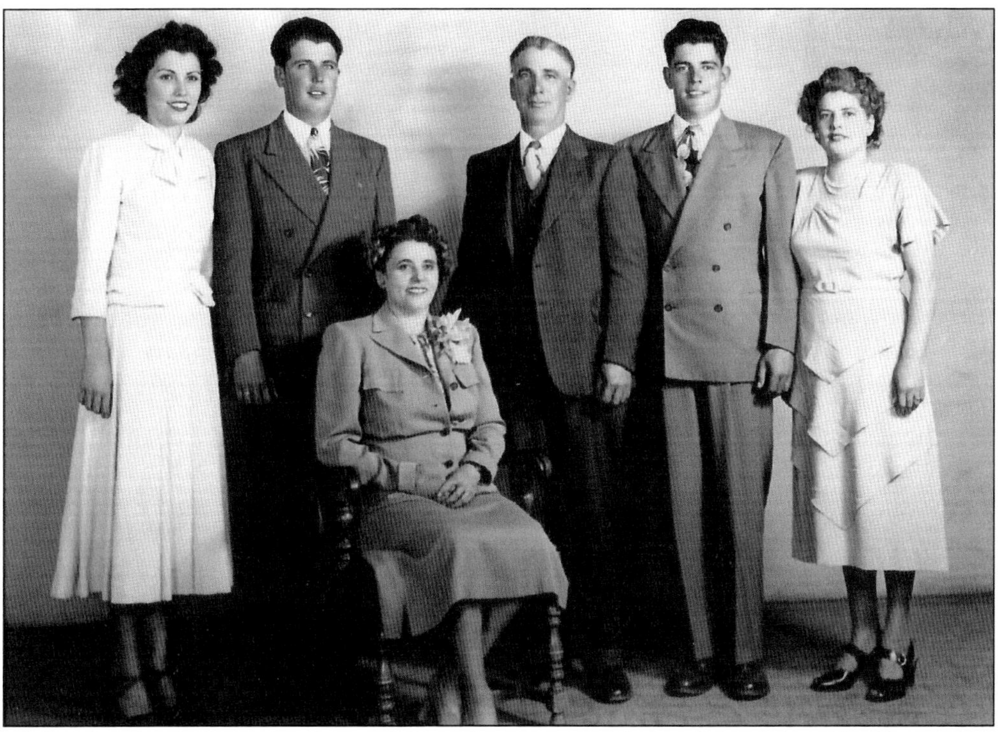

The Maciel family farmed in Warm Springs from 1916 until 1945. After years of hard work, Joe and Annie Maciel bought 10 acres of land, which is now the Franciscan Shopping Center. They farmed walnuts, apricots, and prunes until 1928 and then sharecropped farmland owned by the Sisters of the Holy Names. They are, from left to right, Isabel, Tony, Annie (seated), Joe, Manuel, and Anita. (SVM.)

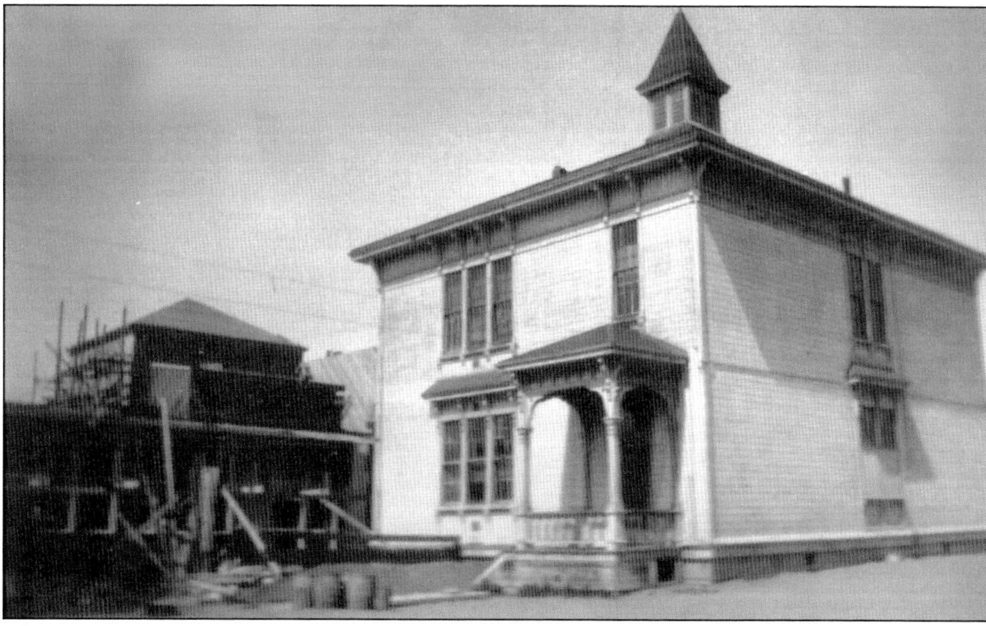

The new Warm Springs School is being built in the background behind the old school. The new school was built partially with Works Progress Administration (WPA) funds in 1936.

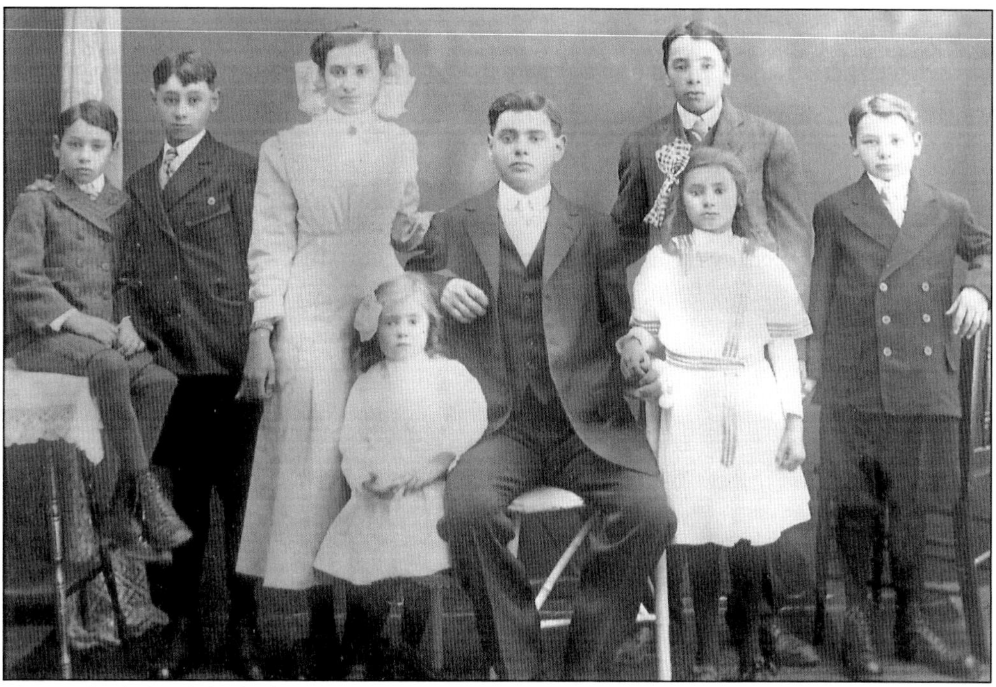

The Andrade family had a farm and a prune-processing center that they shared with their neighbors on Curtner Road. The prunes were dipped in boiling lye water and then moved to trays and put out in the sun to dry. They had to be turned over each day until they were dry enough to sack. Later, they were sold to a prune association in San Jose. Eight of the 10 Andrade children are pictured here. From left to right, they are (first row) Isabel and Mildred; (second row) Ernest, Manuel, Minnie, Joe, John, and William. Alfred and Edward are not pictured.

From left to right, Harry Avila and Richie, Manuel, and Esther Costa wait for the Warm Springs school bus on Landing Road in 1943. Joe Costa's dairy was at the "Y" of Landing Road and the San Jose–Oakland Road. The Alvernaz farm, where Avila lived, was to the south on Landing Road. (HA.)

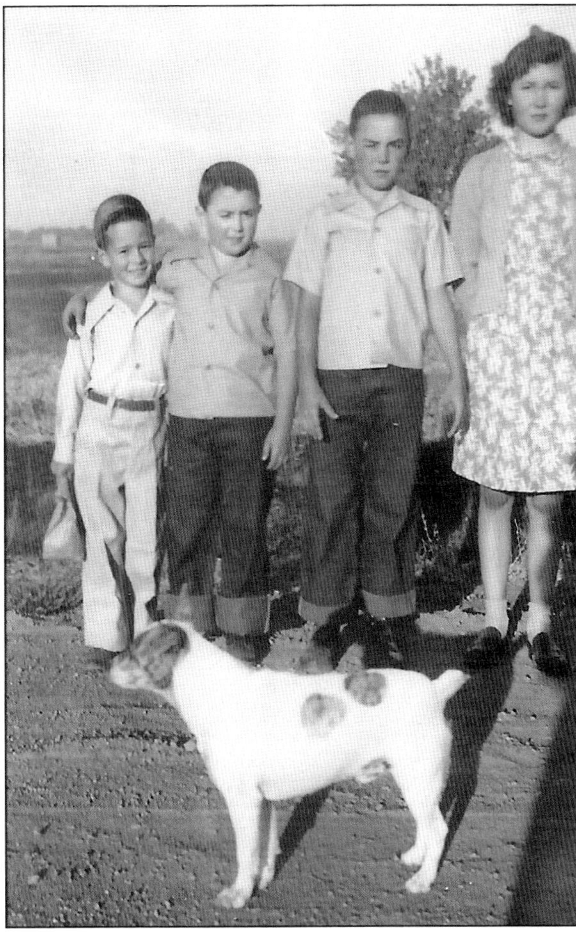

Warm Springs remained a small town and the school had a constant population until after World War II, when it rapidly expanded. Warm Springs Grammar School (below) had an enrollment of 95 in 1947, but by 1960, as more people moved to the area, enrollment more than doubled. (Courtesy Ted Klein.)

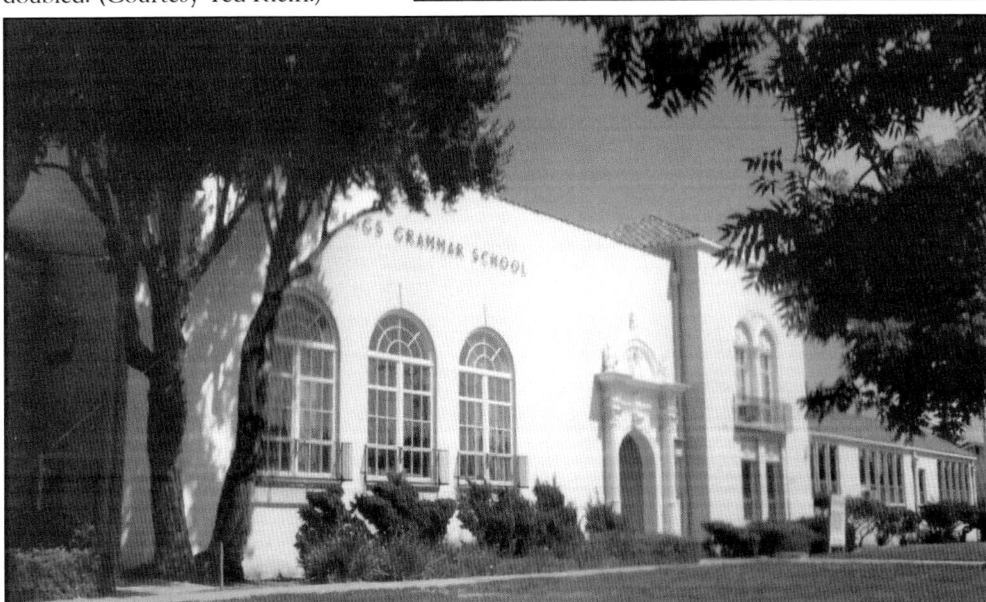

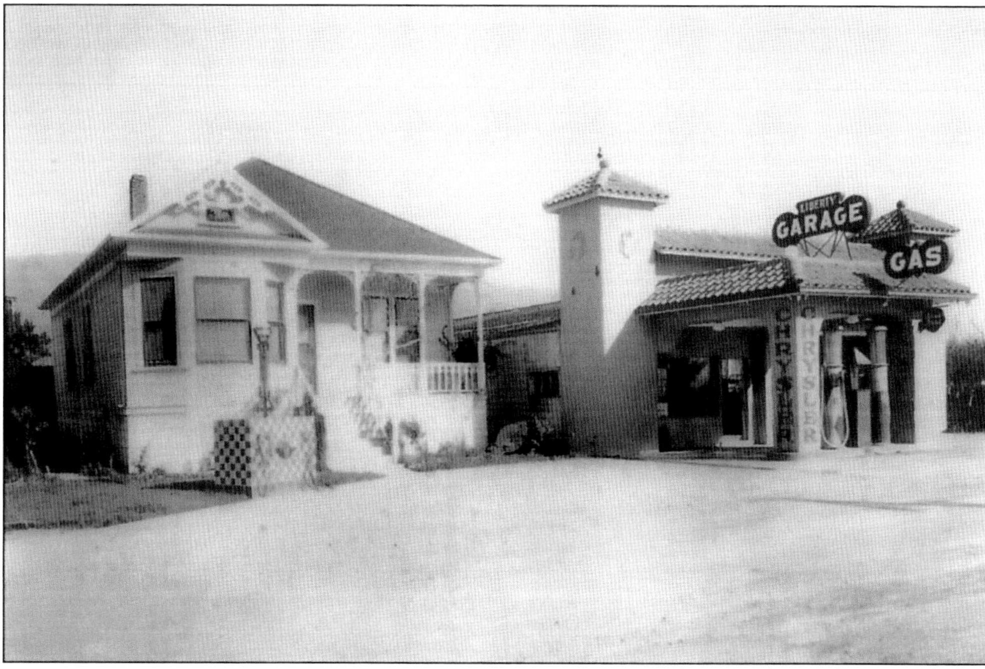


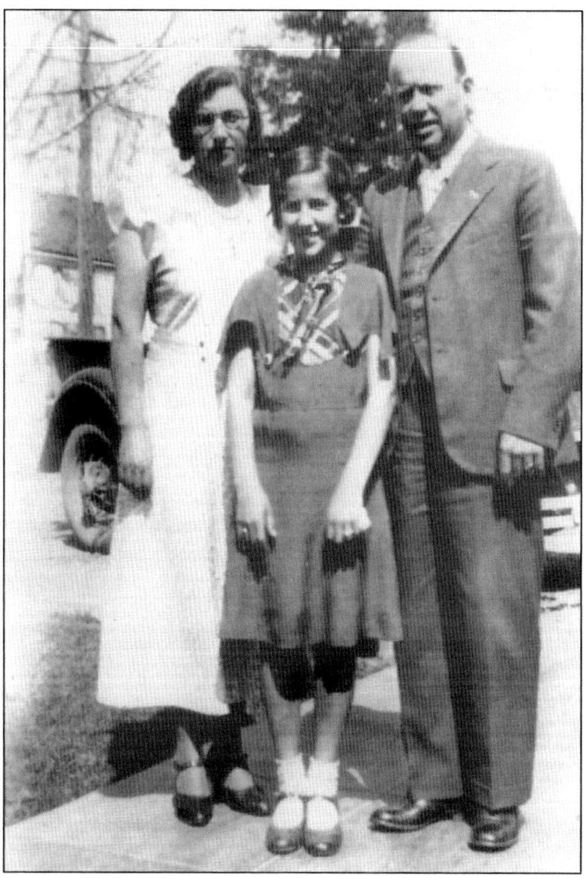

Joseph K. Dutre's home, right next to his Liberty Garage, is seen above around 1930. The buildings were across the street from the Warm Springs Store. Later, Frank and Dorothy Gomes owned the house. (HBH.)

Joe S. and Rosie Brown, the owners of the Warm Springs Store, and their daughter, Evelyn, were very active in the community. Joe belonged to Portuguese organizations, the volunteer fire department, and the school board. Rosie was a member of SPRSI and was a secretary for 25 years. Evelyn was the secretary to the superintendent of Washington High School/Fremont Unified School District from 1942 until she retired in 1983. (SVM.)

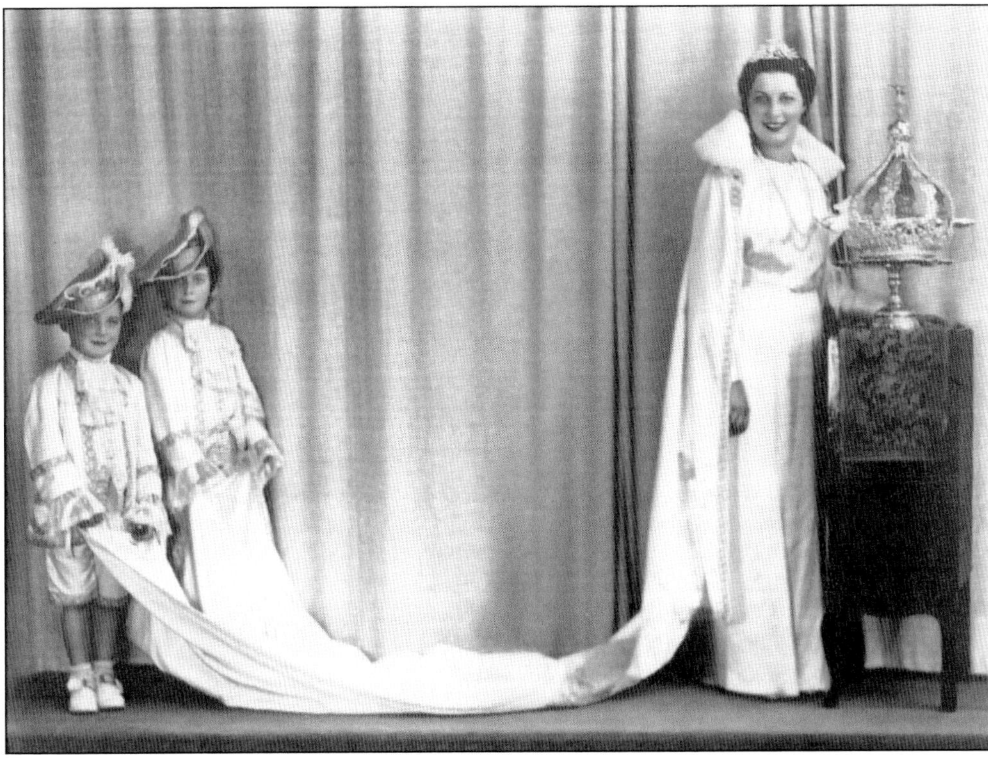

In 1935, the Supreme Council of the IDES (Irmandade do Divino Espirito Santo) sponsored its first festival on 1,972 acres it had just purchased from the former Curtner estate. More than 10,000 people attended. There was a parade with a "queen of queens" and her court, as well as drill teams, marching bands, and other fraternal societies. The queen, Elenore Helen Goularte, is seen above with here attendants (brother and sister) Dan and Mary Goularte holding her cape. (LG.)

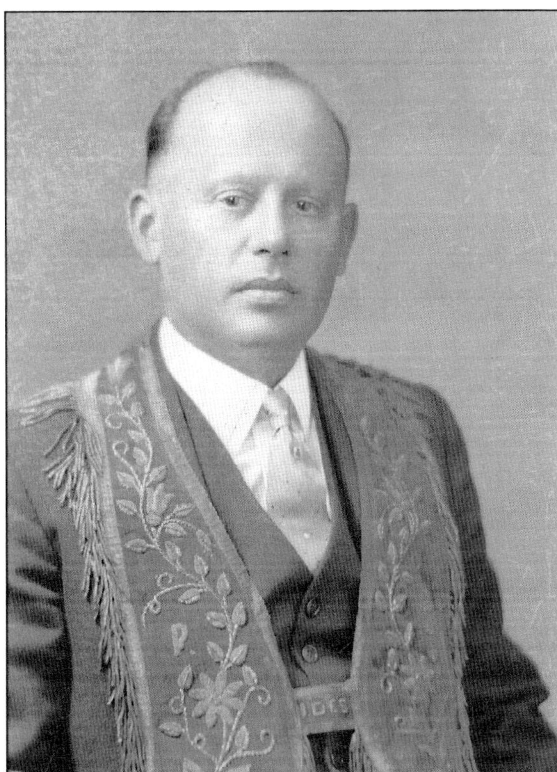

Joe S. Brown is seen here during his time as supreme president of the IDES, a position he held in 1933 and 1934. He belonged to the American Legion Post 195 and several Portuguese organizations, including IDES, UPEC, APPB, and SES. (LG.)

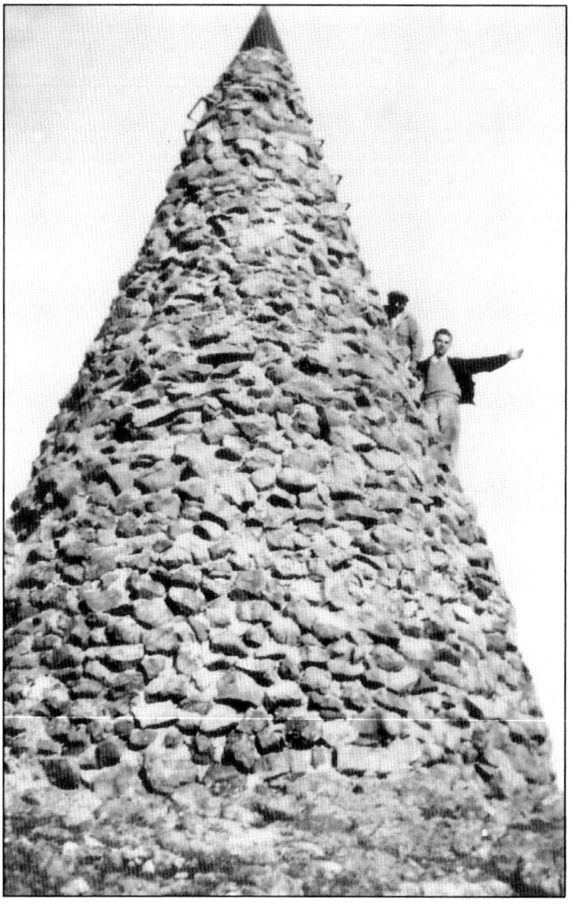

The Alfred Alfonso (A.A.) Moore family owned property behind and to the north of Mission Peak. Moore built this monument at the summit of the peak in honor of his deceased children. The monument had an electric light that shone as a beacon. Here, Anthony Field and an unidentified friend climb to the top of the monument in 1934. It was torn down during World War II so it would not be a marker for possible enemy aircraft activity. (LG.)

Sam Metzger established the first airfield in the area, near today's Warm Springs Boulevard, around 1920. It was adjacent to the Alvernaz ranch on the Martin and Lawrence Murphy property along Landing Road. Several planes of World War I vintage used this field. The Cushing ranch was reported to be the site of a World War II training field. Mae Alvernaz is seen below with an unidentified pilot at Metzger Airfield in 1932. (HA.)

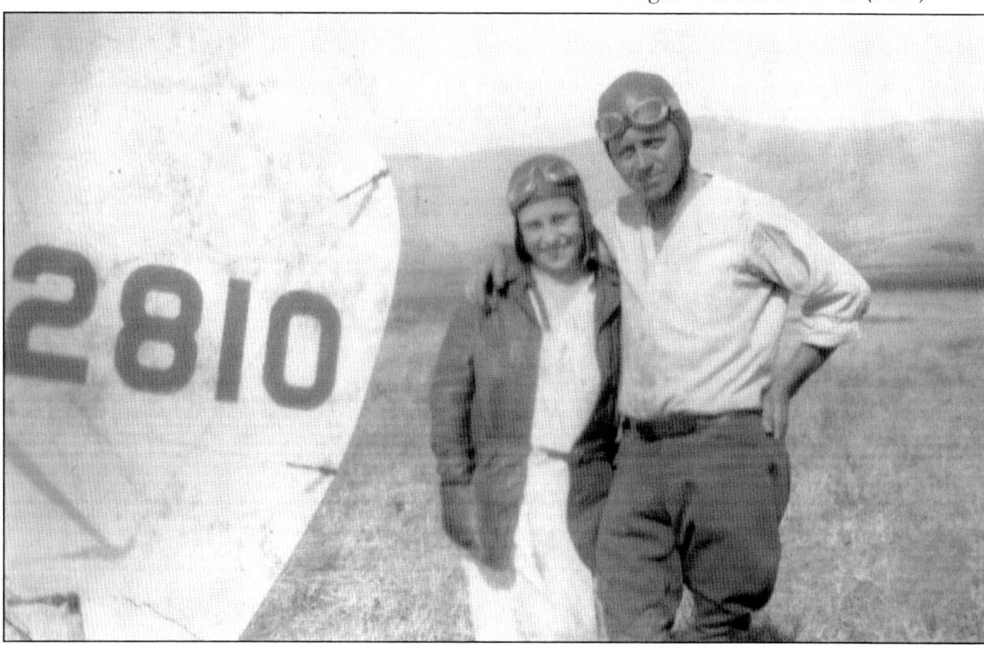

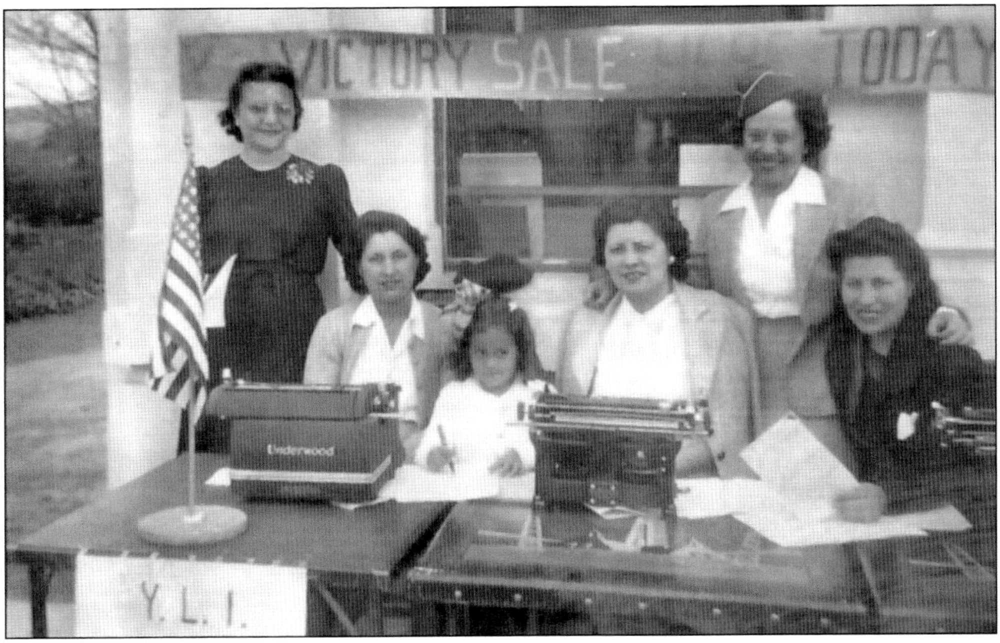


Above, local members of the Young Ladies Institute (YLI) sell World War II bonds to help with the war effort in Irvington in 1944. They are, from left to right, an unidentified woman, Irene Harvey, Carol Anne Rose, Irma Marks, Mae Avila, and Paula Galvin. (HA.)

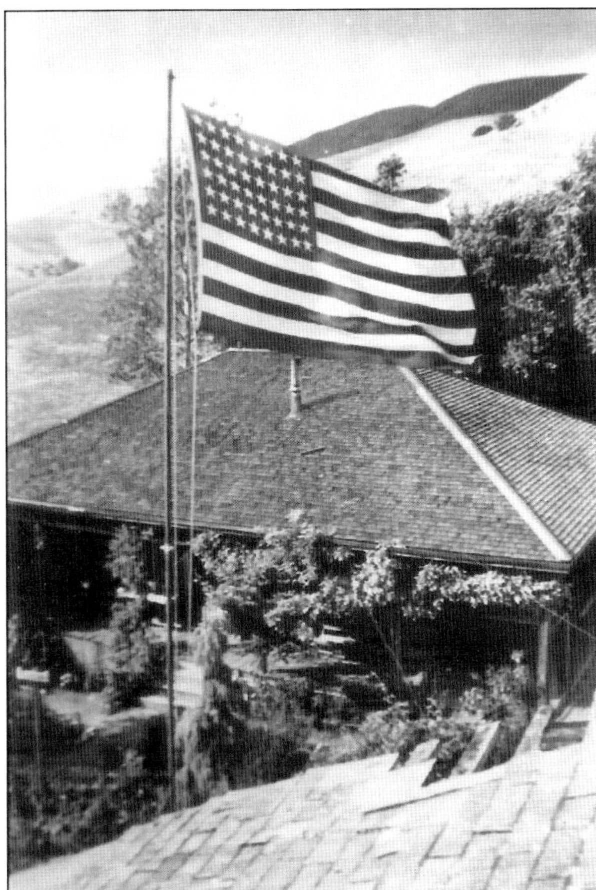

During World War II, many people planted victory gardens and flew the American flag. The Goularte family flew this giant flag every day on their ranch, where they also had a very large garden, fruit trees, and animals.

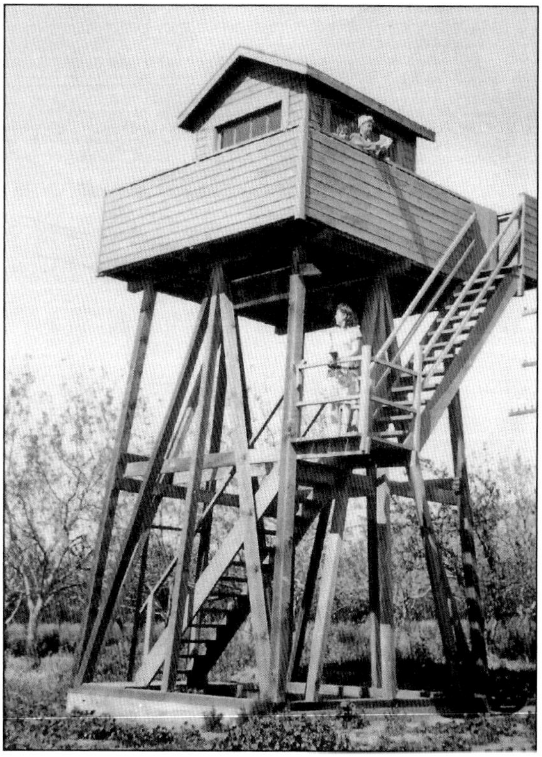

During World War II, citizens took turns watching for enemy aircraft. In 1943, a tower was built in Warm Springs for such a purpose. The post was later commended for a perfect score on its observation test. Volunteers received a certificate "for patriotic devotion to duty in the Ground Observation Corps of the Aircraft Warning Service of the Fourth Fighter Command." Minnie Sarmento Souza and a child are seen here at their post above. Rosiland Sarmento stands on the landing below them. (SVM.)

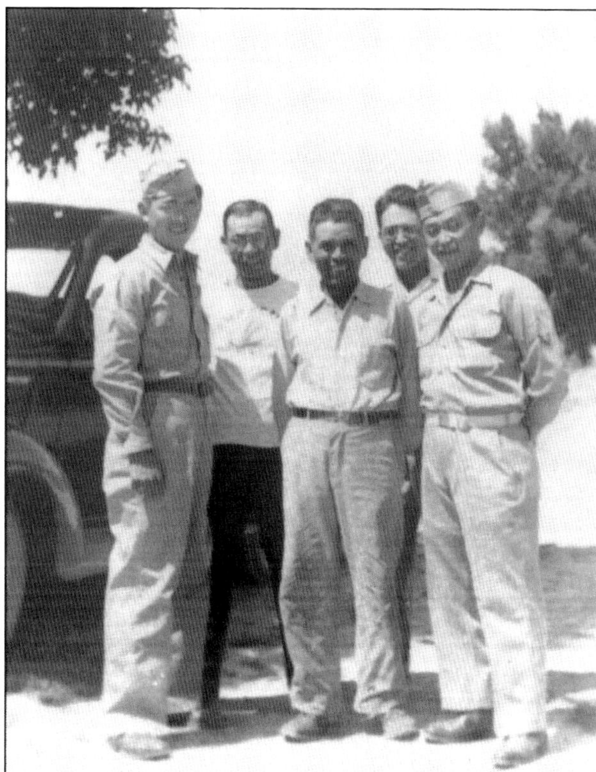

Posing for a family photograph are, from left to right, Henry Kato, Fred Sakuda, Taiju Kato, Yosuto Kato, and Joseph Kato. Because they were Japanese American, the family members were sent to relocation camps in different areas of the United States in 1942, but Joseph and Henry enlisted in the US Army instead. Henry served in England and Joseph served with the famous 442nd Regiment in Europe. He was killed in France in 1944. (Courtesy Wayne and Denise Sakuda.)

# *Seven*

# Cars, Champagne, and Chips

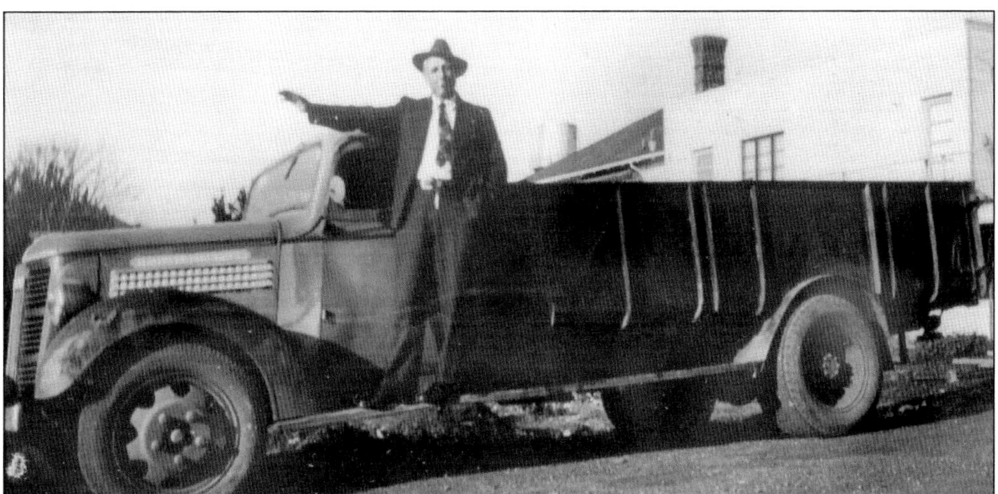

Armando Ramacciotti shows off his swill truck around 1950. He owned and operated the Independent Livestock Company, a pig and cattle feeding farm at the end of Cushing Road, from 1948 to 1978. The company had approximately 2,000 pigs in some 60 pigpens as well as 100 cows on the 24-acre facility. The feed included cauliflower scraps from neighbors at Lloyd Baily Ranch and restaurant scraps from Italian Village Restaurant (now Papillon Restaurant), which was also owned by Ramacciotti. In 1974, health regulations, a lack of potable water, and difficulty obtaining permits to use the land contributed to the family's decision to sell the property. (Courtesy Dino Ramaccoitti.)

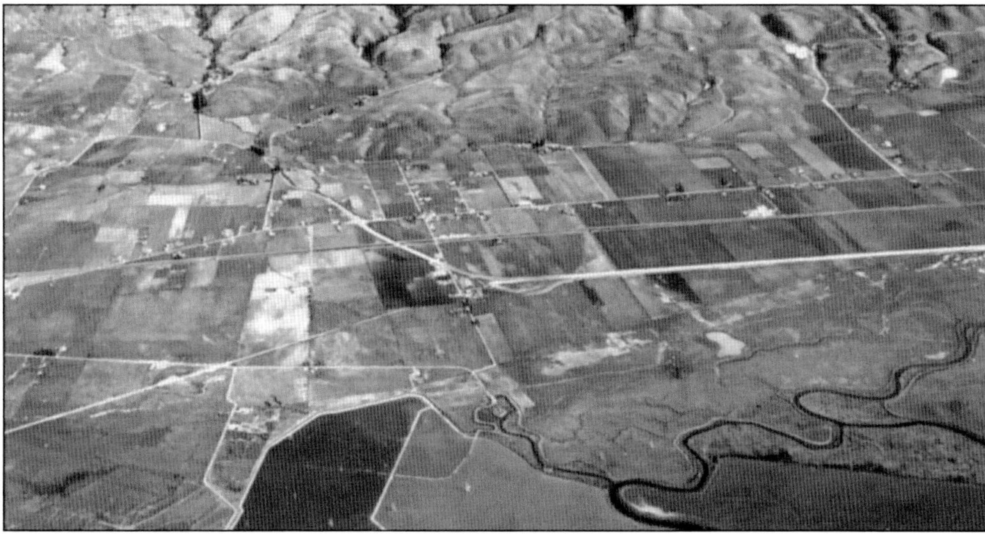

These two aerial photographs of the Warm Springs area illustrate the rapid growth that occurred after 1960. The first aerial (above) looks east in 1955 and shows the farming community of Warm Springs. Hay, grain, fruit, and vegetable farming flourished, with a few stores and gas stations. Mission Boulevard was extended to meet the Nimitz Freeway, which, at that time, started in Warm Springs and continued to San Jose. The Southern Pacific Railroad also runs parallel to Warm Springs Boulevard and the freeway. Farmers pushed for their land to be rezoned to allow them to sell it to sub-dividers, stating that rising property taxes and bad conditions made farming unprofitable. The aerial view below, taken in 1962 looking north, shows the completed Nimitz Freeway. North of the Mission Boulevard exchange, the General Motors assembly plant is being constructed, and to the left of the plant, over the freeway, is the Fremont drag strip. New housing developments had sprung up, including Starlite Hills and the Barlow development, a build-your-own-home development. (Both, MLH.)

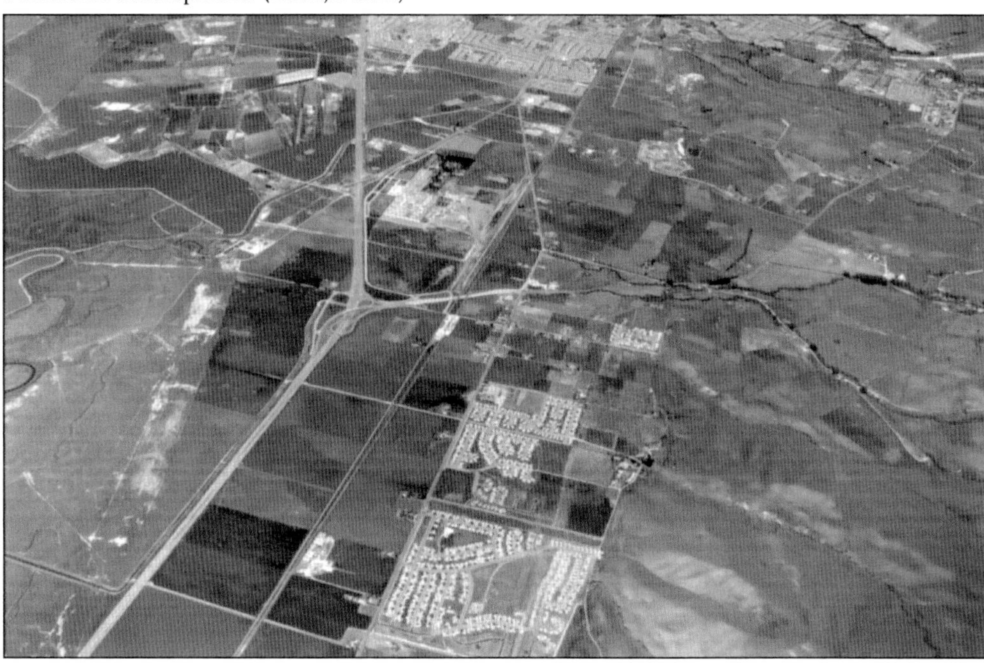

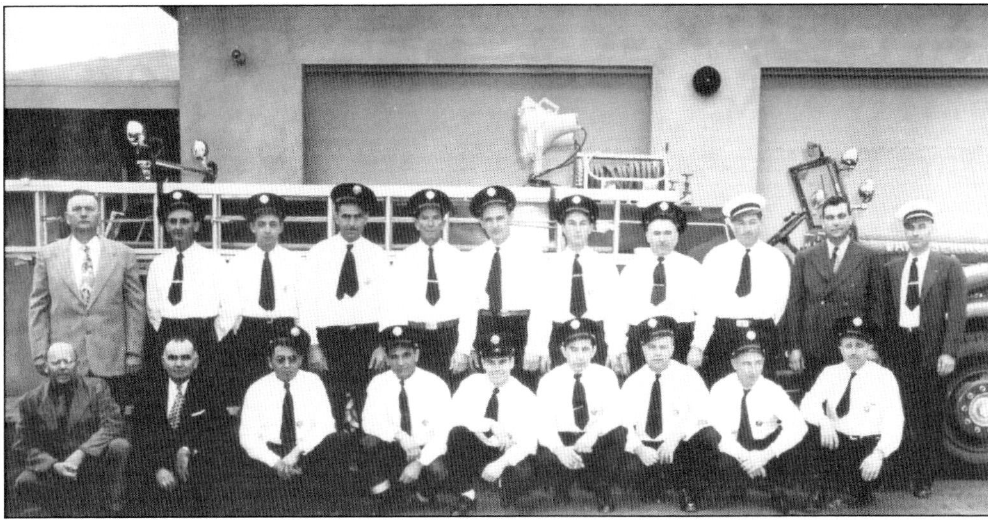

Members of the Warm Springs Volunteer Fire Department pose in front of the new fire engine in 1950. The department included, from left to right, (first row) Joe S. Brown, commissioner; Tony Braga, commissioner; Yasuto Kato; Melvin Leal; Danny Rodrigues; Louis Rodrigues; Alfred Smith; Raymond Garcia; and Joe Bettencourt; (second row) Orville Leitch, commissioner; Joseph Sarmento; Leonard Gonsalves; Jack Santos; Rufio Durazo, commissioner; Joe Wagner; Bill Borba; Joe Oliver; Tony Brazil, assistant fire chief; Tony Vargas, commissioner; and John Souza, fire chief. (SVM.)

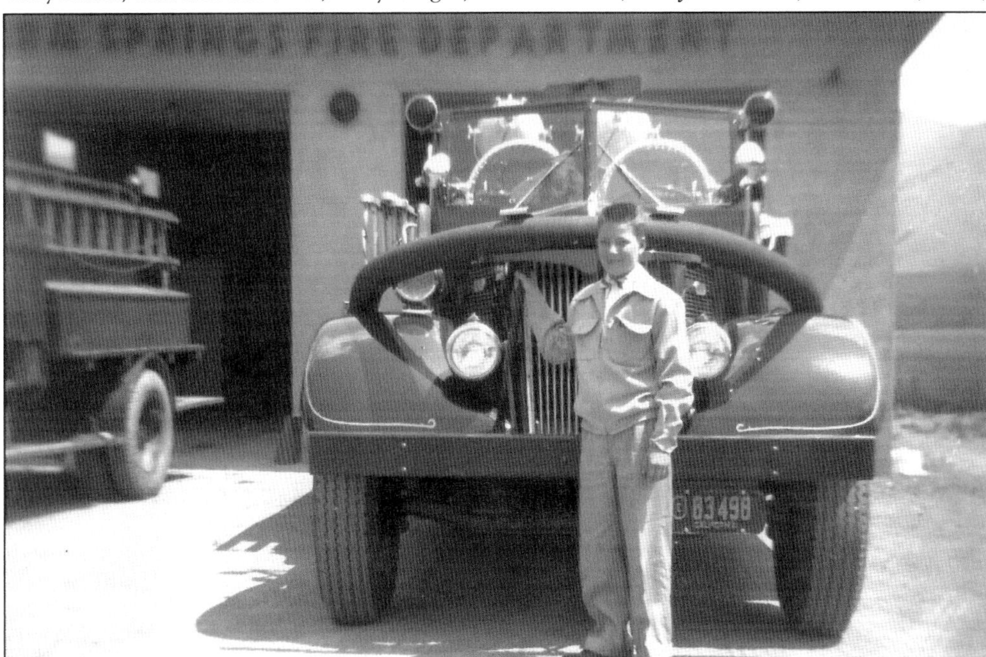

Warm Springs had a volunteer fire department from 1950 until the incorporation of Warm Springs into the City of Fremont in 1956. Leon Gibson is seen here in front of one of the fire engines in 1953. Before 1950, the fire equipment, including the 400-gallon pumper, was housed in Minnie Vargas Souza's sheds. She donated water to the fire department, and the fire horn was attached to her water tank. All fires were reported by a phone call to Minnie's garage, after which Minnie would run across the street to sound the alarm for the volunteers. (DT.)

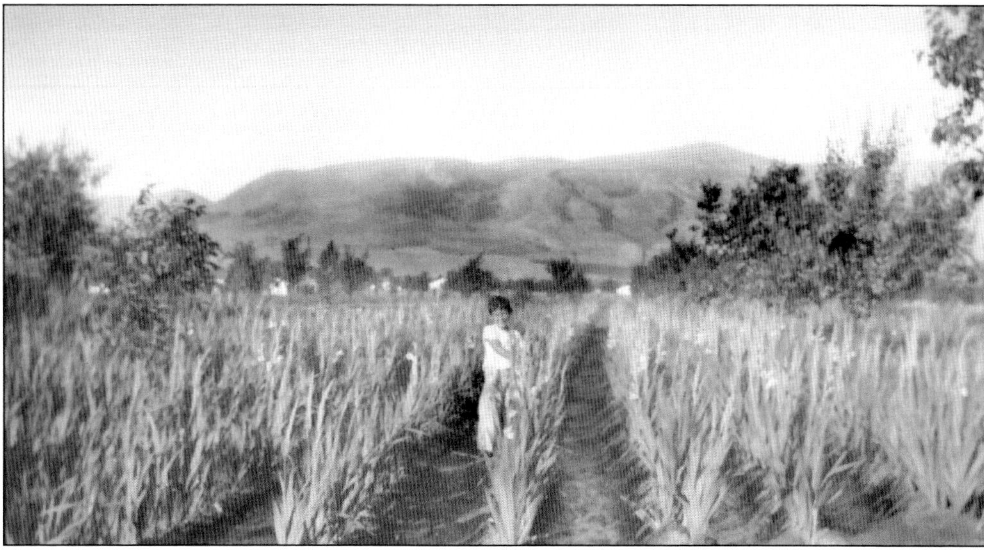

Doug Tavis stands in the middle of his family's gladiola field in 1950. Their flower stand was on the corner of Prune Avenue and Warm Springs Boulevard, on the edge of the property. Antoinette and Tony Tavis bought the property in the mid-1940s and lived there for the rest of their lives. Their son, Doug, sold it in 2000. (DT.)

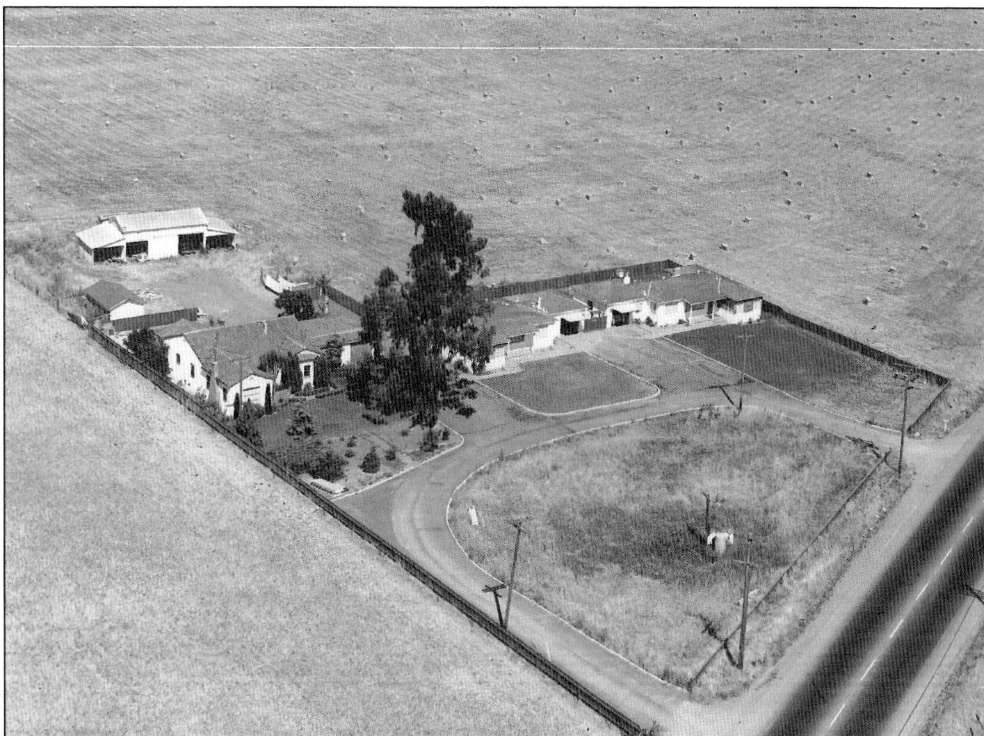

The homes of James, Takea "Tak," and Harold Fudenna are seen here on their 20-acre ranch on Warm Springs Boulevard. The property was part of their extensive farming operation in the 1950s, when they farmed up to 1,500 acres of land they owned and rented. Fudenna Brothers, Inc., was a leading grower, packer, shipper, and marketing organization. (Courtesy Larry Fudenna.)

James Fudenna helps load crates of produce for shipment on an American Airlines airplane. Fudenna's had a packing shed operation in Warm Springs from which it distributed farm produce, especially lettuce and cauliflower, across the United States and around the world. (Courtesy Larry Fudenna.)

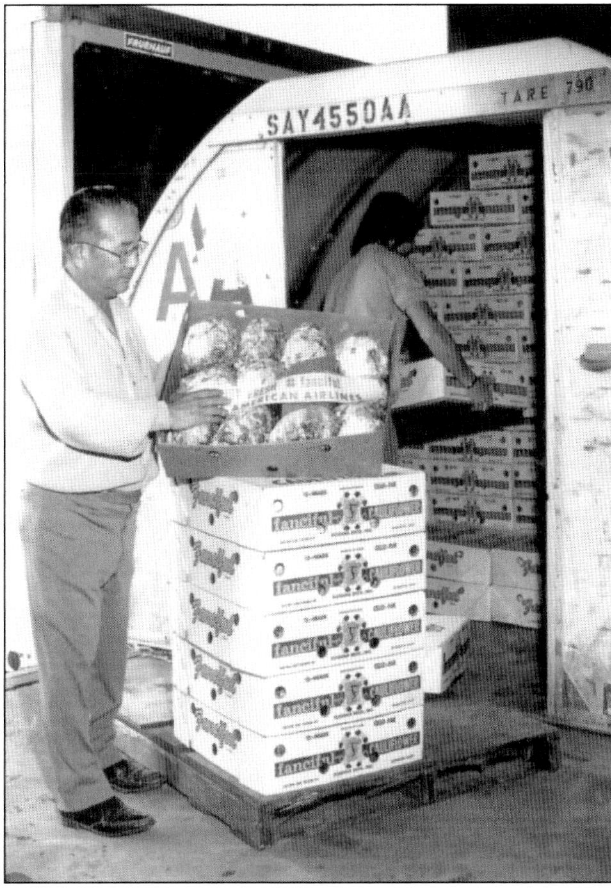


Ice was a commodity that allowed produce to be shipped longer distances. In 1950, Hugo Miller created an ice-crushing system and a vacuum cooling system used on a truck, which permitted him to go into packing sheds and onto fields. Miller and John Nicholson started Glacier Ice Company in 1975 and moved its headquarters to Warm Springs in 1992. Their long-haul truck is seen below. (Courtesy Floyd Miller.)

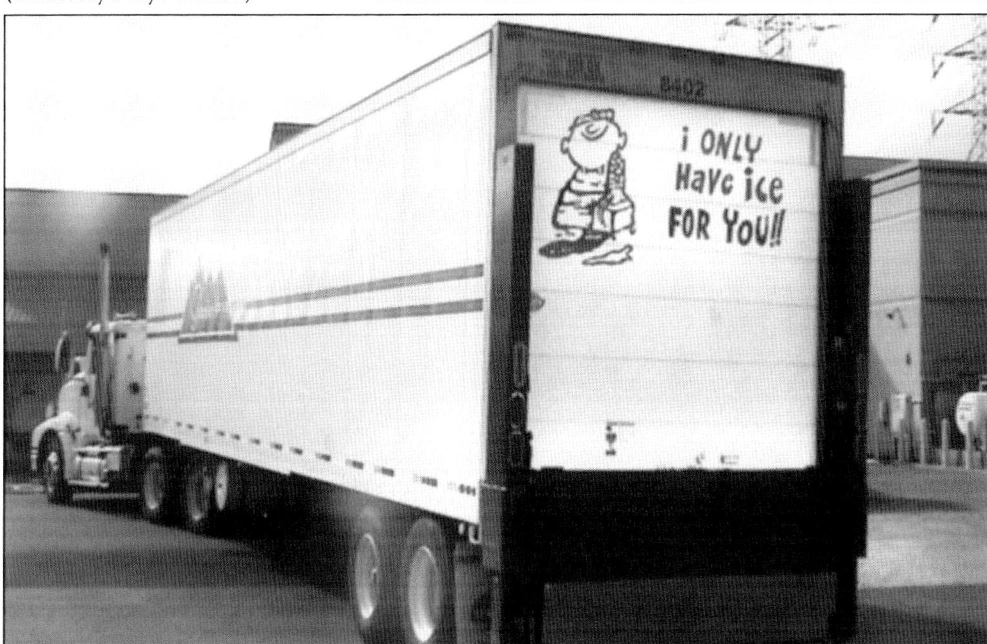

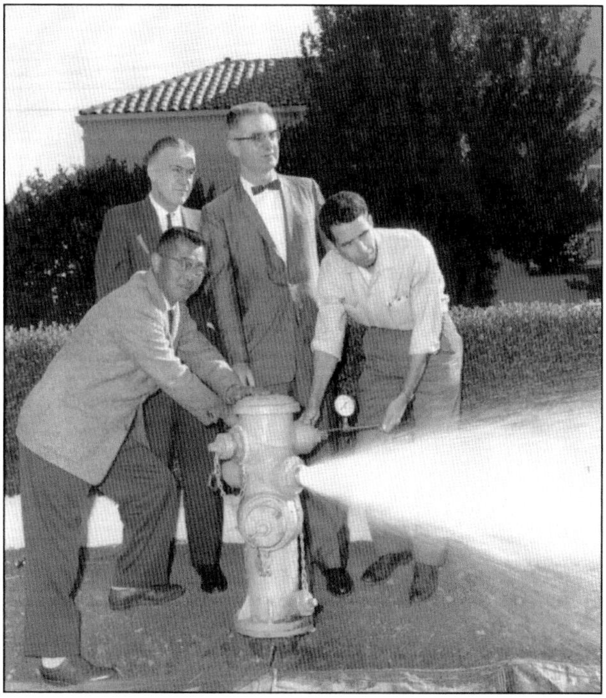

Getting enough water to customers was a continuous problem. The Alameda County Water District offered a more permanent solution. Here, members of the Warm Springs community and the Alameda County Water District celebrate the new water system. From left to right, they are Henry Kato, president of the Warm Springs volunteer fire department; John Pihl, water district director (1956–1960); Matt Whitfield, water district general manager (1953–1977); and Leonard Silva. (MLH, George Oaks Collection.)

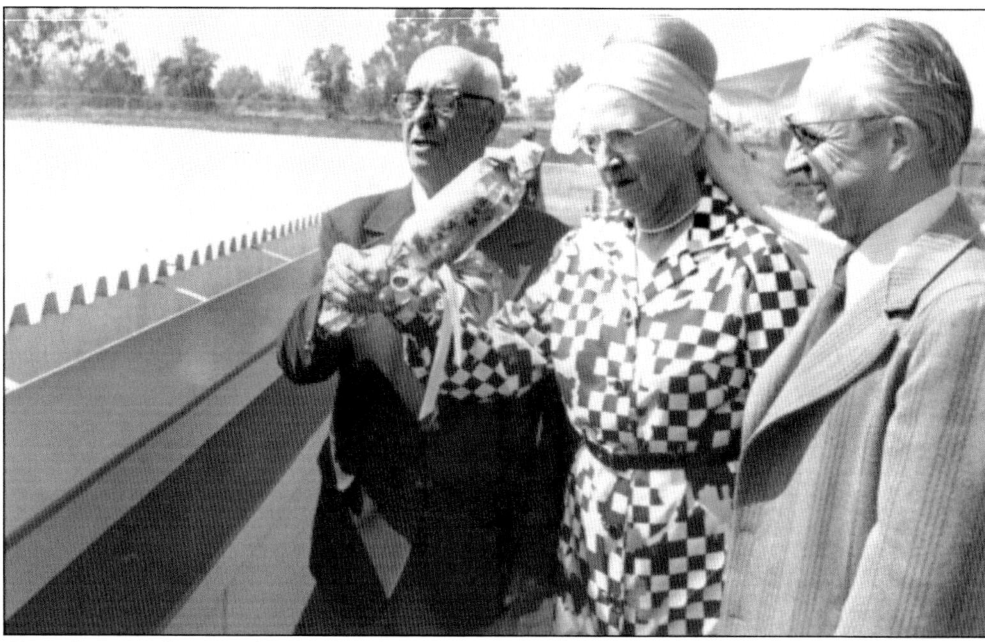

This photograph was taken at the dedication of the A.E. Alameda Reservoir of the Alameda County Water District (ACWD) in Warm Springs, where Paseo Padre intersects Curtner Road. This backup reservoir was named after Anthony "Tony" Alameda to commemorate his service on the water board from 1962 to 1969. Seen here in 1972 are, from left to right, Tony and Pauline Alameda and Harry Brumbaugh, the director at the time. Other Warm Springs reservoirs include the Hidden tank, created in 1979, the Vineyard Heights tank, created in 1987, and the Avalon Hills tank, created in 1996. (DV.)

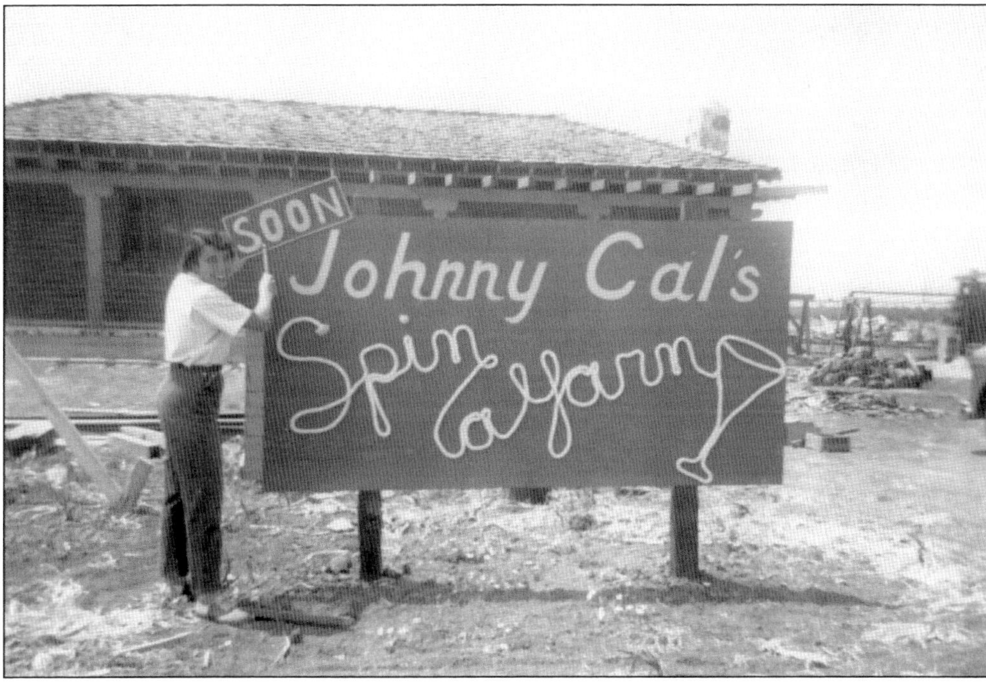


John Calcagno, the former owner of Central Chevrolet in Centerville, purchased land on Highway 17 in 1951 and hired Randy Griffin to build a cocktail lounge. Billy Calcagno and Alberta Nunes George helped with the interior design. When John Calcagno asked George to come up with a name for the lounge, she created this logo and sign, naming it Spin a Yarn because Calcagno was a great storyteller. (Courtesy Alberta Nunes George.)

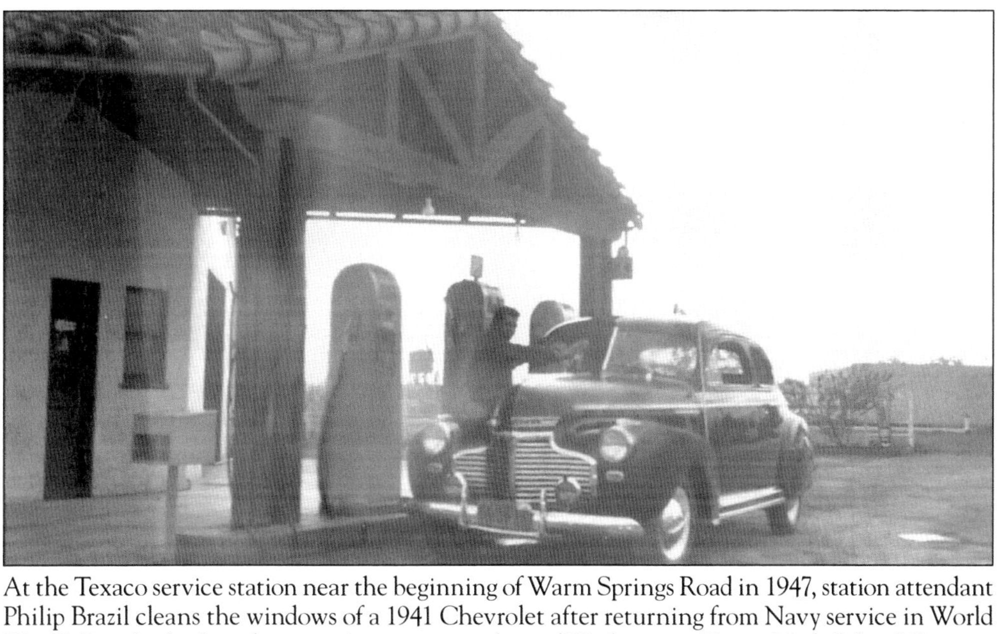

At the Texaco service station near the beginning of Warm Springs Road in 1947, station attendant Philip Brazil cleans the windows of a 1941 Chevrolet after returning from Navy service in World War II. Brazil, who later became the superintendent of Washington Union High School District, worked here part-time while going to school. (Courtesy Philip Brazil Jr.)

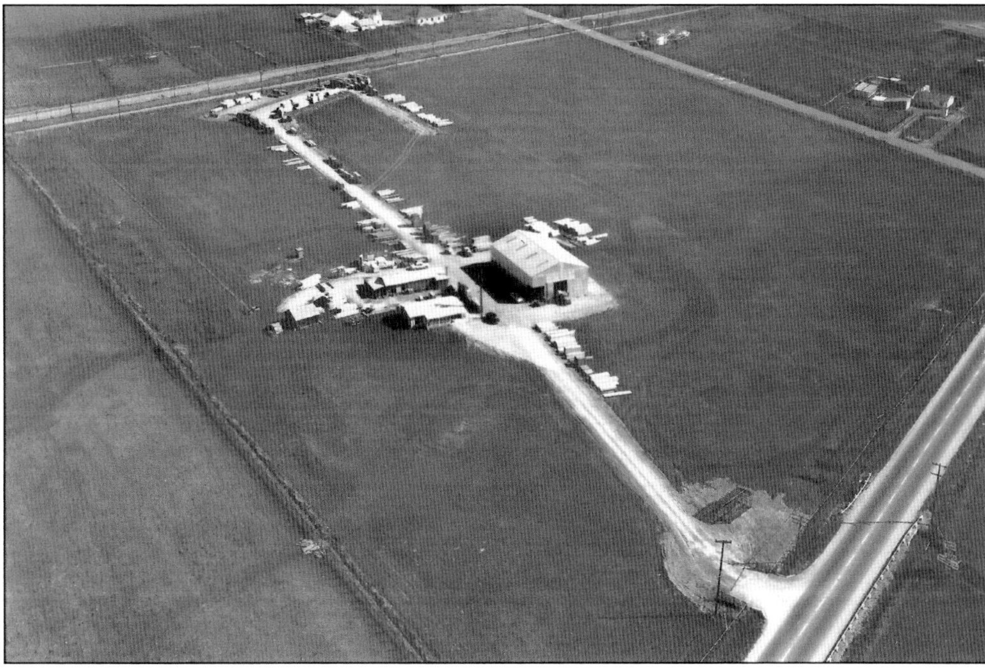

The Warm Springs Lumber Company was established in 1953 and grew from a plot of bare land to a major retail and wholesale distributor of lumber in the East Bay. The firm maintained a variety of modern mechanical equipment, including an automatic rafter cutter, forklifts, lumber carriers, pickups, and 10-wheelers to serve the needs of contractors. (DT.)

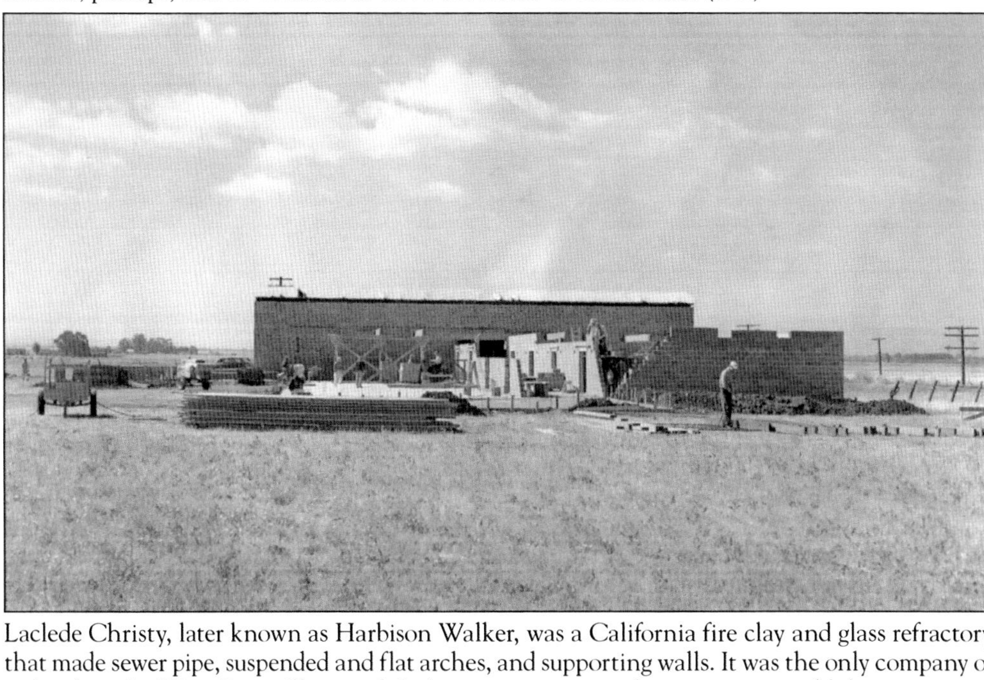

Laclede Christy, later known as Harbison Walker, was a California fire clay and glass refractory that made sewer pipe, suspended and flat arches, and supporting walls. It was the only company of its kind on the West Coast. Shamrock Industries, a paper products company, sold the property to Laclede Christy, and it began construction on this factory in 1954. Frank Vargas was an employee. (Courtesy Nancy Margherita.)

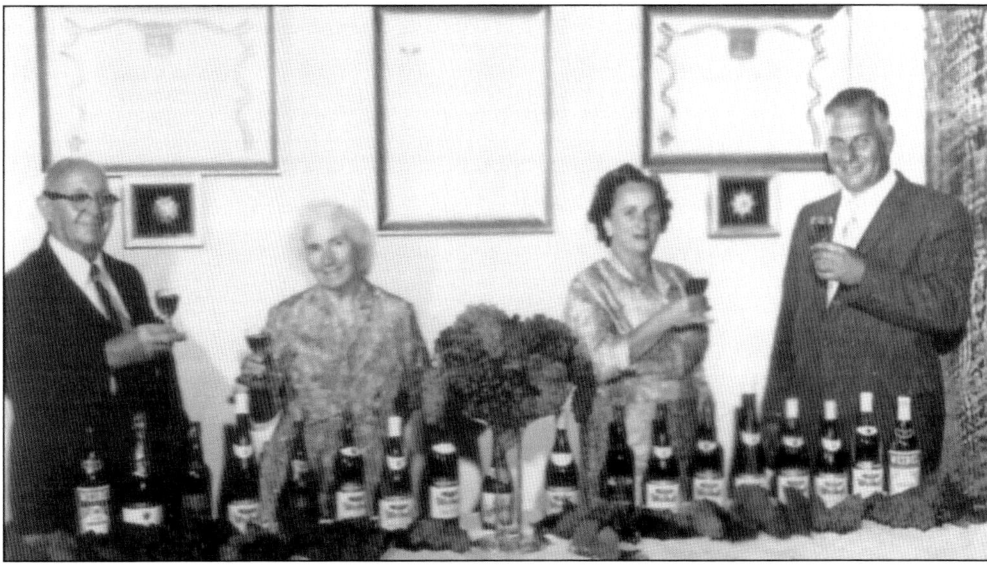

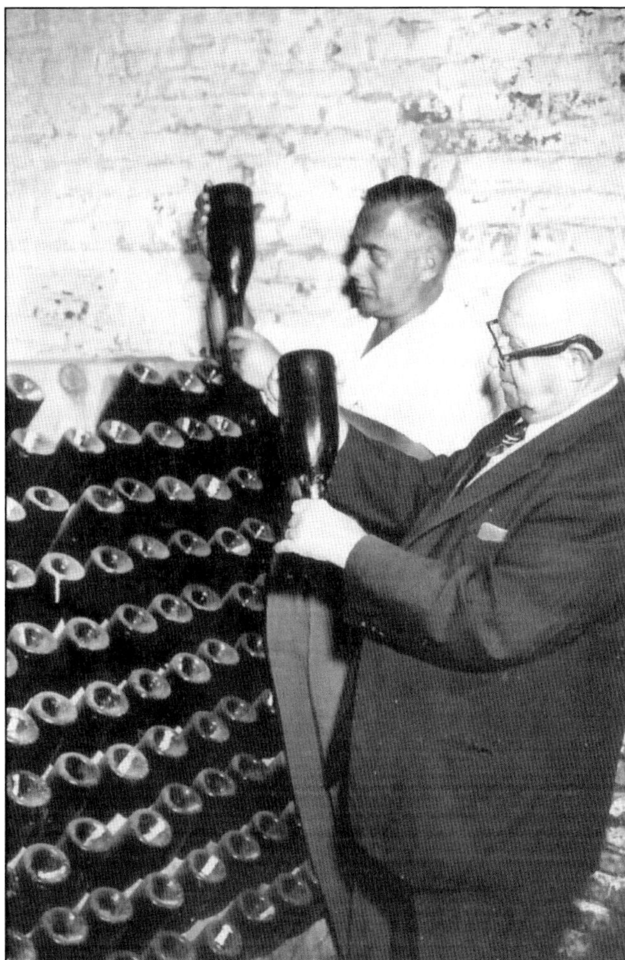

Rudolf E. Weibel and his son, Fred Weibel, founded Weibel Champagne Vineyards in Warm Springs in 1945. Rudolf came to California from his native Switzerland with his wife, Elise, and two of his children, Jeanette and Fred (another daughter remained in Switzerland). Rudolf and Fred saw the future of California wines and produced champagne in San Francisco. In 1945, they decided to locate their winery on approximately 100 acres of the former Stanford family property, an ideal place to establish a vineyard. They pulled out the old worn vines and replanted, bringing many cuttings from France in 1948. They restored some of the Stanford buildings and installed a cooperage. Above, from left to right, Rudolf; his wife, Elise; Fred's wife, Hulda; and Fred raise a toast surrounded by various Weibel products and awards the vineyard received. At right, Rudolf and Fred inspect bottles of champagne for secondary fermentation on "A" racks. (Both, MW.)

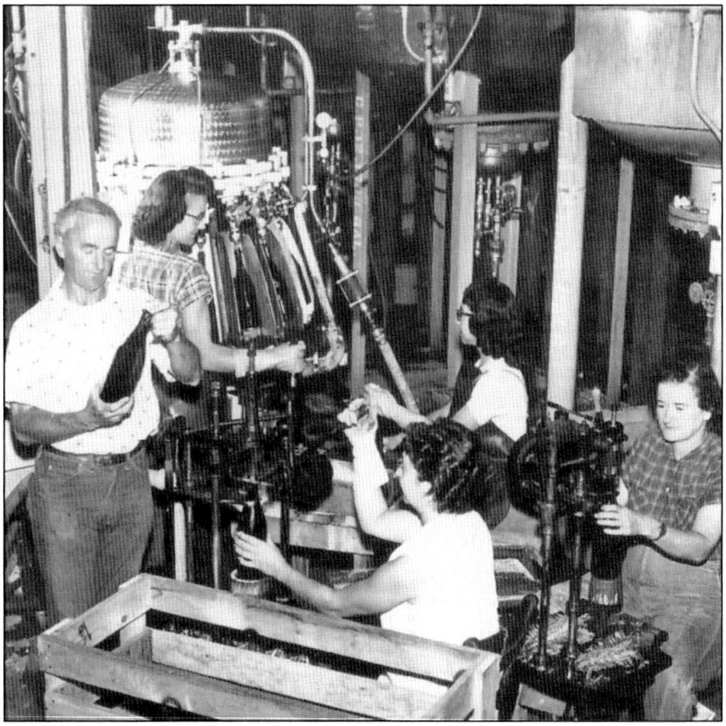

New winemaking equipment was installed at the Weibel vineyard in 1945, and the first champagne from the vineyards was marketed in 1952. In the 1960s, the Weibel winery produced more champagne than any other producer in California and won more than 650 awards. Here, Oscar Habluetzel (left), Fred Weibel's brother-in-law, checks the champagne bottling process. One woman is running the bottling machine, another is corking, and another is wiring the top of the bottle and attaching foil. (MW.)

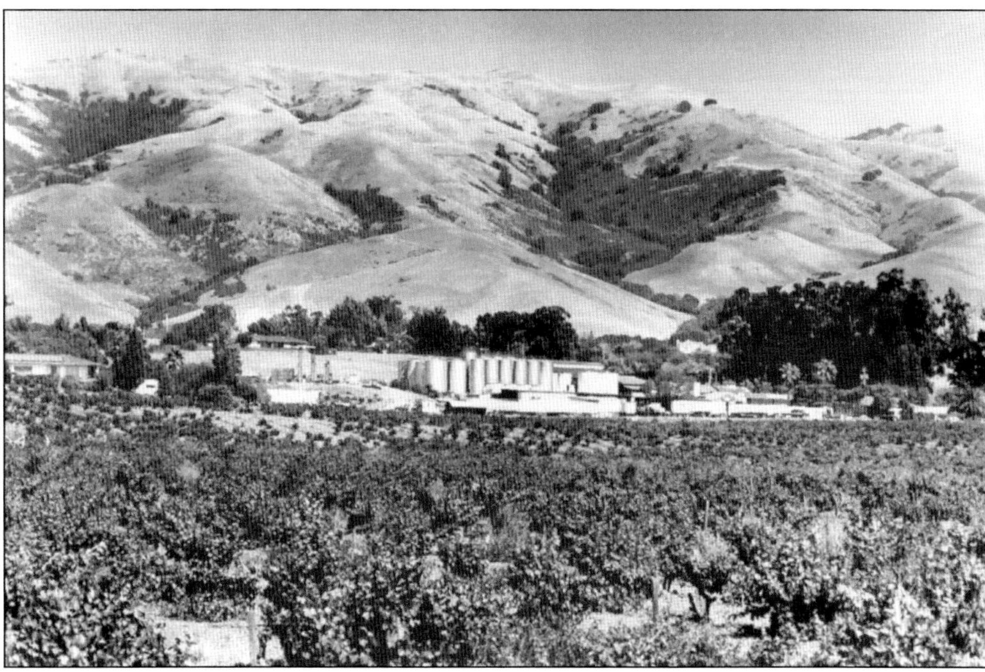

The Weibel Champagne winery and vineyard is seen here in the 1970s. On the far left is Fred Weibel's house, a ranch-style home in the middle of the vineyard. The crushing operation is to the left of the giant storage tanks. Above the crushing area is the house of neighbor Jessie Goossen. The "old" Stanford winery buildings are to the right. Rudolf and Elise Weibel's home was across from the tasting room.

The Weibel Hacienda tasting room was built in 1958. The newest addition to the champagne vineyards, it was a place for visitors to relax and sample wines. A state historical marker inscribed "Leland Stanford Winery" was on the front of the building. (MW.)

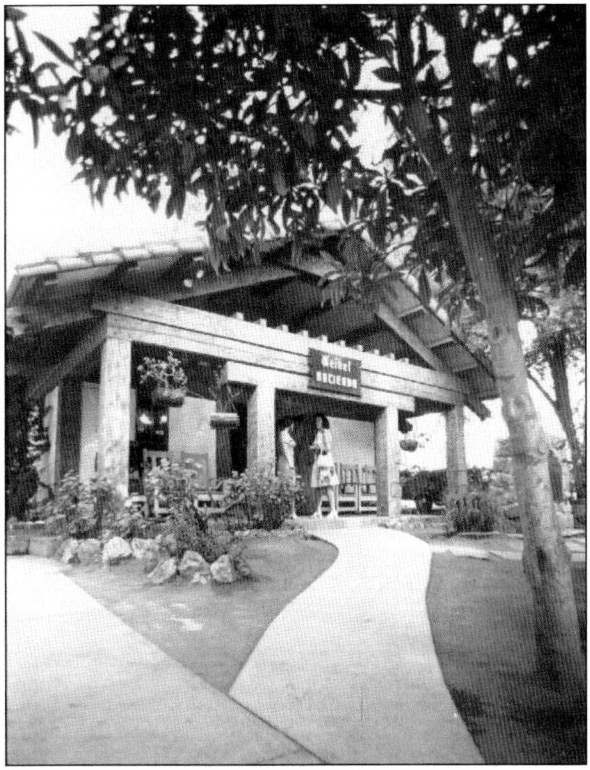

Below, fashion designer Kay Cantonwine poses for a photograph with Groucho Marx. The grapes may be plastic and the bottle may be straw, but the label and neckband are authentic. Cantonwine sold these hats nationally to specialty shops and leading department stores, giving Weibel, already California's largest champagne producer, wide national exposure. (DV.)

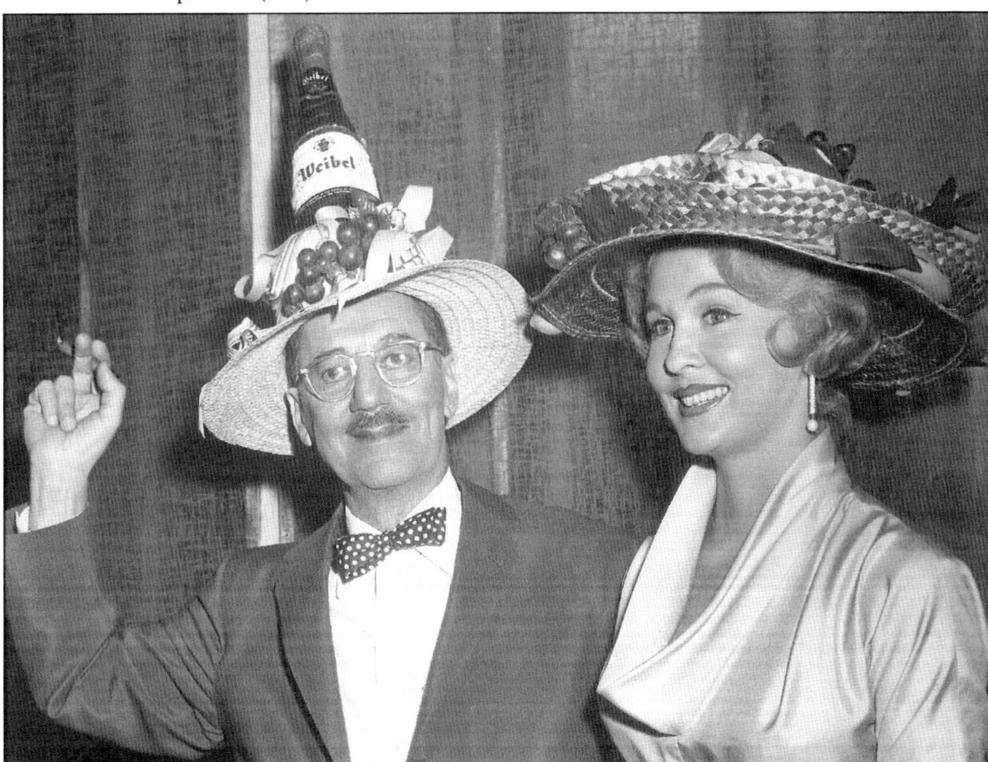

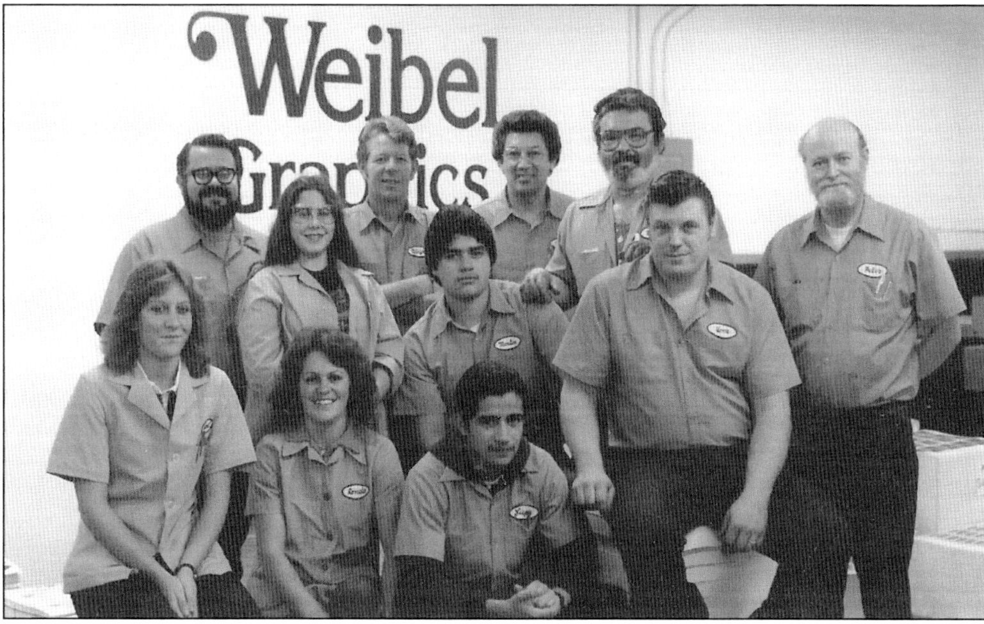


After a fire in 1960, Weibel created its own print shop to get its labels printed quickly. The print shop crew posed for this photograph after it moved to a newer facility in Newark. From left to right are (first row) Ronda ? and Lupe Arroyo; (second row) Jennelle ?, Lynne Jensen, Martin Aroyo, and Tom Vuich; (third row) Brad Jensen, Wayne ?, Wally Verret, Peter Avalos, and Peter Hall. (Courtesy Lynne Wright.)

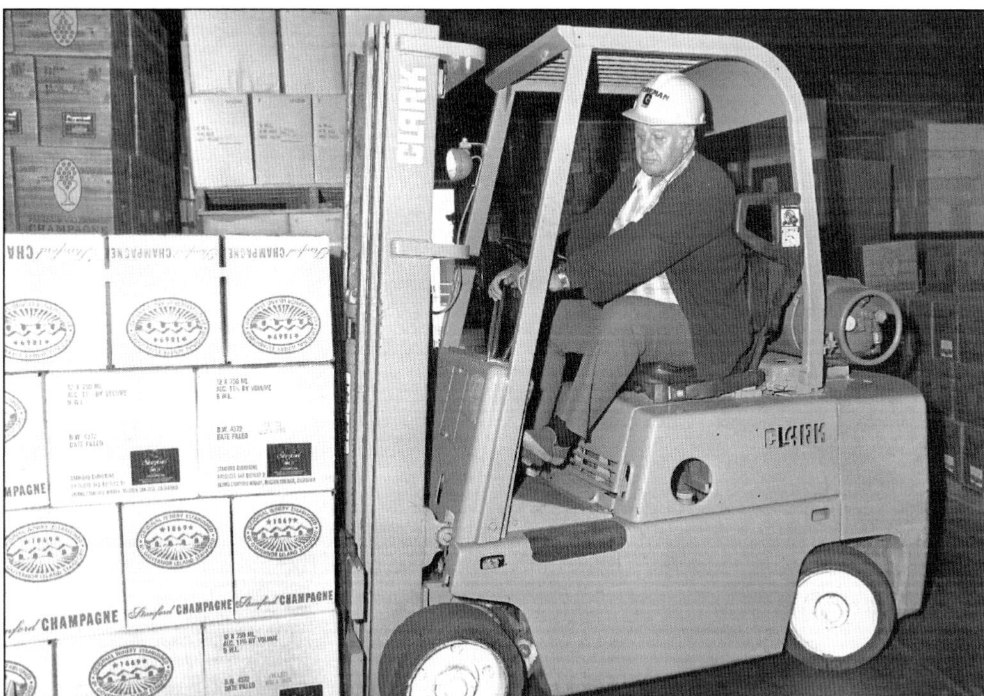


Fred Weibel continued to work at the winery for years, loading wine cases on trailers and railroad cars. Here, he moves a pallet of one of the winery's most popular labels, Stanford Champagne. (MW.)

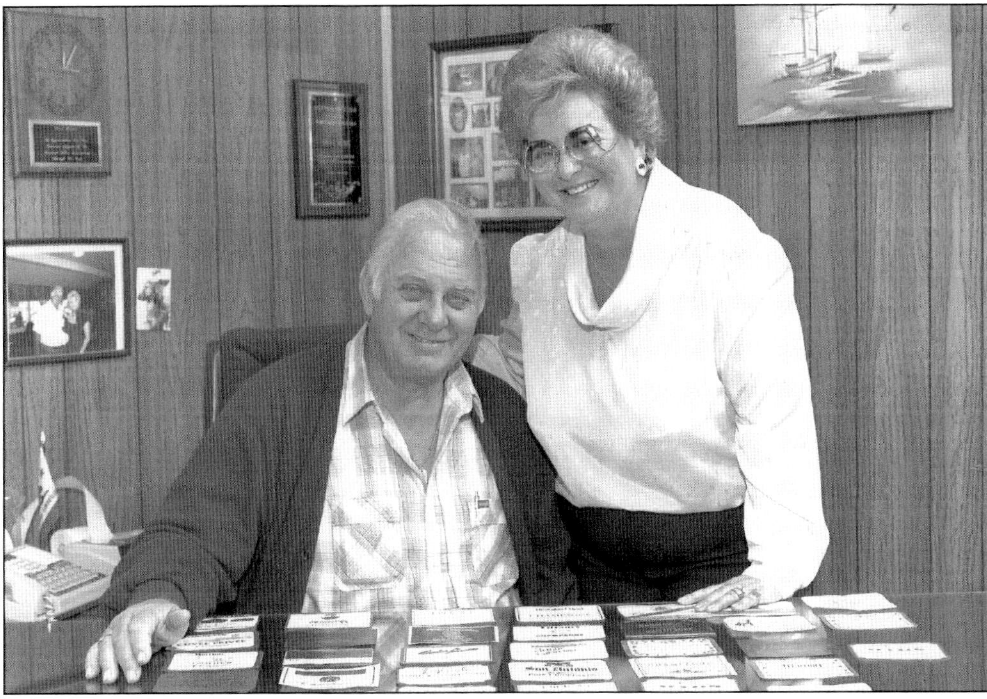

Fred Weibel is seen here with his second wife, Marlene, looking at assorted wine and champagne labels in the company office. The photograph behind Fred to his left shows him posing with Zsa Zsa Gabor, who was the spokesperson for their green Hungarian wine. A special emerald green dress was made for Zsa Zsa to represent the wine. (MW.)

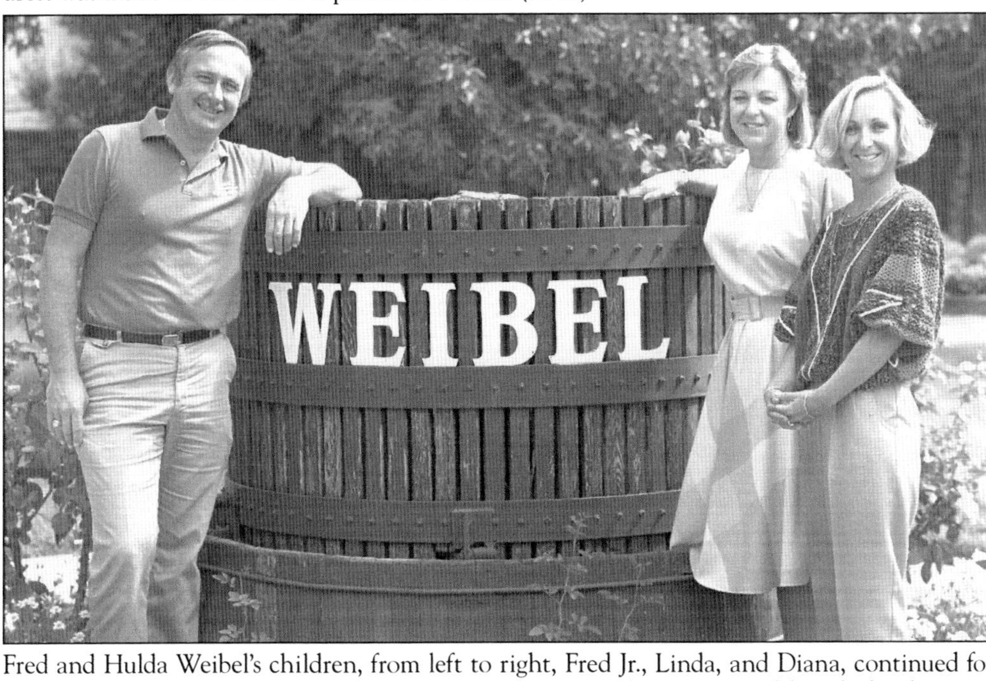


Fred and Hulda Weibel's children, from left to right, Fred Jr., Linda, and Diana, continued for some time in the wine business. Fred Jr. still runs the family company, although development pressures forced him to relocate the winery. (MW.)

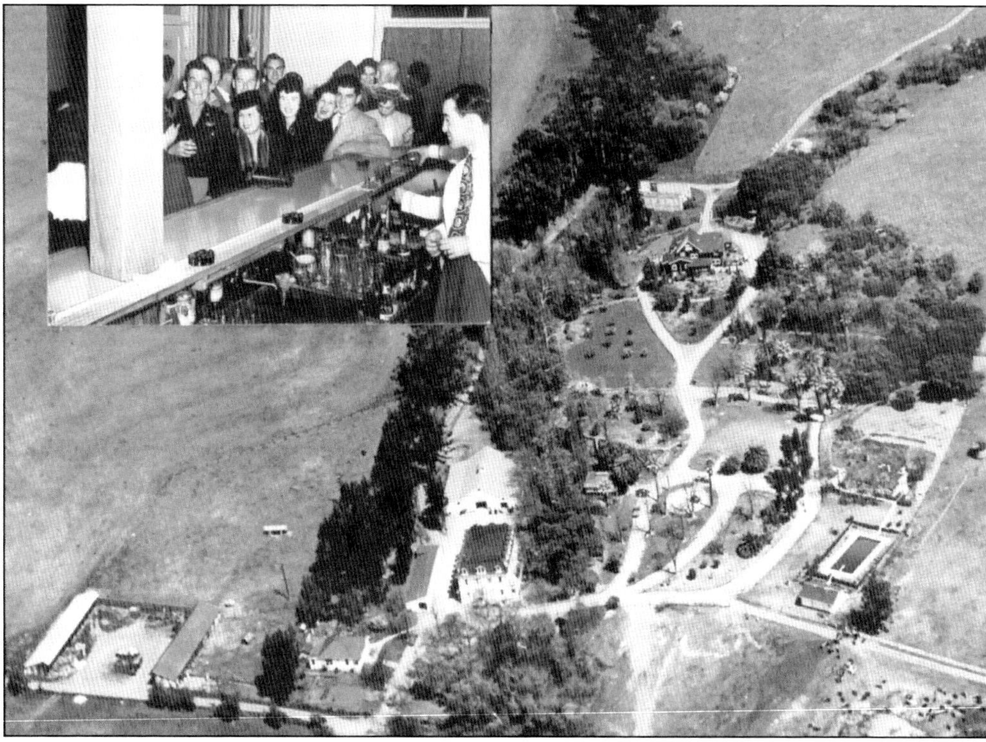

The Hidden Valley Dude Ranch opened on September 8, 1945. This aerial view shows the old Warm Springs Hotel (also known as the Cohen Hotel) in the center foreground, with the swimming pool on the right. The famous fountain and the former Stanford residence are just above it. The inset photograph in the upper left shows customers enjoying the festivities at the hotel's bar.

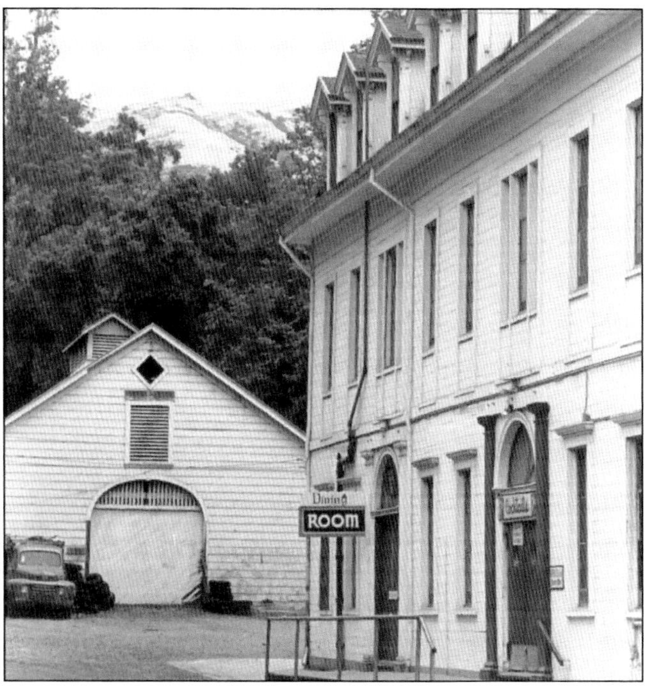


The Cohen Hotel and stables were the centerpiece of the Hidden Valley Dude Ranch, seen here in the 1970s. Fred Goossen, the owner, was very fond of horses and made them an important part of the ranch. He also sponsored many rodeos. The stable was large and well built, with box stalls for the "guest string" of 36 horses, which were rotated regularly between the barn and the pasture.

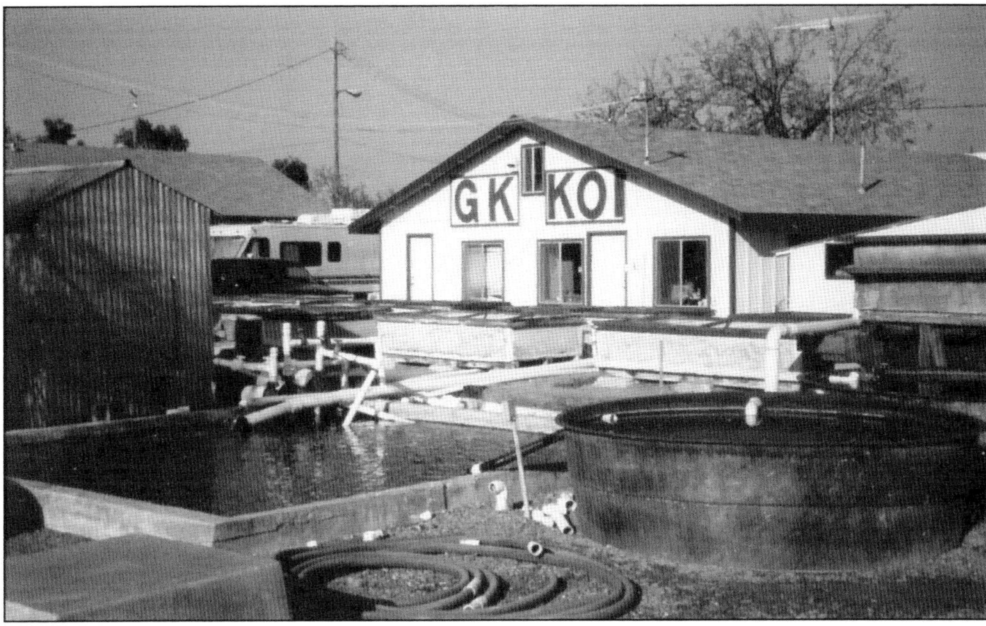


G.K. Fish Hatchery raised and sold koi just across from the Spin a Yarn from 1970 until 2003. Gerry and Diane Klinke sold ponds, filters, and fish supplies and installed and repaired filter systems. It was a unique niche business serving the entire Bay Area. The business was formerly a chicken ranch owned by Mr. and Mrs. Keyes. The Keyeses' egg-processing building was used as a sales room by the Klinke family, who showcased fishponds in front. (Courtesy of Diane Klinke.)

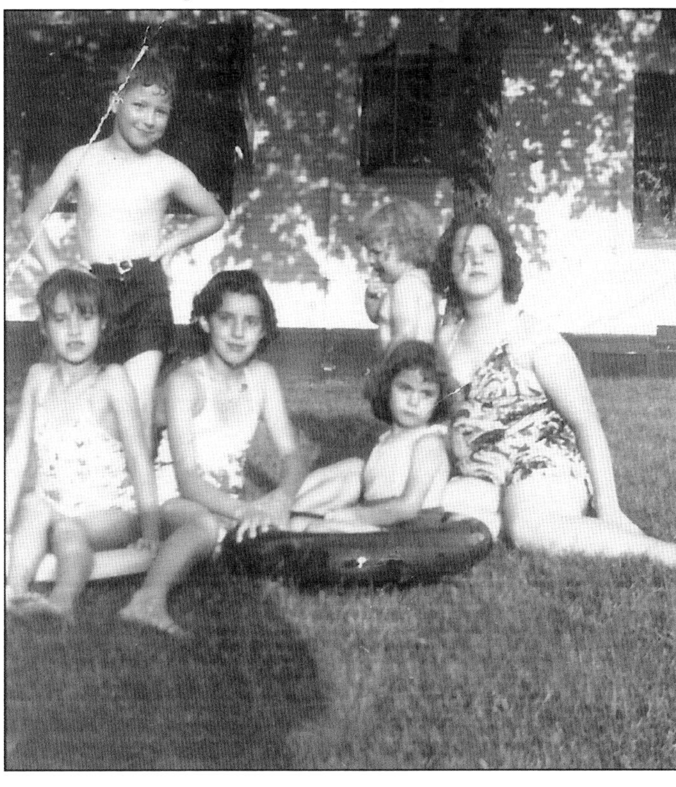

Families spent a lot of time cooling off at the large Hidden Valley Ranch pool. These children are sitting on the grass up behind the pool with the caretaker's residence in the background in 1949. From left to right are (first row) Patsy ?, Billie Ann ?, and Diane Gibson; (second row) Leon, Barbara, and Jeanette Gibson. Jeanette worked at the ranch so she could ride the horses. (DT.)

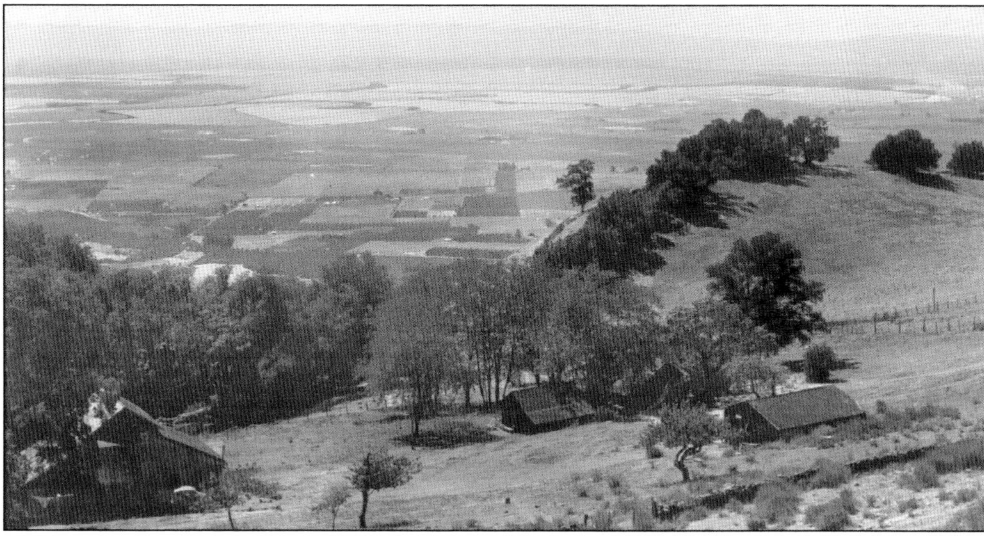

Just above Hidden Valley Dude Ranch, about a mile towards Mission Peak, was the McClure Ranch, also known as Peak Meadow Ranch. A.A. Moore willed it to his daughter Margaret in 1928. This 1938 photograph shows the ranch nestled in a grove of locust trees, with a spring and a canyon to the south (left) and "The Flat" to the north (right). Warm Springs farmlands are below. (RM.)

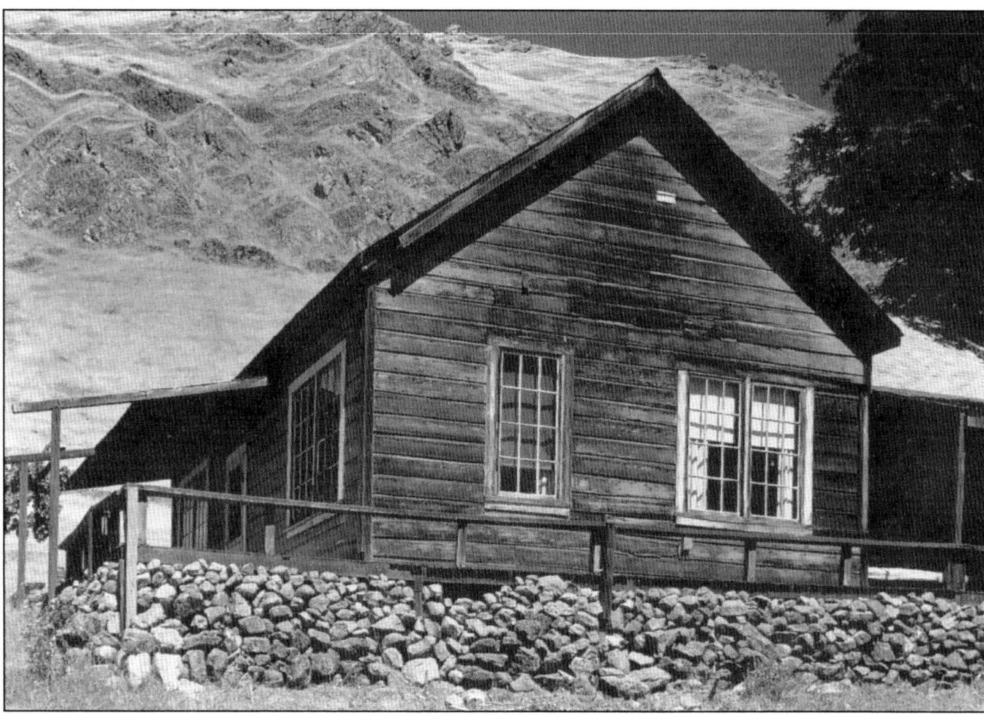

According to Roan McClure's *Mill Creek Road*, Thomas Millard built the main residence on Peak Meadow Ranch in 1855. He planted grapes on "The Flat," but they died during the grape root-rot of the 1870s. Millard died at the ranch in 1923. Margaret McClure had the main residence remodeled with plans from architect Noble Newsom in 1928. The house is seen here with its surrounding porch and the slopes of Mission Peak in the background. (RM.)

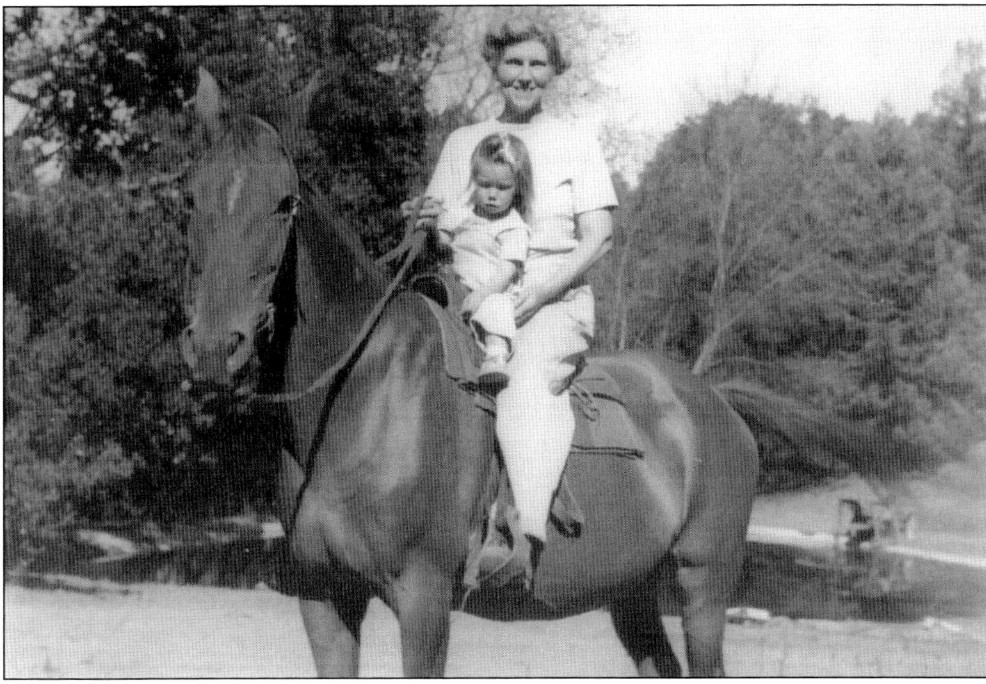

Margaret McClure and her granddaughter, Torrence, are seen above on a horseback trip to the Moore Rancho, north of Mission Peak on Mill Creek Road, in 1945. McClure stayed at Peak Meadow Ranch and drove a buckboard down to Mission San Jose to do her shopping. Years later, she drove a jeep to town. For 53 years, the McClure family used the ranch as a second home and had many good times living the ranch life. (RM.)

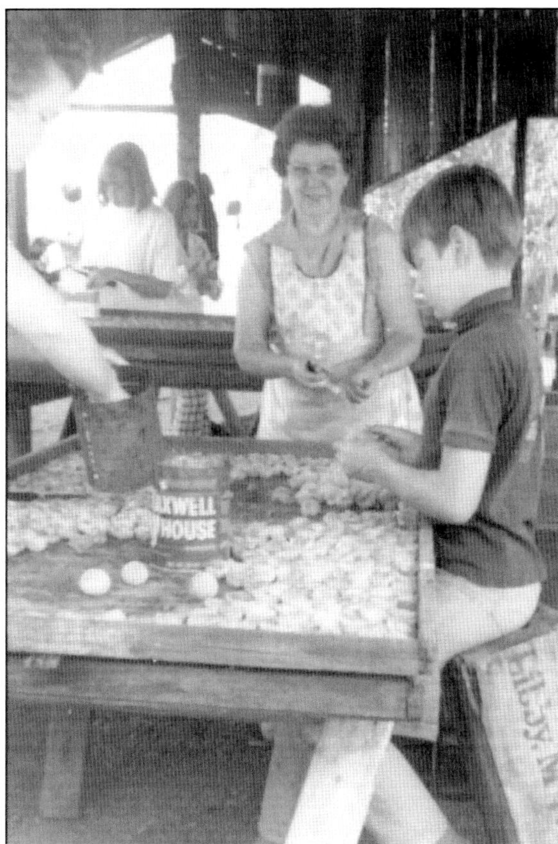

In the late 1960s, Donald and Bob Brazil went into the apricot and walnut farming business and became the largest dried-apricot producer in northern California. They ran two huge cutting sheds, one in Warm Springs and the other in Milpitas. Jan Brazil is on the far left, partially out of the photograph, and Adeline Vargas Swartz is looking into the camera. The unidentified children were some of the up to 300 children hired during the summer season to cut apricots. (SVM.)

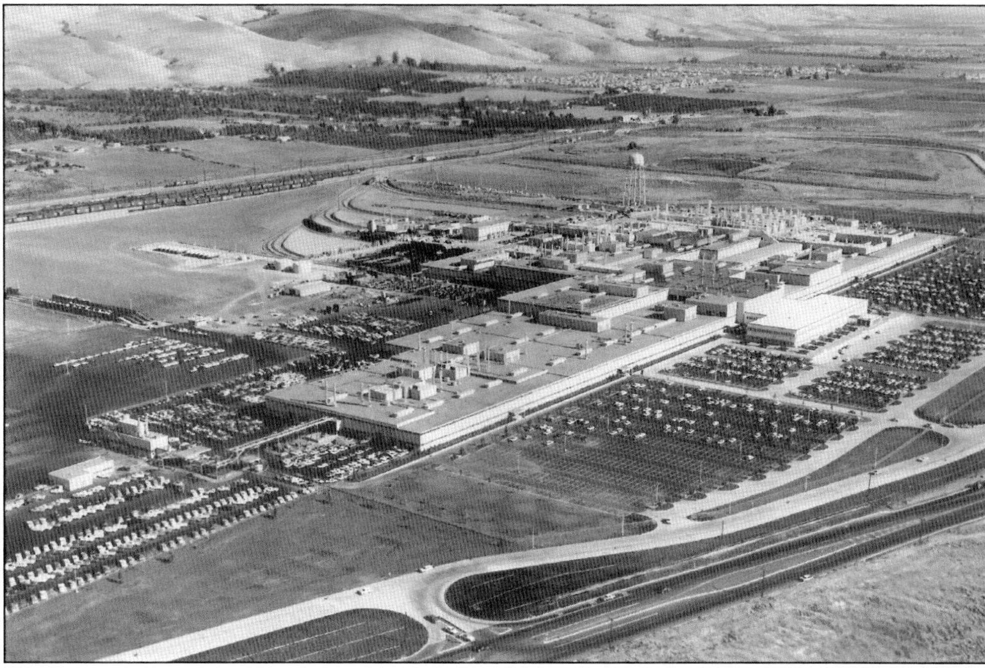

The new two-million-square-foot General Motors assembly plant in Fremont was located on a 411-acre tract. The ground-breaking ceremony was in 1961, and the plant quickly began producing Chevrolet and GMC trucks, Chevrolet Chevelles, Pontiac Tempests, Oldsmobile F-85s, and Buick Special passenger cars in 1963. Employing 4,100 people, the Fremont plant was the first GM facility to produce four different lines of passenger cars and two lines of trucks under a single roof. (JB.)

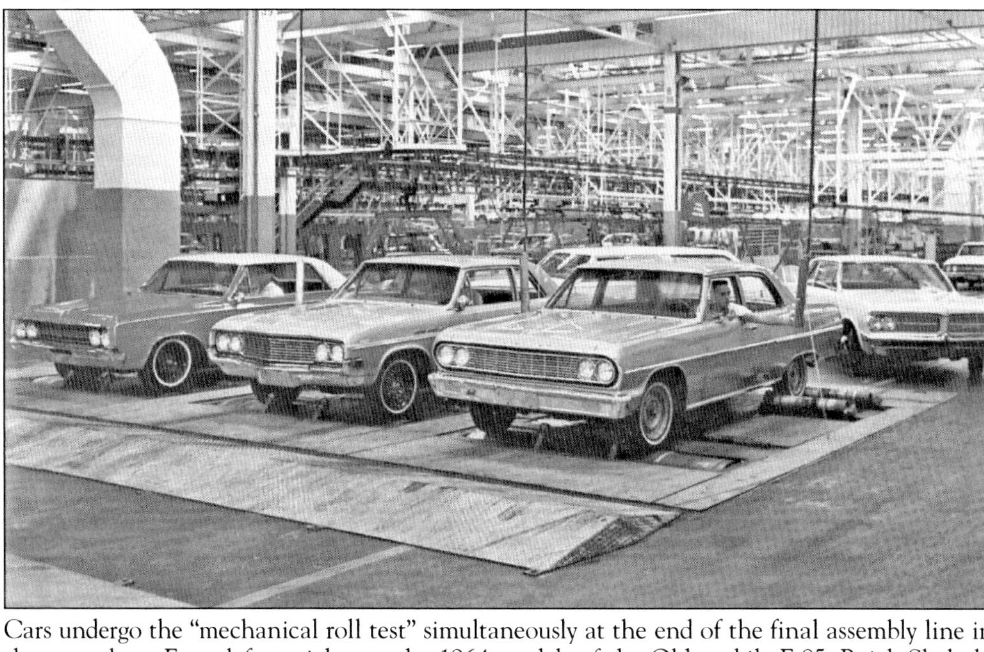

Cars undergo the "mechanical roll test" simultaneously at the end of the final assembly line in the new plant. From left to right are the 1964 models of the Oldsmobile F-85, Buick Skylark, Chevrolet Chevelle, and the Pontiac Tempest in the back right. (JB.)

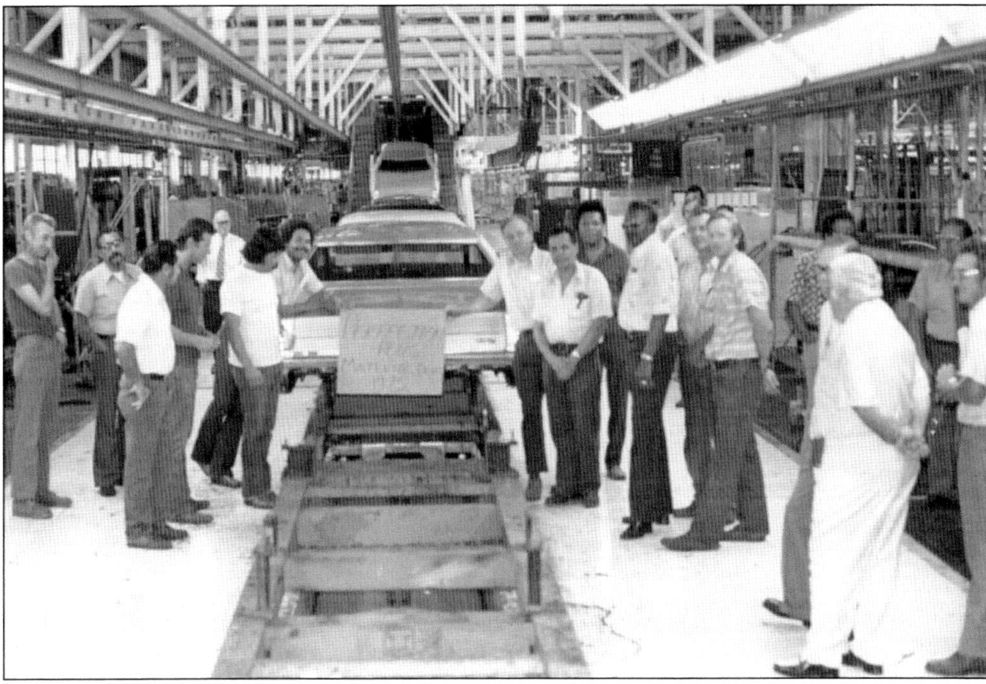

A "perfect build out" was when no repairs or changes were needed as a car came off the assembly line. The proud workers in this 1975 photograph include, from left to right, Bob Butler, unidentified, Benny Gutierrez, James Nixon, unidentified, Ralph Valasco, Charlie Tubbs, Clay Brand, L. Nunes, Walt Flowers, Jim Holmes, and 10 unidentified employees. (Courtesy James Nixon.)

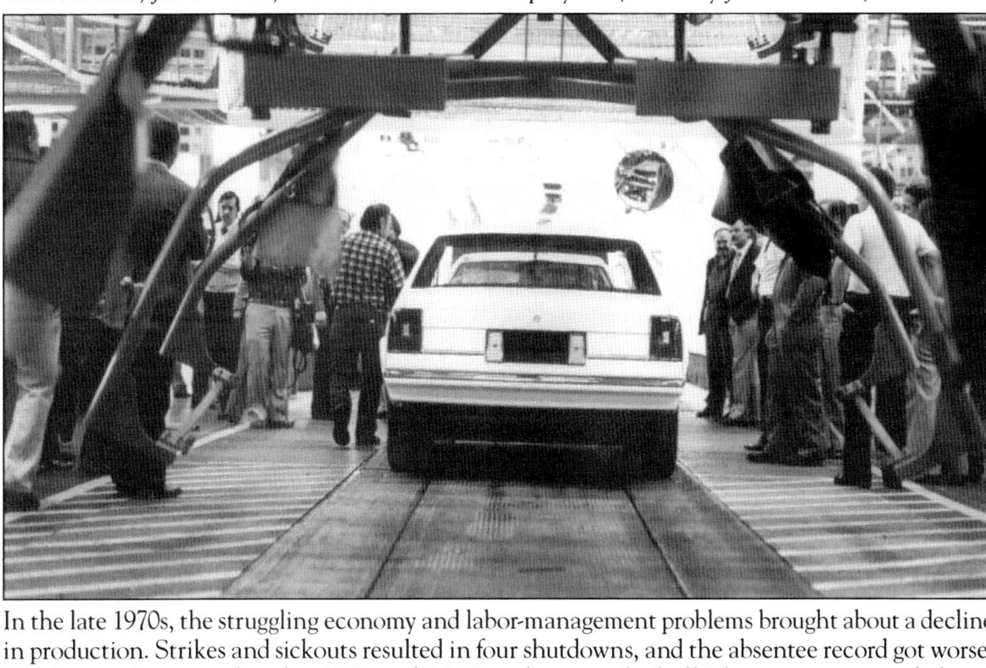

In the late 1970s, the struggling economy and labor-management problems brought about a decline in production. Strikes and sickouts resulted in four shutdowns, and the absentee record got worse. The last truck was produced in 1981, and 2,200 workers were laid off. The company struggled, and the plant's decline continued. After 18 years of production, the plant closed indefinitely in 1982, leaving 2,500 employees without a job. This white Oldsmobile Ciera was the last car produced.

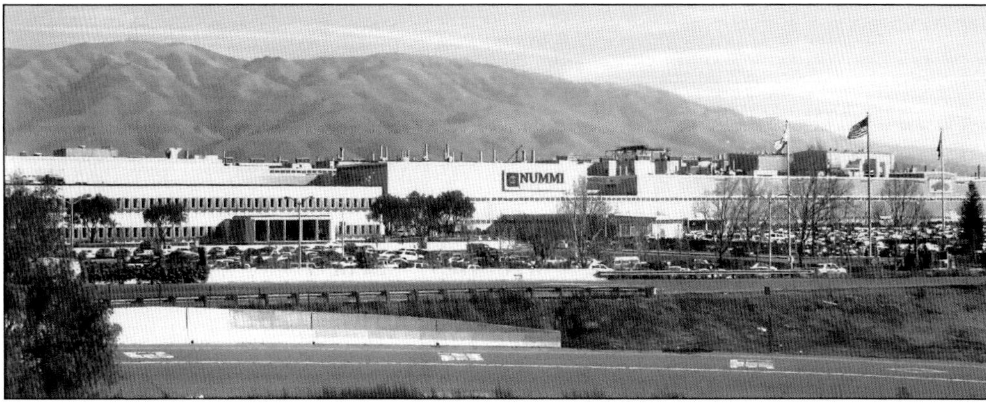


New United Motor Manufacturing, Inc. (NUMMI), a joint venture between General Motors and Toyota, was established in 1984 and replaced the former GM plant. Under the Japanese philosophy, the Toyota production system made many changes at the plant, which had about 5,100 employees. NUMMI operated from 1984 to 2010. Full production—two shifts making 940 cars per day—was reached on April 14, 1986. The Nova was built from 1984 to 1988, and the Toyota Corolla FX was built from 1986 to 1988. The one-millionth car was produced on January 29, 1991. The NUMMI plant is seen above in 1990. Below, at the debut of the new Chevy Nova in April 1985, are Shoichiro Toyoda of Toyota and Roger B. Smith of General Motors. (Above, MLH; below, courtesy Al Minard.)

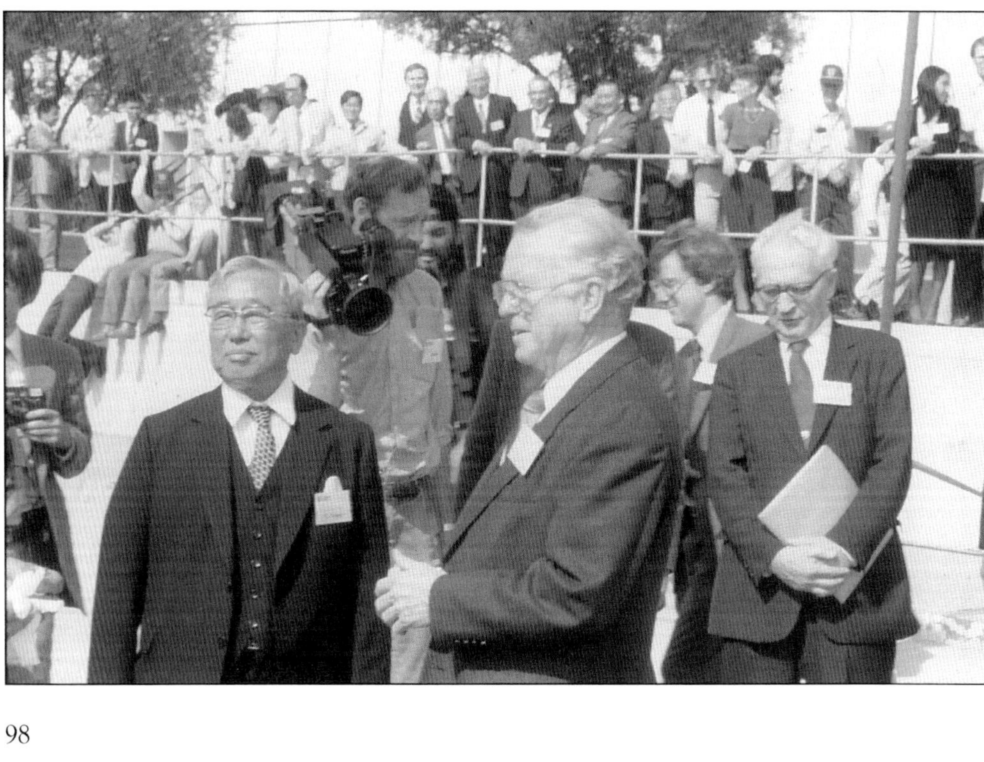

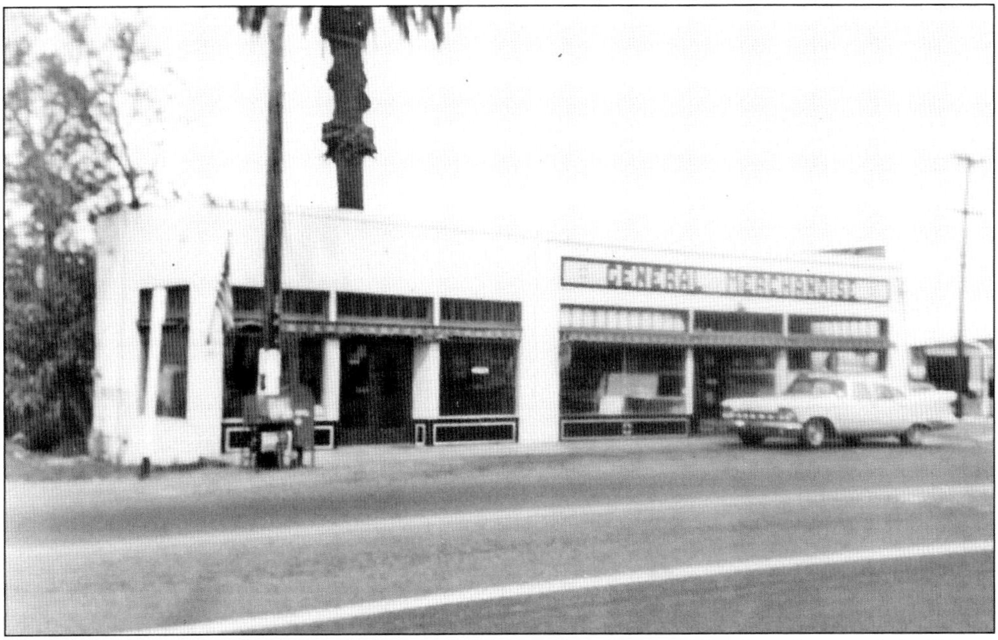

In the early 1960s, Warm Springs began to change drastically. The demolition of the Warm Springs Store is representative of that change. In this photograph, taken from Warm Springs Boulevard in 1966, the Browns' store is about to be demolished and replaced by the Hebel Union Service Station, owned by Herman and Bette Hebel. The palm tree behind the store today is on the corner of Warm Springs Boulevard and East Warren Avenue, a reminder of days gone by in Warm Springs.

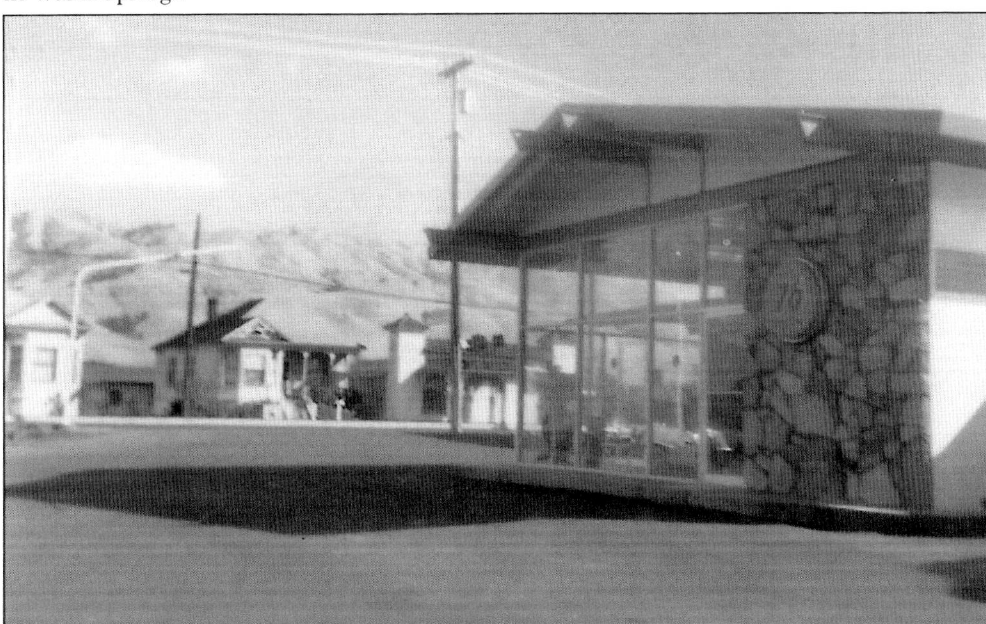

When the 76 gas station was built, the area around it was modernized, with sidewalks and a widened Warm Springs Boulevard. The Hebels operated the station from 1966 until they retired in 1993. (HBH.)

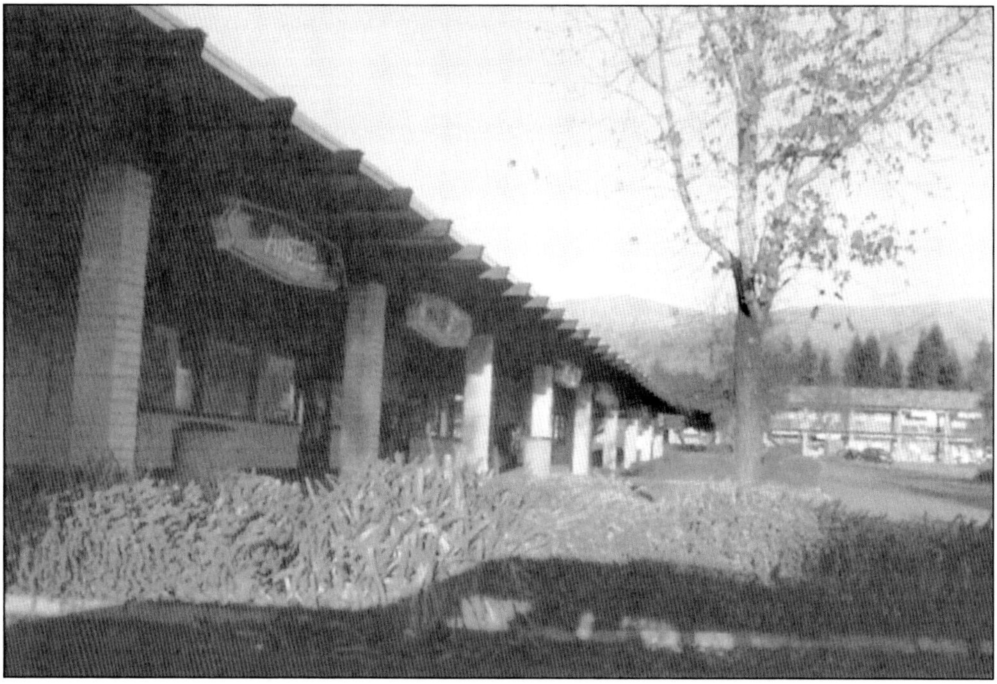

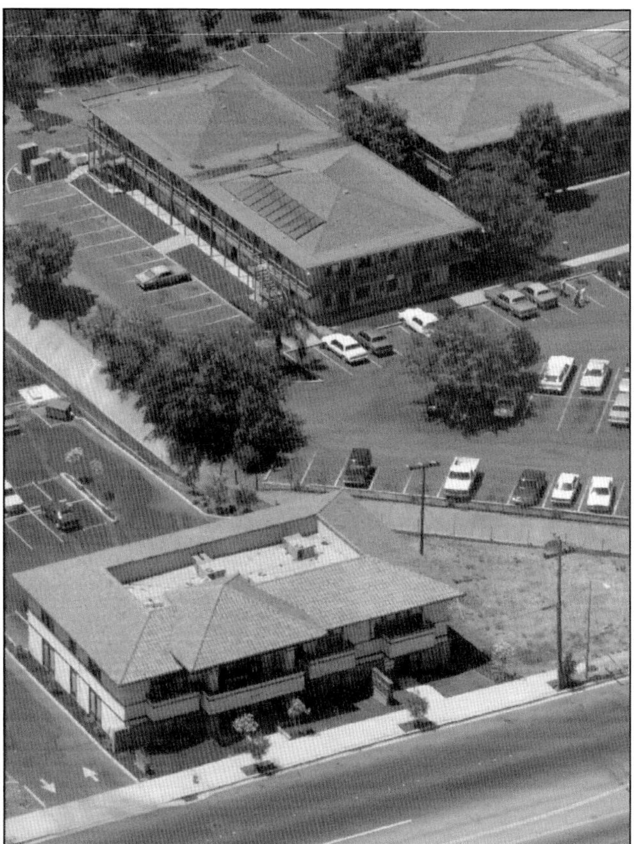

Joe F. and Anna Vargas bought 33 acres of land from James Leitch in 1910. Francisco Lane in Warm Springs was named after the middle name "Francisco," which all of the Vargas children used. The land around Francisco Lane and the Franciscan shopping center, seen above, was once owned by four of the Vargas children: Alvino, Annie, Tony, and Joe. (PH.)

This aerial photograph shows part of the Franciscan Shopping Center, with Dutra Realty, built in 1985, in the foreground. This bustling center was originally built around 1970 and housed Chateau Gourmet, Flair Market, Martin's Hair Salon, a donut shop, a dry cleaner, the South 40 Club, which was opened in 1970 by Jim Adams, and a gas station. (Courtesy Dutra family.)

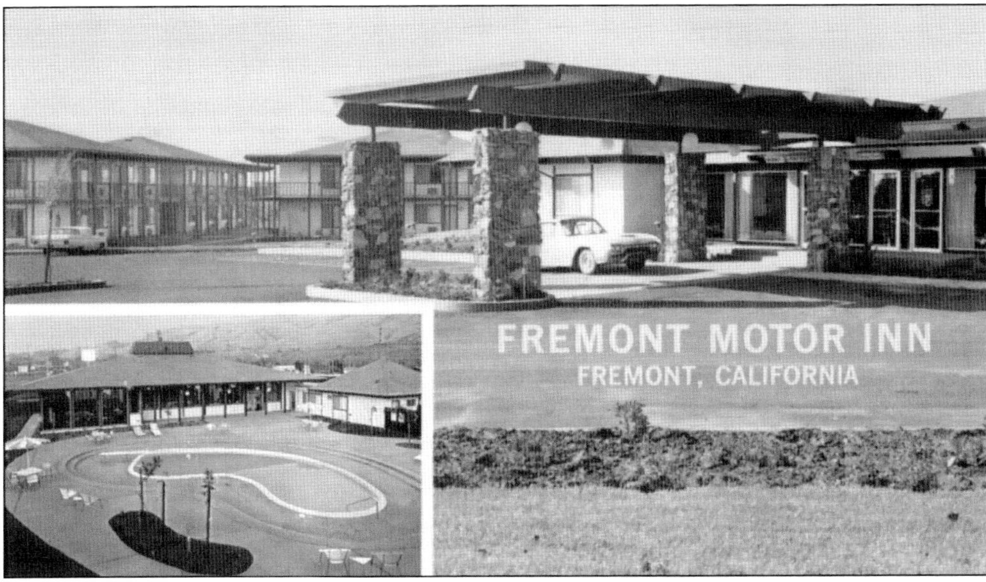


Built in the mid-1960s, the Fremont Motor Inn was the first modern motel in the Warm Springs area. On the corner of Warm Springs and Mission Boulevards, it advertised "restaurant-banquet facilities, cocktail lounge, room service, heated pool, 'magic fingers' massaging beds. Coffee in rooms." This 1966 postcard shows the motor inn complex with the Mission hills in the background. Meetings of the Rotary Club, the Moose Lodge, and the Lions Club were held here. (MLH.)

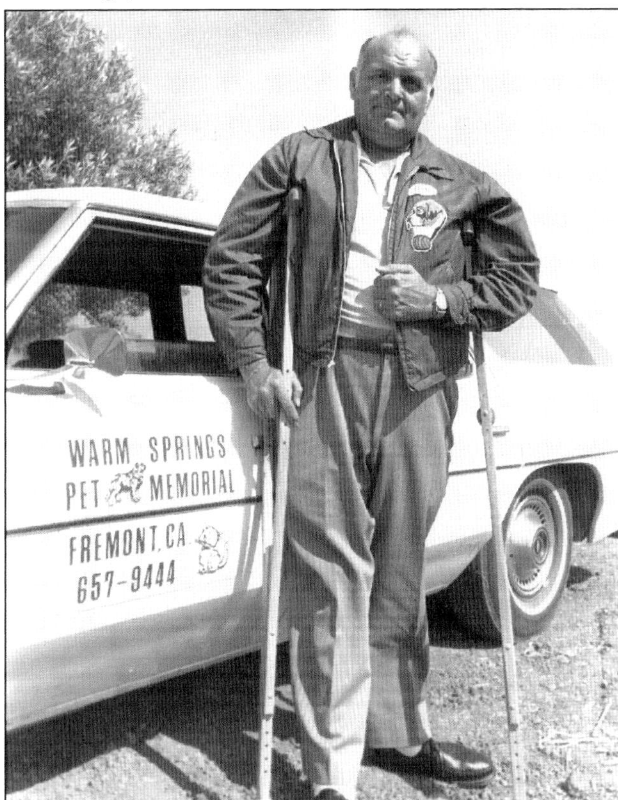


Warm Springs Pet Memorial was on the west side of the Nimitz Freeway on Braga Street near West Warren Avenue.

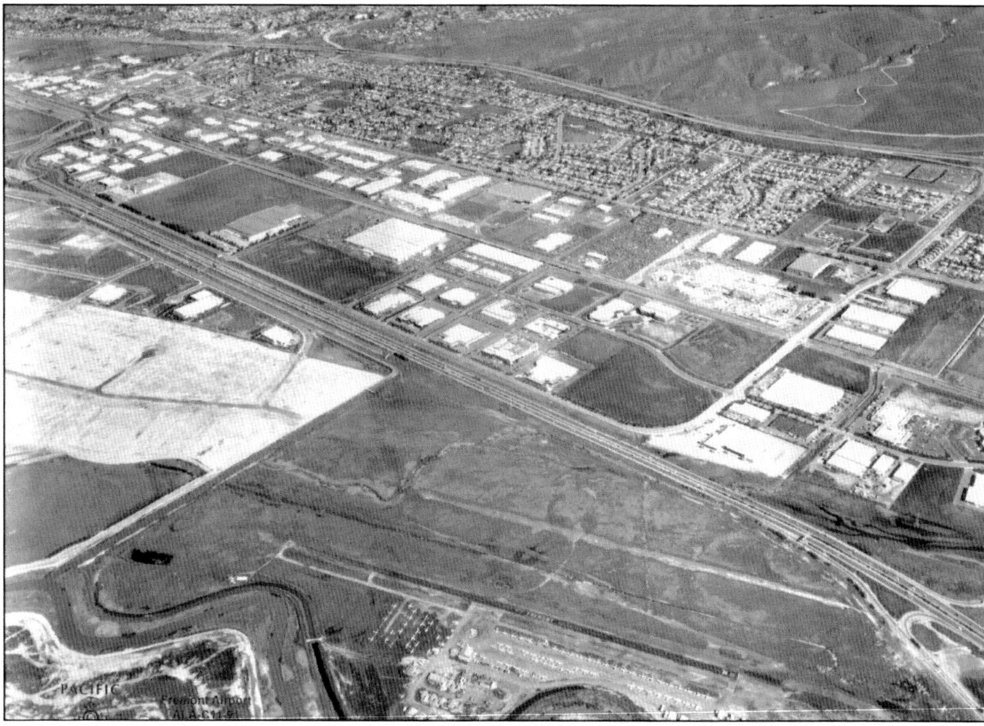

This aerial photograph from 1985 shows the southern part of Warm Springs. The airport is on the bottom, with the 880 freeway running north to south, parallel to Warm Springs Boulevard and the 680 freeway. Industrial development is west of Warm Springs Boulevard and north of the airport. The housing and commercial developments are between the two freeways. (Courtesy Celebrate Fremont Collection.)

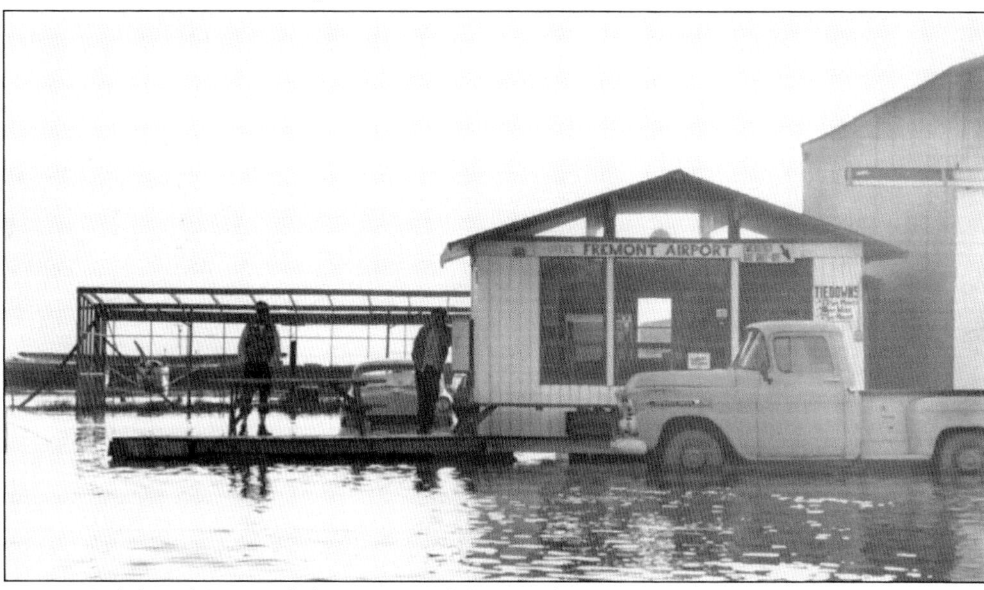


In 1947, Ralph and Betty Salisbury operated the Northern California Soaring Association at the Warm Springs Airport (later the Fremont Airport). It was reported by some pilots to be a little short, sometimes a bit rough, and subject to floods, as seen in this late-1950s photograph. (MLH.)

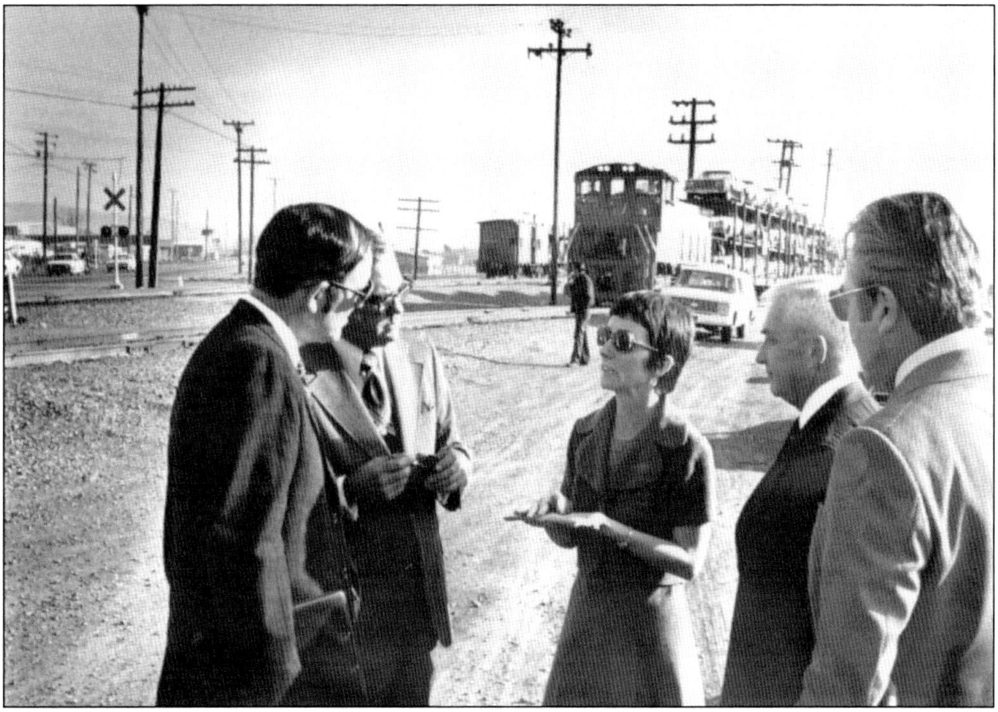

The Bradley Baez Overpass was built to minimize train accidents at the double railroad crossing on Grimmer Boulevard. Here, representatives from various public agencies discuss the project. From left to right are Tom Blalock, Leon Mezzetti, Jan Stillwell, and two unidentified men. In the background are Warm Springs Road and railroad cars loaded with vehicles from the GM plant. (DV.)

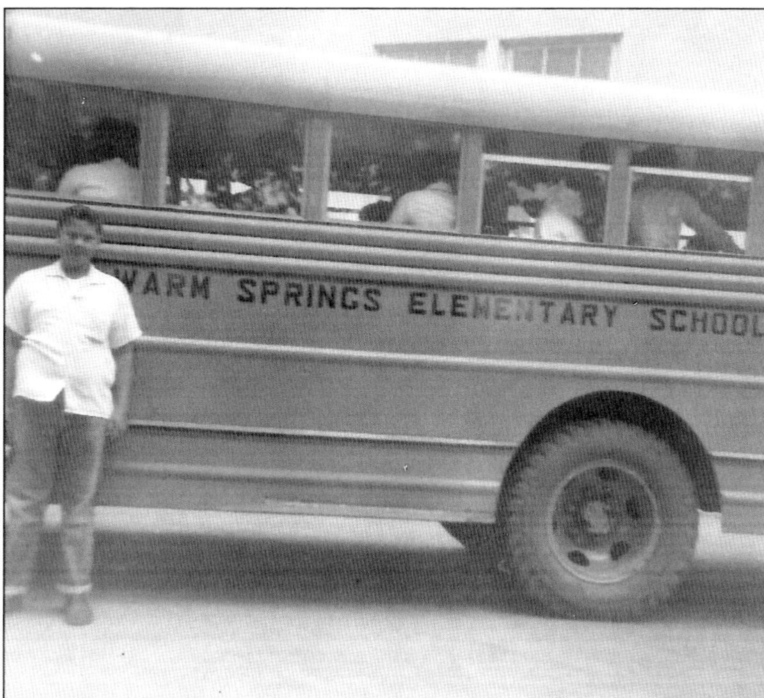


Kenneth Benge stands in front of the familiar site of the Warm Springs school bus around 1956. Sid Treleavin was the bus driver at the time, and his wife was the cook at the school. (DT.)

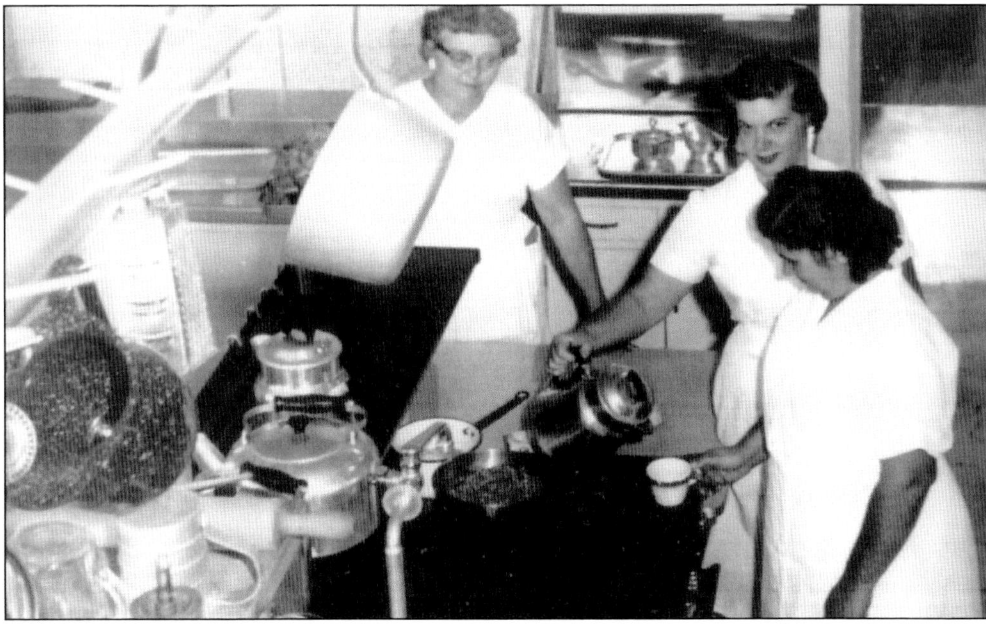

The Warm Springs school cafeteria was added in 1953. Here, cafeteria workers prepare lunches for the students in the modern kitchen in 1960. Lorraine Dias is in the middle looking at the camera, and Elsie Duarte is on the right. (SVM.)

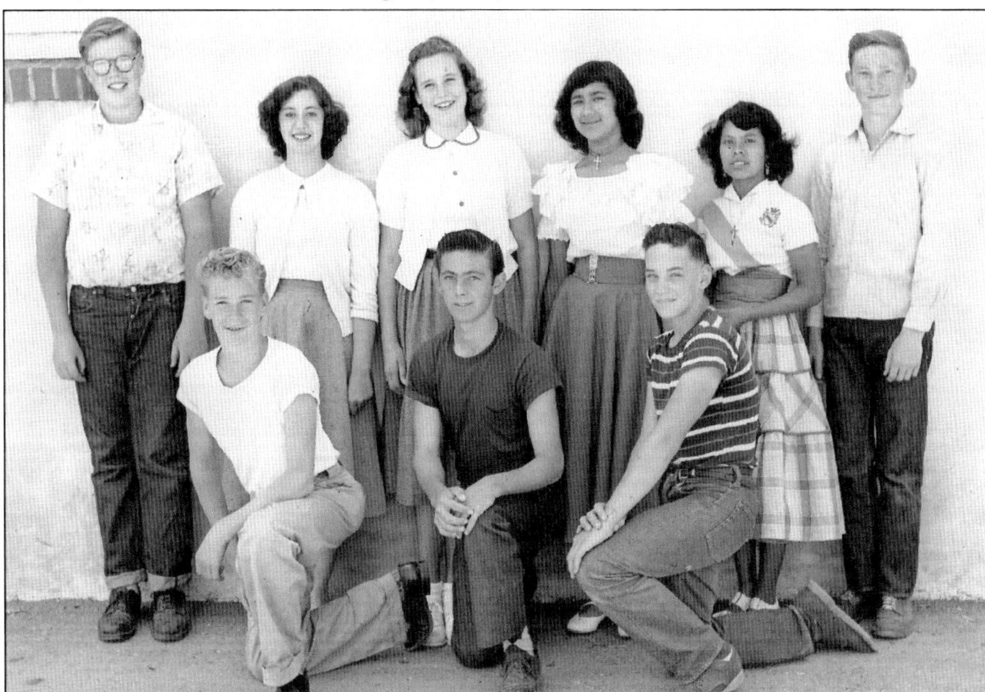

Warm Springs School still had a relatively small enrollment in 1954, as seen in the size of its eighth-grade graduating class. From left to right, the class included (first row) Claude Yeakey, Jerry Vargas, and Pat McClough; (second row) Clifford Moilan, Nancy Coehlo, Dona Leak, Rosa Espinoza, Ruth ?, and Philip Kinzli. (Courtesy Nancy Margherita.)

Marion Moilan (left) and Emily Bettencourt prepare for a PTA function in 1957. Both were very active in the PTA and in other Warm Springs organizations. Moilan was also active in the 4-H Club, the Warm Springs Chamber of Commerce, and the local Democratic Party. Bettencourt was the grand director of the Benevolent Society of California and a member of the SPRSI and hosted many meetings at her home in Warm Springs. (Courtesy Jane Huber.)

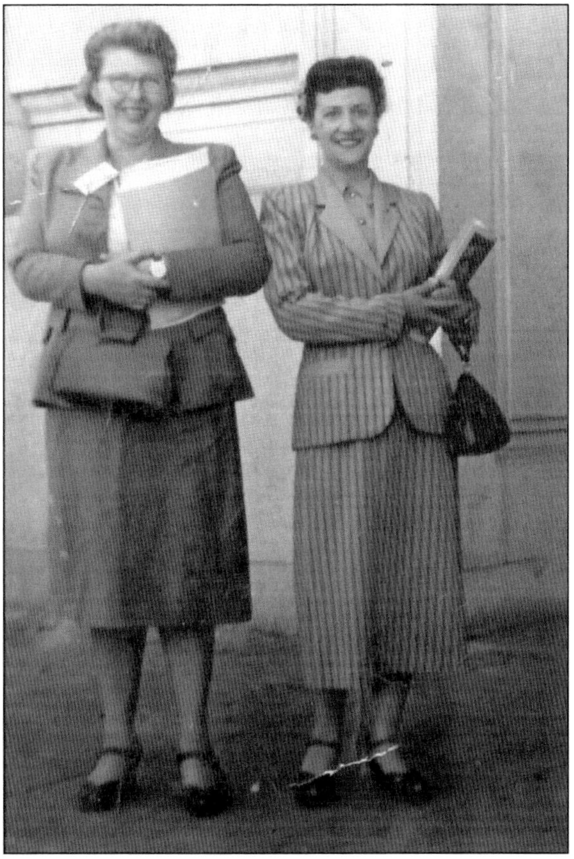

Below, Orville Leitch, the clerk of the Warm Springs Elementary School board, hands a diploma to Jane Moilan at the 1958 eighth-grade graduation ceremonies. Leitch often stopped by the school in his farming overalls to the delight of the children, who enjoyed seeing his friendly face. Leitch, Orville Gibson, and Tony Vargas were responsible for the daily operations of the school and its personnel. (Courtesy Jane Huber.)

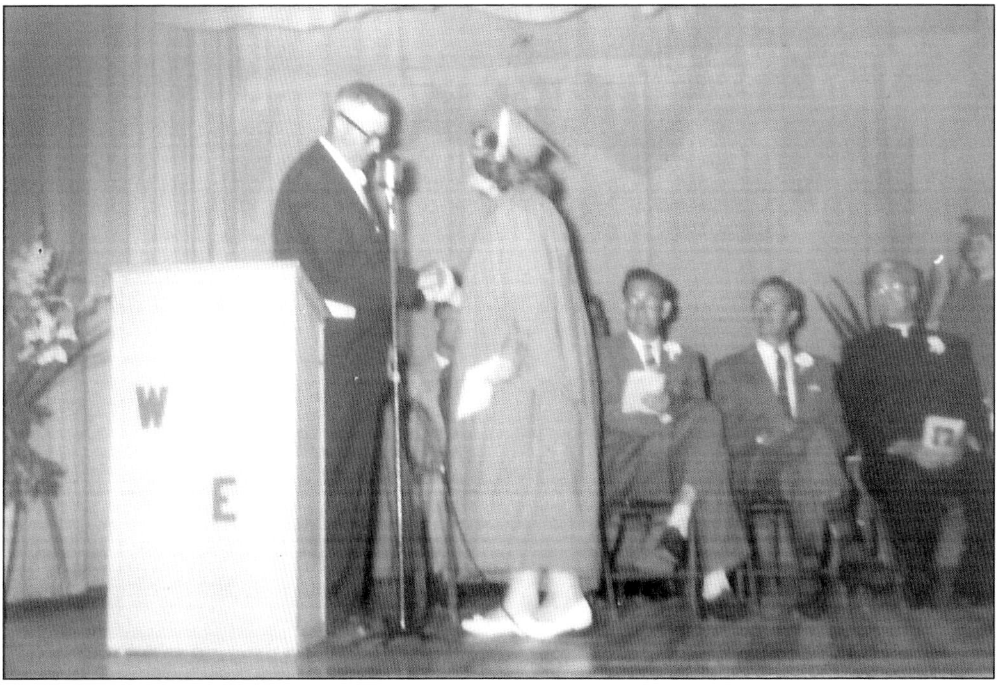

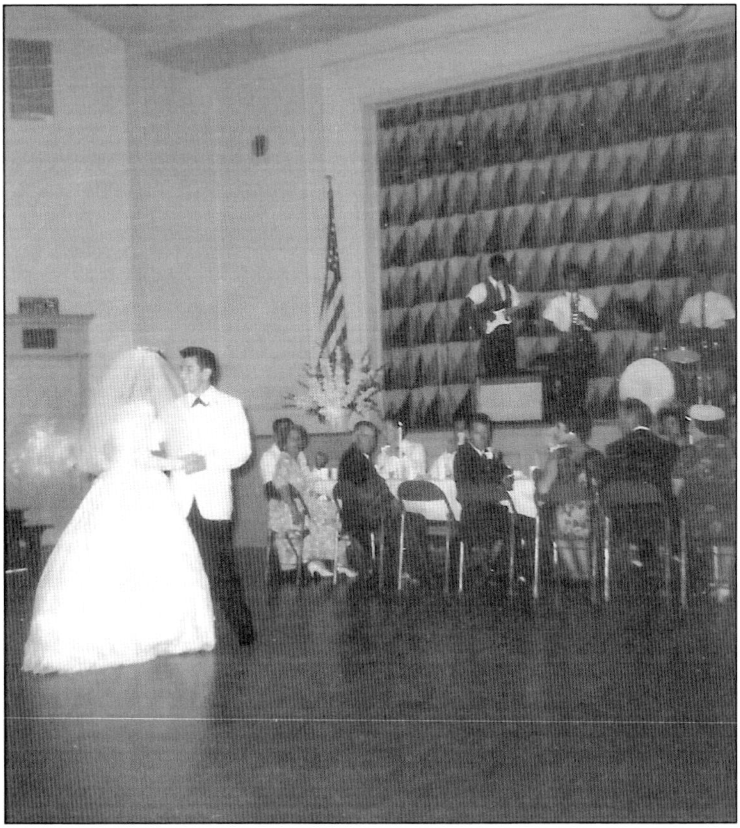

The Warm Springs School has been a cultural center for the area for more than 120 years. Seen here in 1963 is likely the last wedding between two graduates of the school, Doug and Barbara Tavis. The couple dances to the music of Doug's band as the guests enjoy the festivities. (DT.)

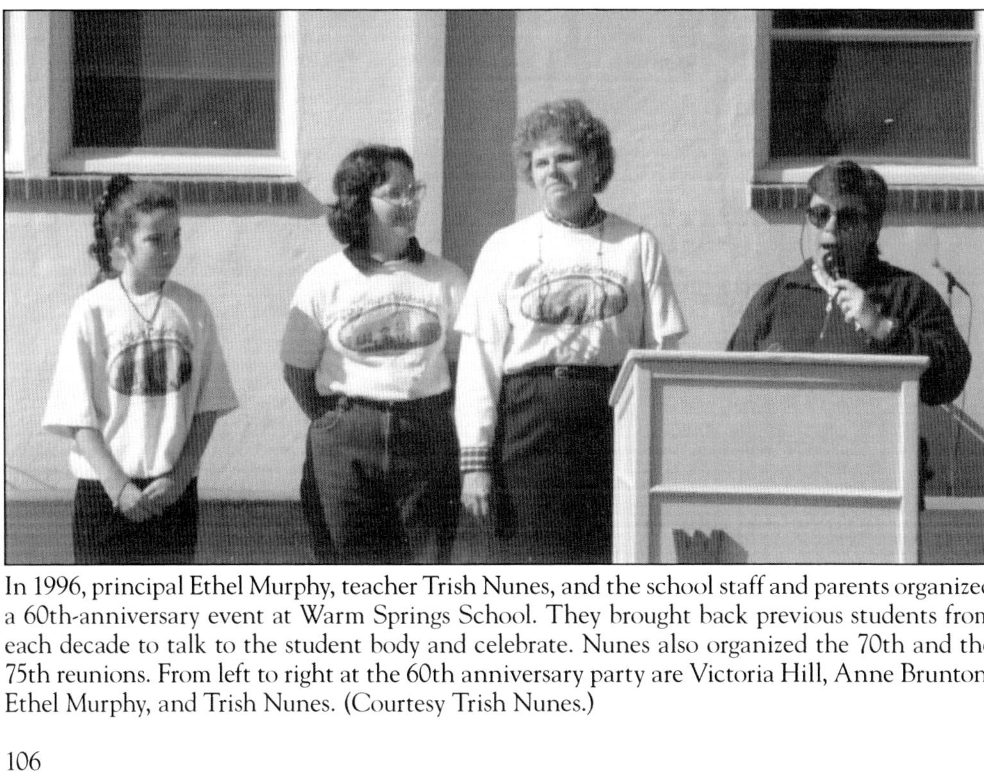

In 1996, principal Ethel Murphy, teacher Trish Nunes, and the school staff and parents organized a 60th-anniversary event at Warm Springs School. They brought back previous students from each decade to talk to the student body and celebrate. Nunes also organized the 70th and the 75th reunions. From left to right at the 60th anniversary party are Victoria Hill, Anne Brunton, Ethel Murphy, and Trish Nunes. (Courtesy Trish Nunes.)

Nancy Curteman was an innovative teacher at Leitch School. Her outdoor class project, "Our Tree," and the science center in her classroom were widely recognized. Curteman and her class were featured on the public television station KQED in 1976. Here, she works outside with her students on one of her many class projects. (Courtesy Leitch School.)

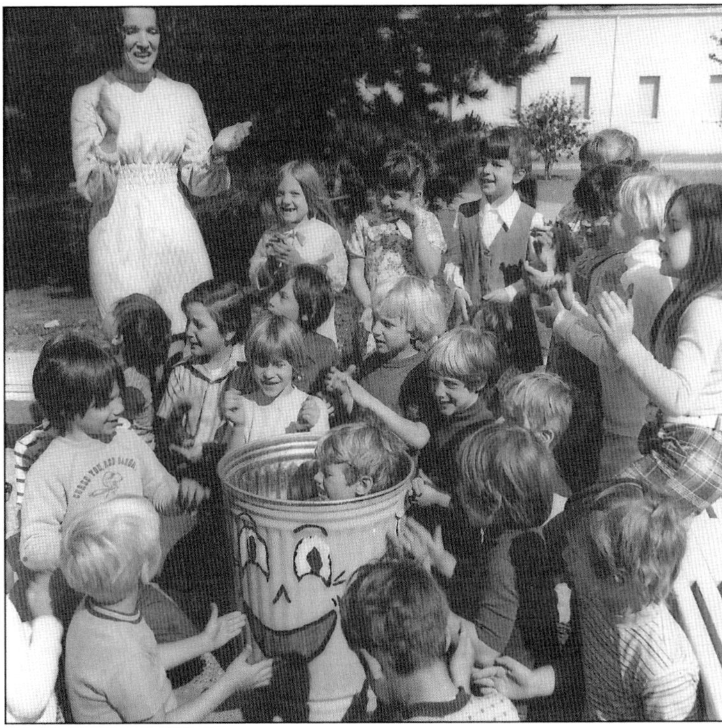

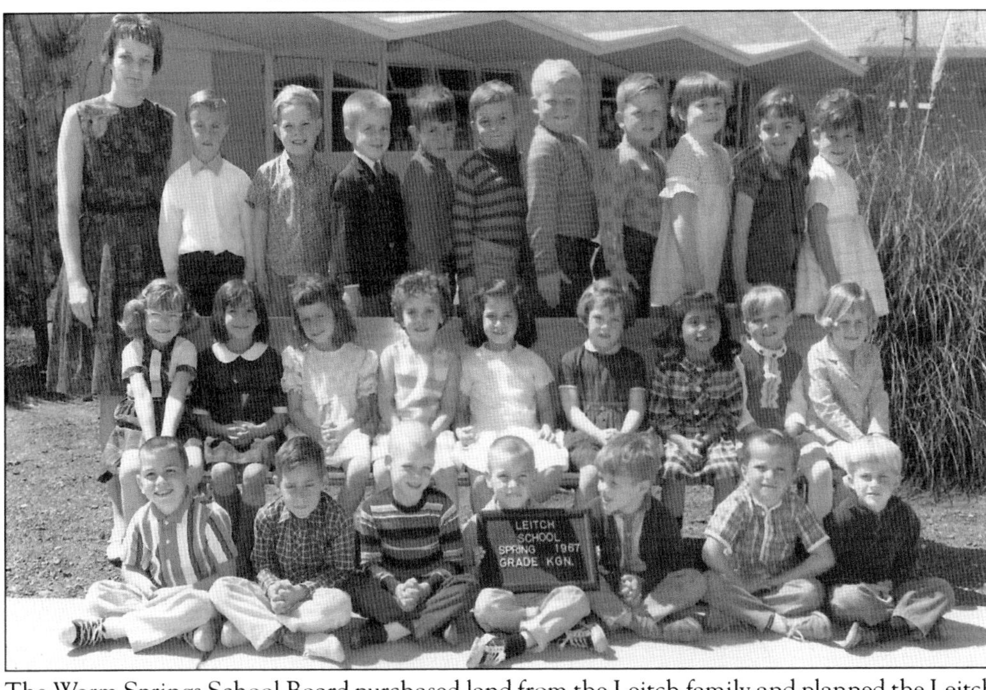


The Warm Springs School Board purchased land from the Leitch family and planned the Leitch Elementary School, which opened in 1965, as part of the newly formed Fremont Unified School District. John Lanthier was the first principal, followed by James Howden. Ann Shepherd was the school secretary for many years. The members of this 1967 kindergarten class were 51 years old in 2012. (Courtesy Leitch School.)

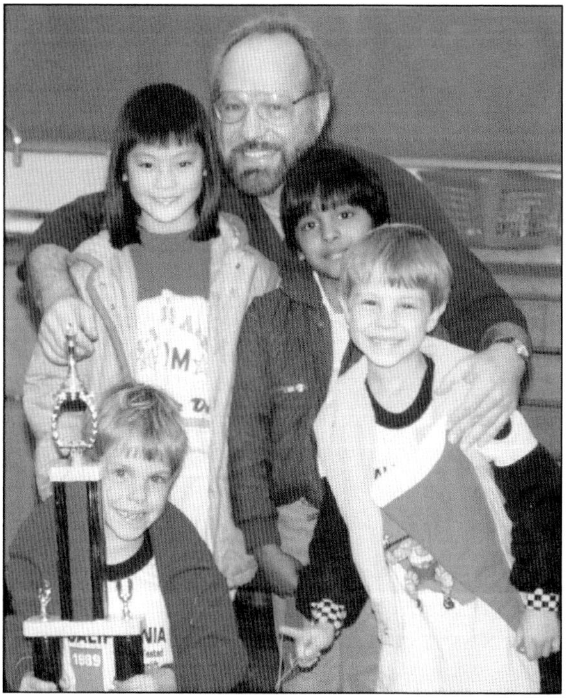

Dr. Alan Kirshner, a history professor from Ohlone College, set up the Weibel Chess Club at the school in 1989 and continues to run it through the auspices of the Parent-Teacher Organization. He is seen here with the primary school division at the California State Championship in 1989. They took fifth place that year and first the next. From left to right, they are Micah Fisher-Kirshner, Jennifer Chen, Dr. Kirshner, Rathnam Kumarappan, and Tov Fisher-Kirshner. (Courtesy Dr. Alan Kirshner.)

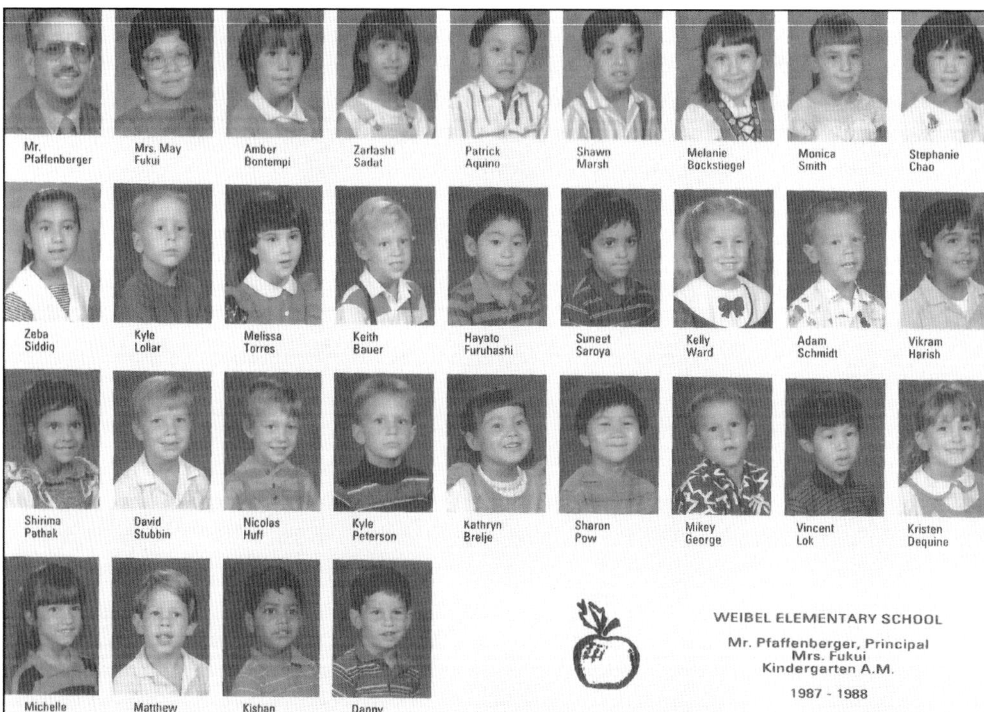


Weibel School, named for Fred Weibel Sr., opened in 1987 with a student population of more than 700. It was a state-of-the-art school, with a new computer lab of 18 new Apple IIGS computers, which parents paid for with $28,000 that they raised. George Pfaffenberger was the first principal. May Fukui's first kindergarten class is seen here. (Courtesy Weibel School.)

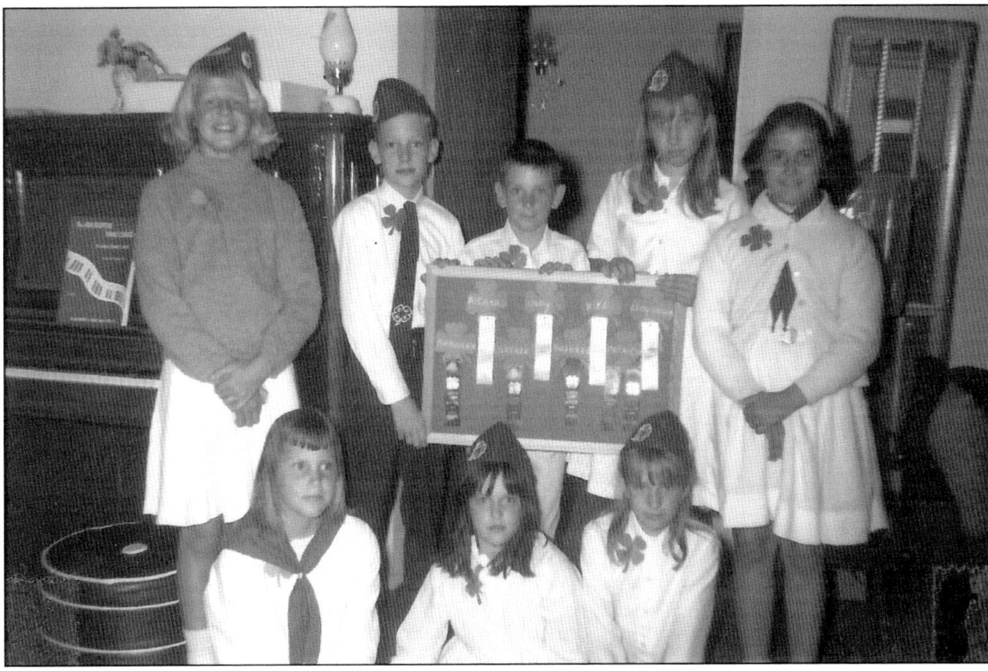

The first 4-H group in Warm Springs was formed in 1944, with Jimmy Coehlo as president. Members of the Warm Springs 4-H are seen here around 1970 at a ribbon show. The members of the group told how they won their ribbons at judging day. The children are, from left to right, (first row) Judy Seiber, Uoydena Aguilar, and Sherri Russell; (second row) Shenee Andrew, Richard Girling, Mike Oliver, Barbara Russell, and Patricia Flietz. (MLH.)

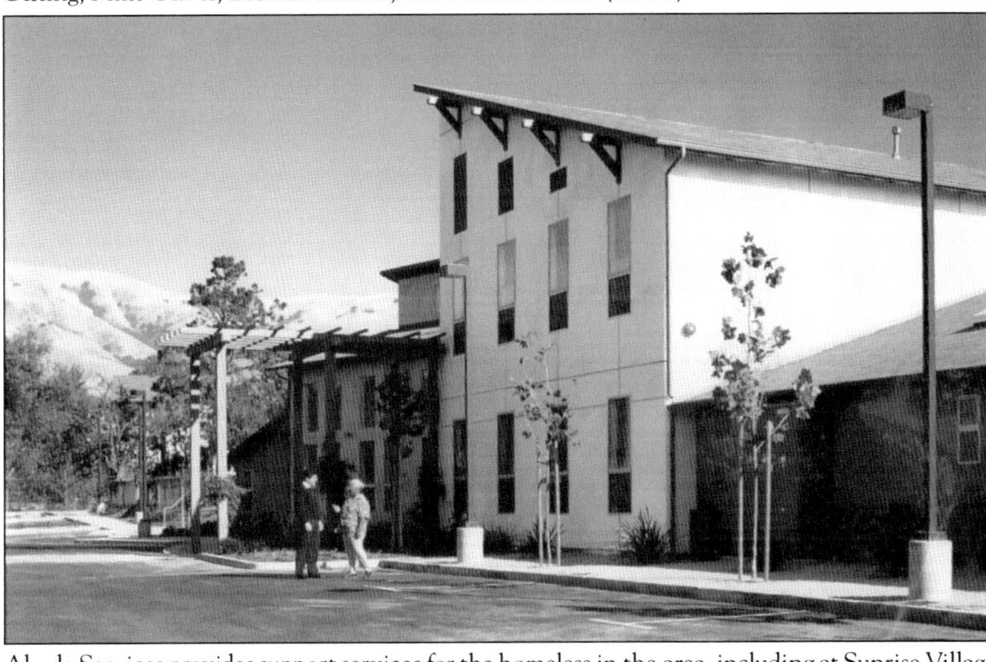

Abode Services provides support services for the homeless in the area, including at Sunrise Village in Warm Springs. Jose Sanchez (on the left) and an unidentified person are seen here in front of the new facility in 1996. (Courtesy Abode Services.)

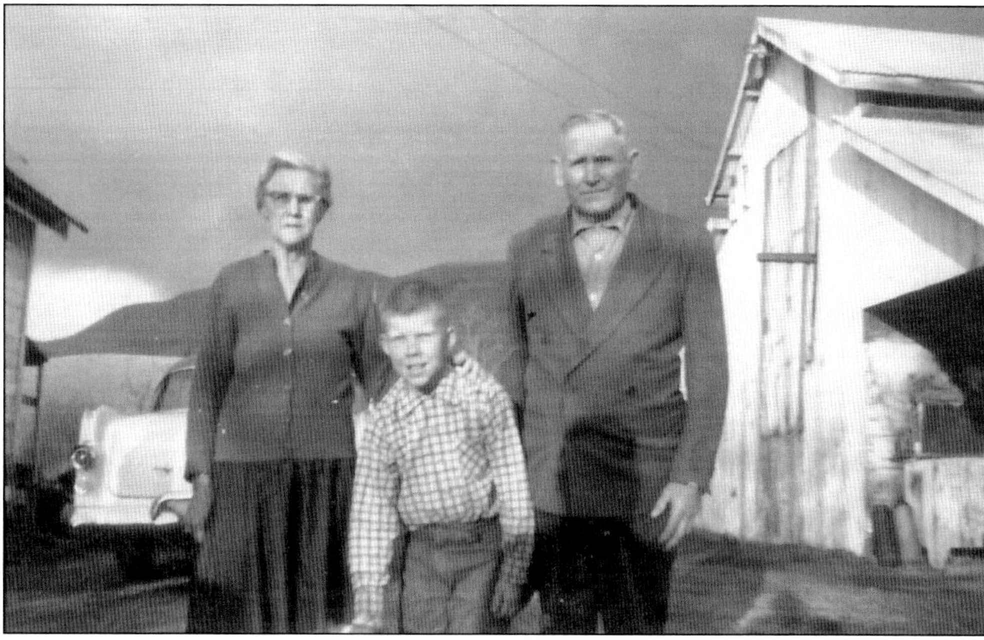

John Breitweiser poses with his wife, Mabel, and his step-grandson, John Moilan, in 1957, with his barn on the right and his home on the left. His father, Charles, arrived in Warm Springs in 1861 and purchased land from the Higuera family. John lived all of his 88 years on the home site that his father bought. (Courtesy Jane Huber.)

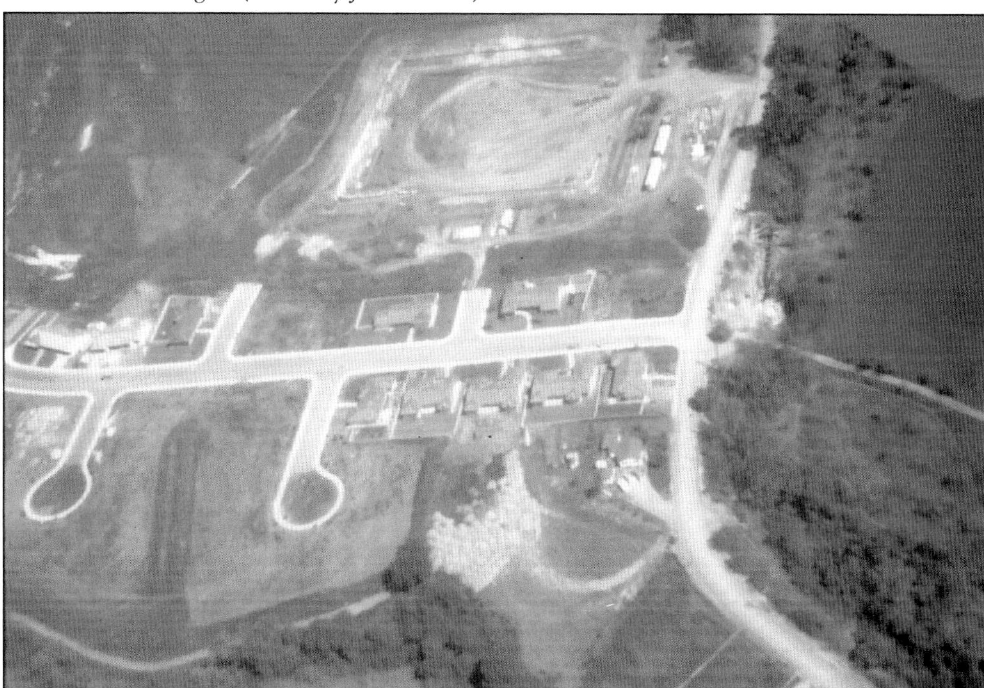

This aerial view shows the Moilan farm, just at the corner of Curtner Road. John Breitweiser's adjacent property was developed into the Glenmoor Hills subdivision. Just above the home excavation site is the construction of the A.E. Alameda Reservoir. (Courtesy Jim Reed Collection.)

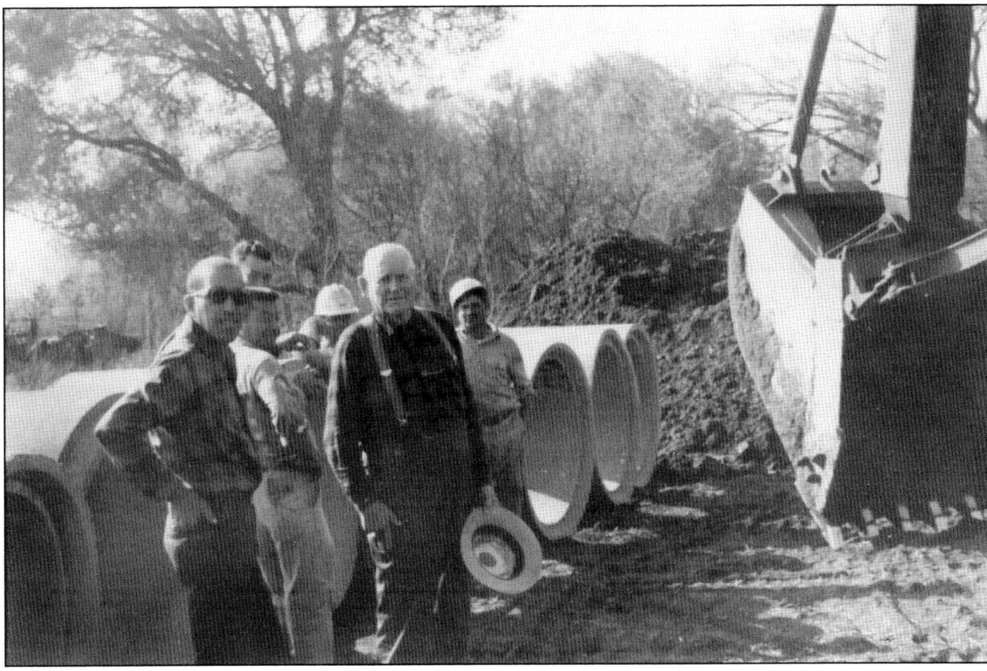

John Breitweiser (center) came to inspect the development of Glenmoor Hills in 1962. He had sold his property but still lived next door with his stepdaughter and son-in-law, Wayne and Marion Moilan. (Courtesy Jim Reed Collection.)

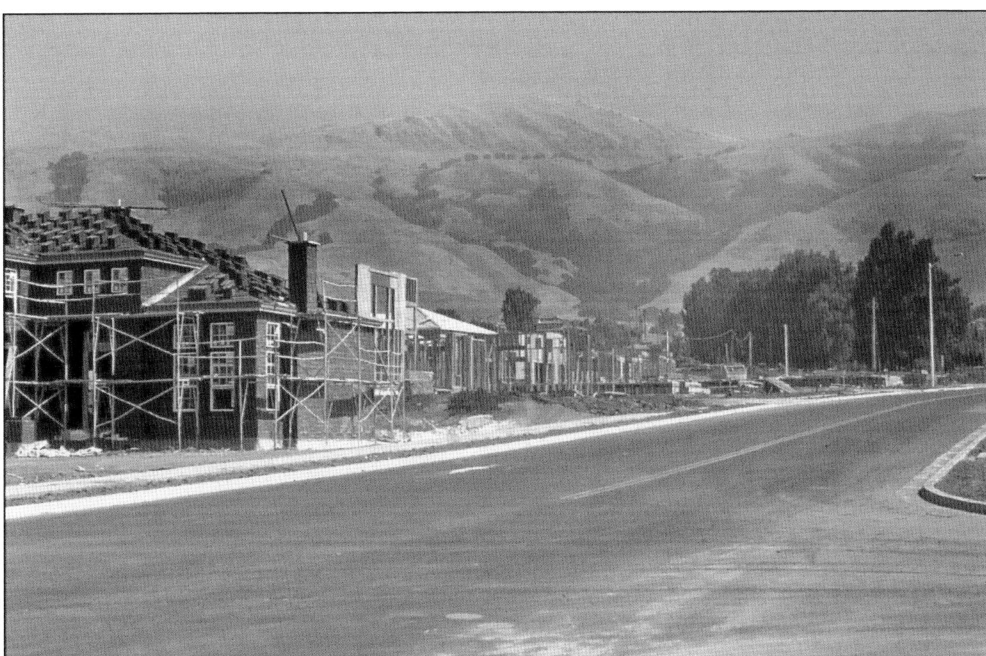

This is familiar in the development of Warm Springs, as new houses are built on Stanford Avenue, the approach to the former Weibel Winery and Hidden Valley Ranch. (PH.)

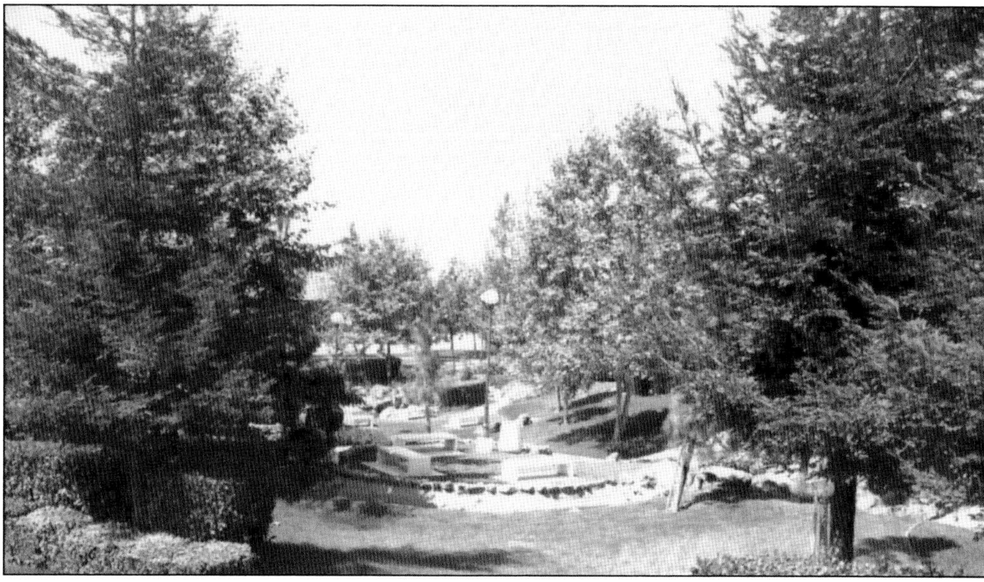

Due to its proximity to Silicon Valley, Warm Springs has attracted many high-tech companies, including Diablo Systems, a division of Xerox, which came in 1982; Apple, which opened in 1984; and Lam Research, which had a small office on Warm Springs Boulevard. In 1987, Steve Jobs opened his third company, NeXT, in Warm Springs. In 1992, Tim Berner-Lee used a NeXT computer to create the Internet. In 1993, NeXT closed its hardware division, and in 1996, it was purchased by Apple, which was run by Jobs. Today, Hurricane Electric occupies two buildings where Apple used to manufacture print circuit boards, including the one at 760 Mission Court. The Apple campus in Warm Springs, which closed and moved to Elk Grove in 1992, is seen above. Early NeXT products are below. (Both, MLH.)

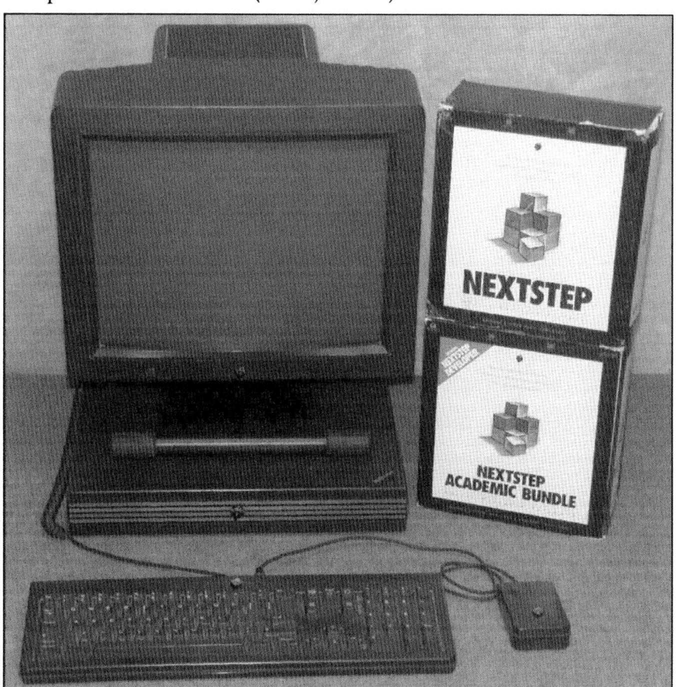

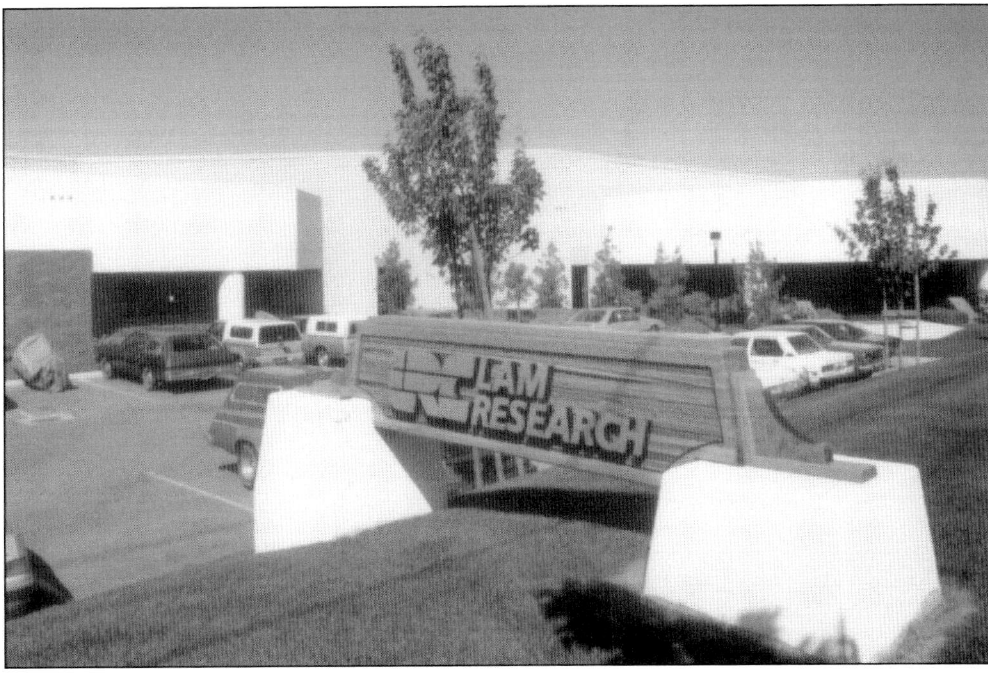


The original facility of Lam Research on Warm Springs Boulevard is seen here in the late 1980s. (Courtesy Lam Research.)

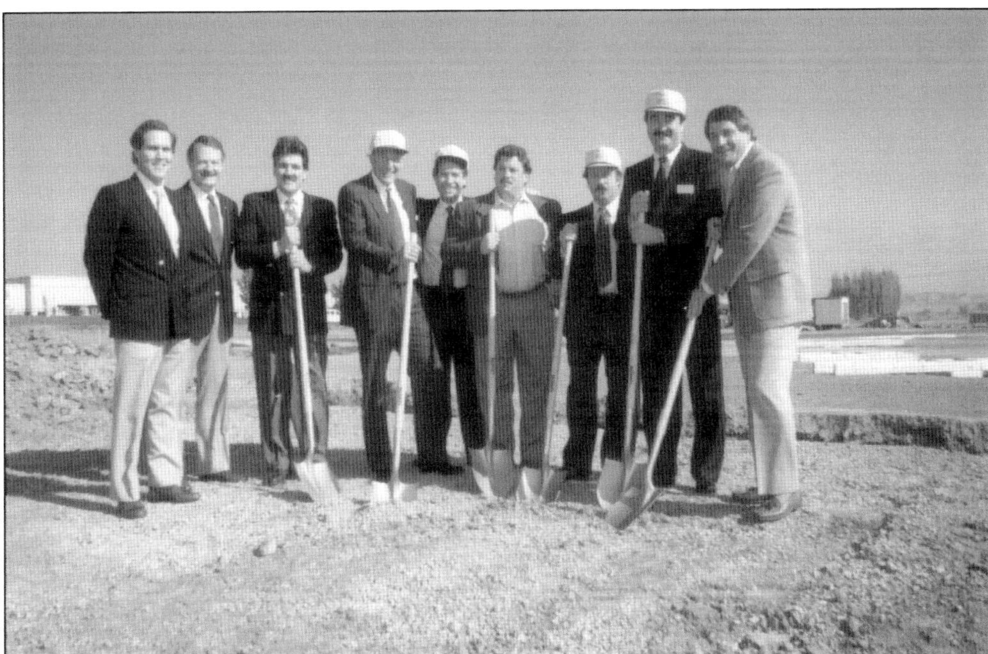

In the 1990s, Lam Research was growing at an amazing pace. The campus on Cushing Parkway expanded throughout the decade to accommodate more than 1,000 new employees. Lam Research executives and local dignitaries are seen here at the 1994 ground-breaking for Lam's new campus on Cushing Parkway. (Courtesy Lam Research.)

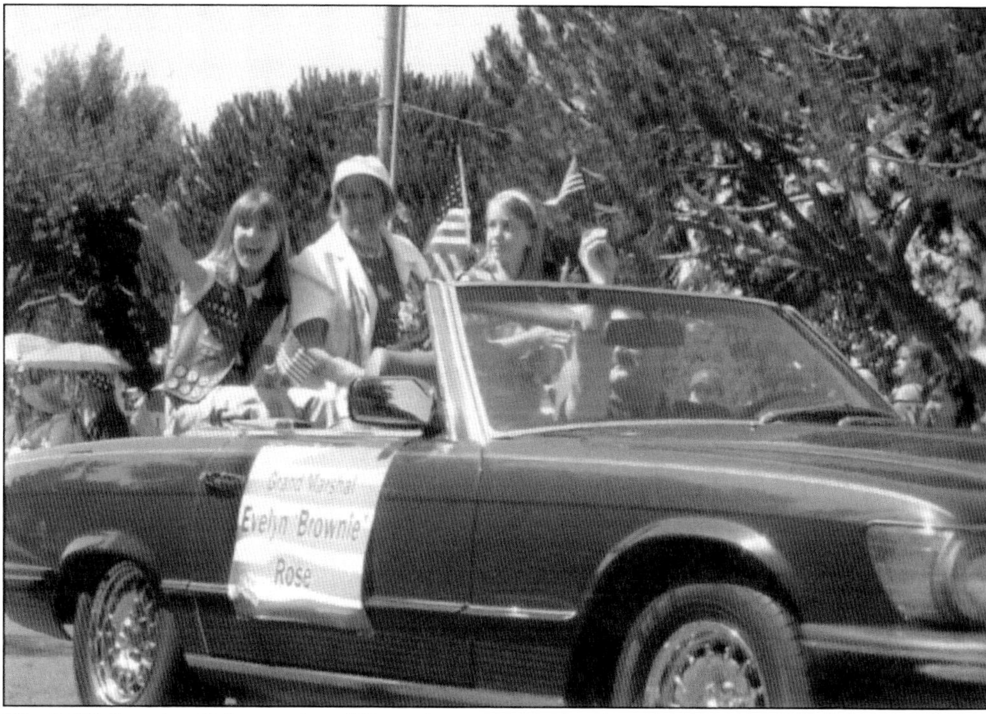


The 2009 Fourth of July parade in Warm Springs brought the community together in celebration. Evelyn "Brownie" Rose, probably the oldest person born and still living in Warm Springs, was the grand marshal. Rose served many terms as president of SPRSI, including during the 50th, 75th, and 100th anniversaries of the club. (HBH.)

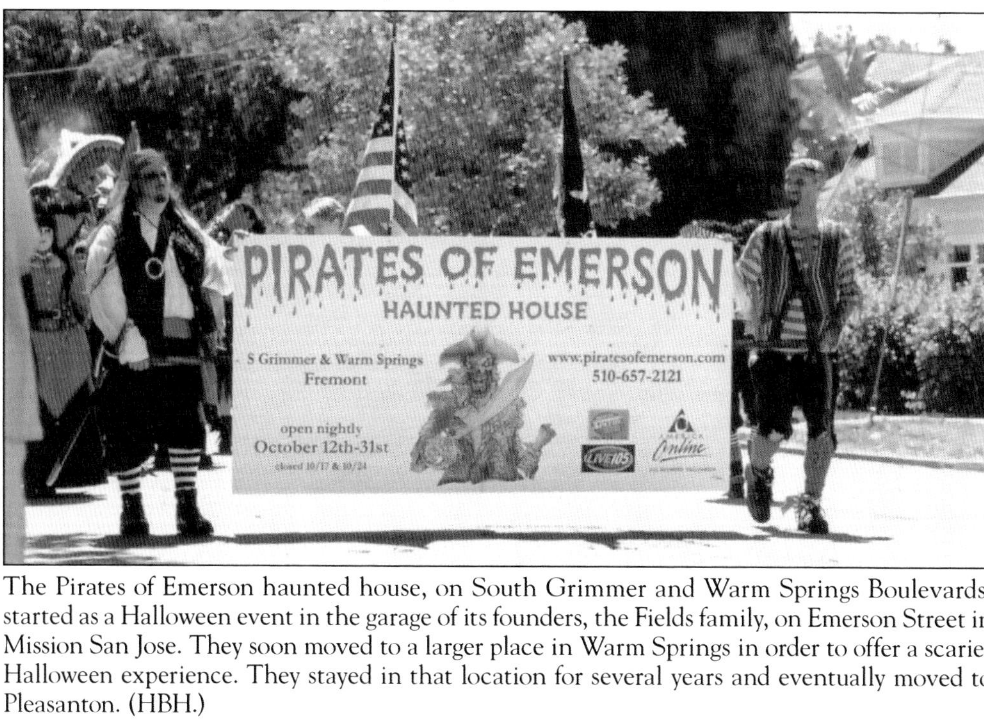


The Pirates of Emerson haunted house, on South Grimmer and Warm Springs Boulevards, started as a Halloween event in the garage of its founders, the Fields family, on Emerson Street in Mission San Jose. They soon moved to a larger place in Warm Springs in order to offer a scarier Halloween experience. They stayed in that location for several years and eventually moved to Pleasanton. (HBH.)

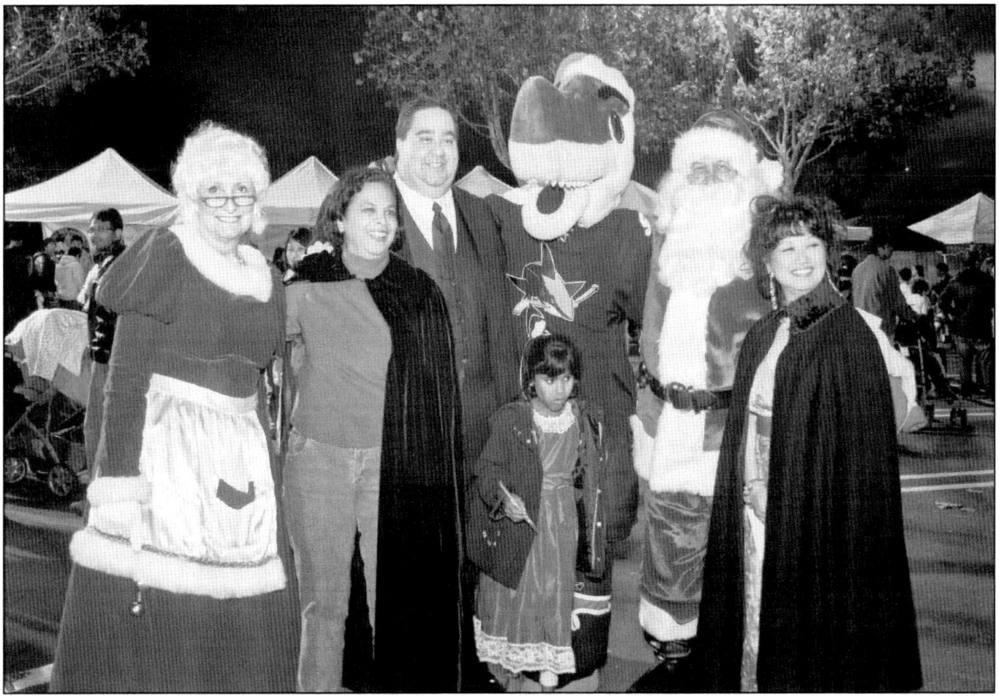

The Warm Springs Business and Community Association started its first annual tree-lighting ceremony at Saki's Spin a Yarn in 2004. The Fremont Warm Springs Sunrise Rotary Club also supports the event. Here, Fremont city council members and others gather for the celebration at the Warm Springs Plaza Shopping Center in 2011. From left to right are an unidentified woman, Anu Natarajan, Bill Harrison, Anjali Natarajan, Santa Claus, and Sue Chan. (Courtesy Don Brown.)

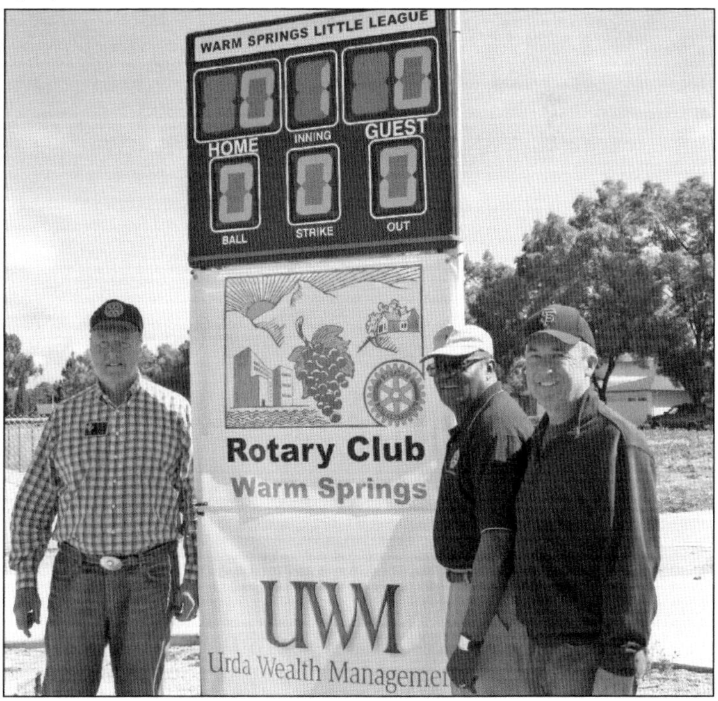


The Warm Springs Rotary Club was formed in 1988 by Stan Allen of the Fremont Chamber of Commerce. Later, Allen formed the Fremont Sunrise Rotary Club, and the two clubs merged in 2010. The Fremont Warm Springs Sunrise Rotary Club donated this Little League score board in 2011. Present for the occasion were, from left to right, Loren Harper, district governor; John Blakely, president in 2009–2010; and Mike Kearns, president in 2010–2011. (Courtesy Don Brown.)

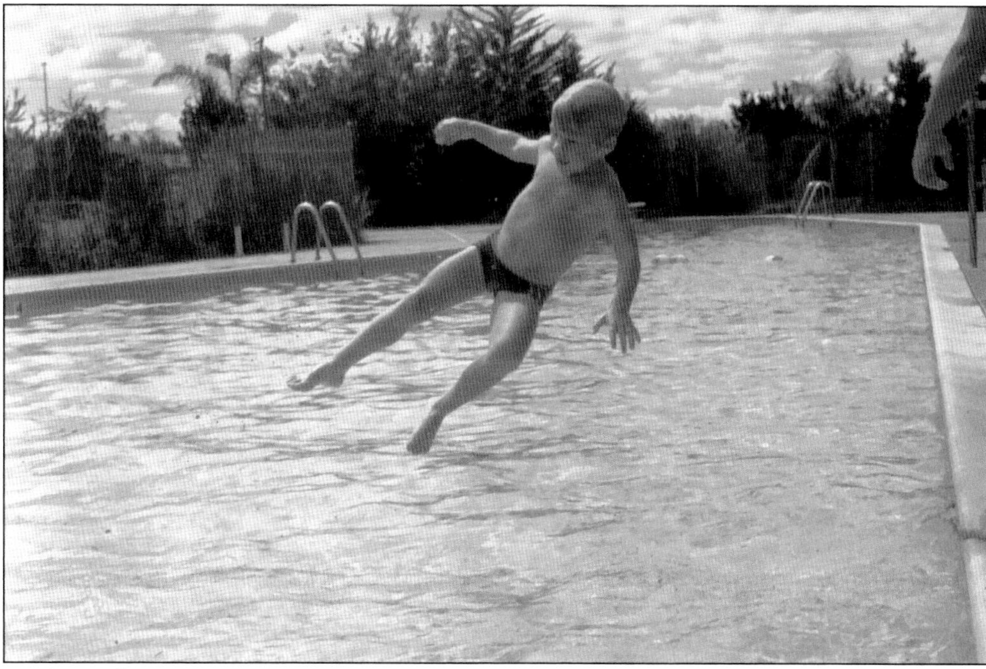

Starlite Hills was one of the first developments in Warm Springs, with its first phase completed in 1962. The Cabana Club, which opened in 1967, was part of the development and featured a pool in the shape of California. It was also home of the Gators swim team. Here, Darreell Soren Brice flies into the pool in the late 1960s. (Courtesy Ted Brice.)

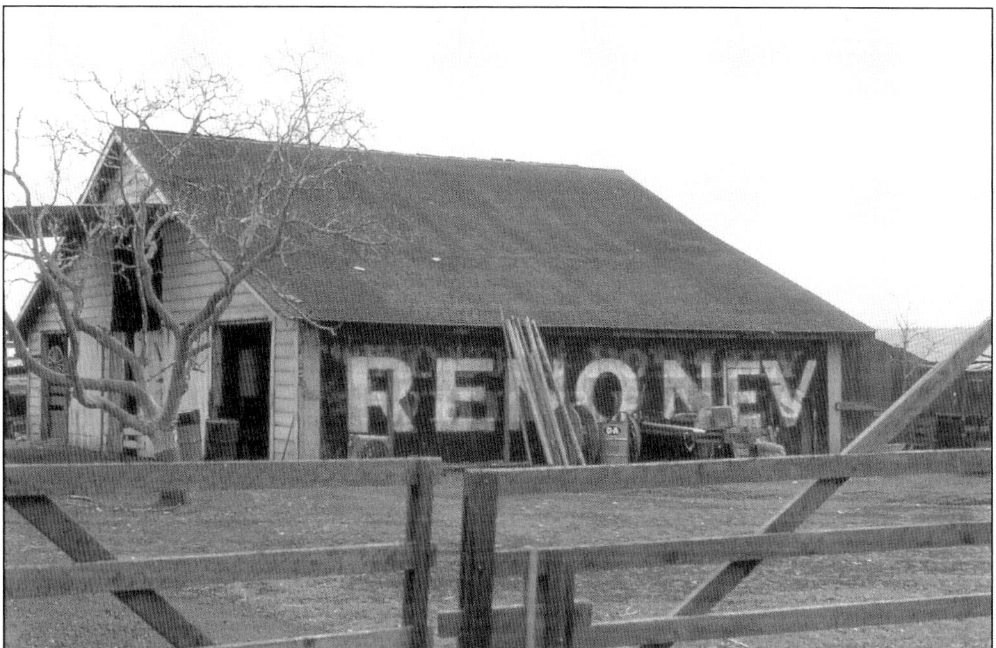


It was common practice for advertisers to rent space on a farmer's barn to publicize their product, or in this case, their town. Reno, Nevada, was touted as a city one needed to visit. (PH.)

# *Eight*

# Preservation and Restoration

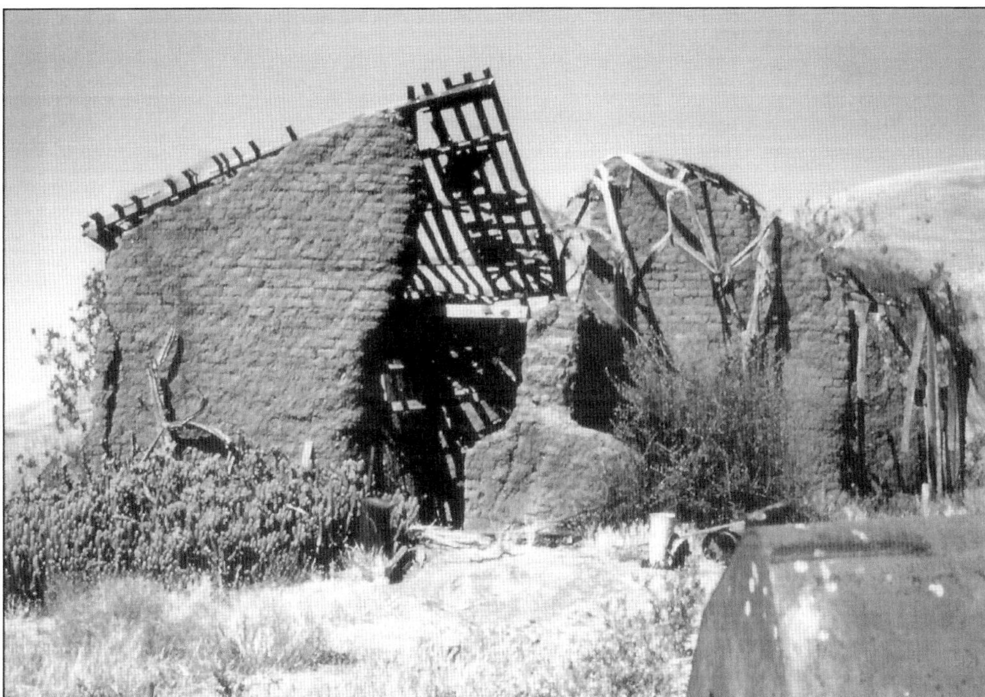

The Higuera Adobe was in ruins by the late 1970s. Only portions of the walls remained standing, and a few rotten boards were all that was left of the roof. It was described by one writer as a "pile of dried mud." A huge crack continued to widen and split the structure. The cactus in front of the adobe was planted by the Goularte family in the 1930s. The Fremont Historical Resource Committee designated the Higuera Adobe as a primary historic resource under the leadership of Dr. Robert Fisher. Land development proposals came and went until Ponderosa Home Development Company bought the property and contributed acreage, the adobe, and funds for the restoration of the adobe to the City of Fremont through the dedication process. The adobe is a symbol of what the community has done to preserve a historical treasure.

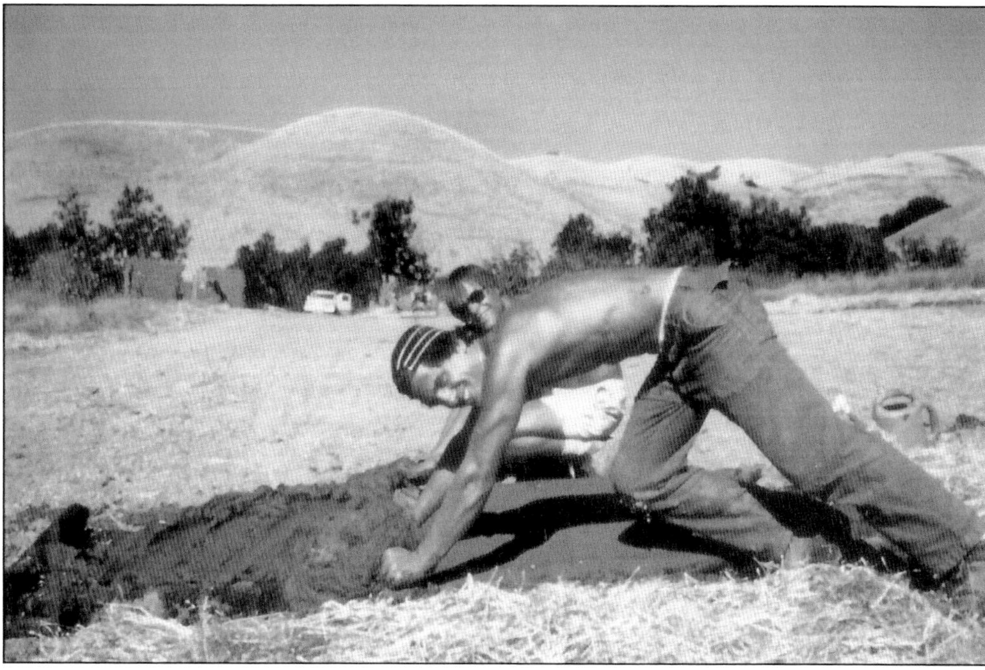

In 1977, the Fremont City Council approved a contract for an accurate restoration of the 1840 Galindo-Higuera Adobe. The architect, Gil Sanchez, personally participated in the deconstruction, the reconstruction, and the experiments to get the correct mixture of clay and sandy soil for the adobe bricks. Charles Buckley was the contractor. Above, workers mix the adobe soil used to make the 7,500 bricks needed for the walls. It took a month for each brick to dry. The contractor used historic-style nails, window glass salvaged from old buildings, and wrought hinges on the front door. Below, a forklift was used to lift the adobe bricks to the top of the wall as workers finish the wall construction.

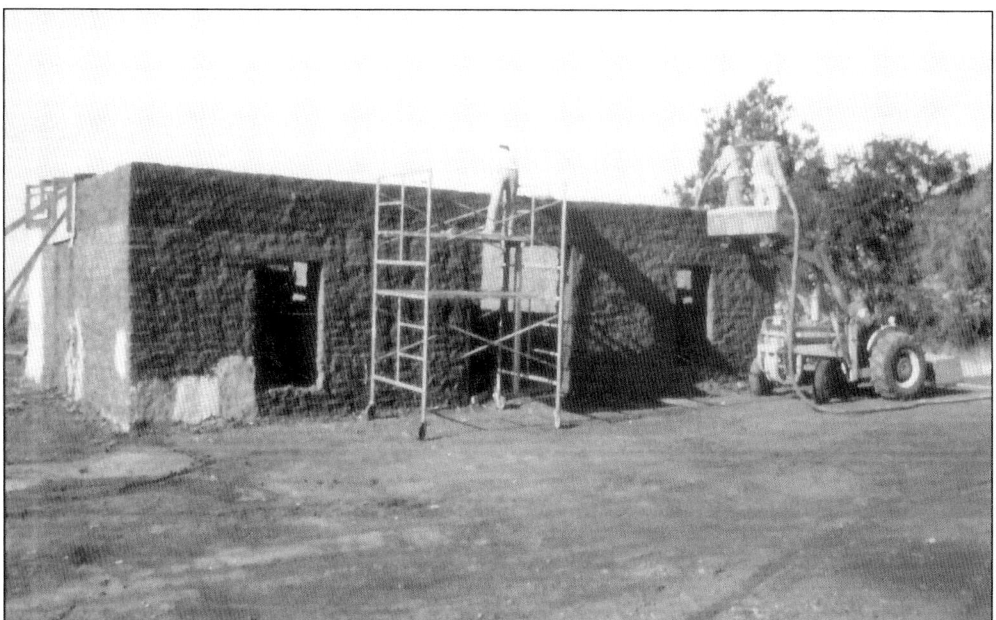

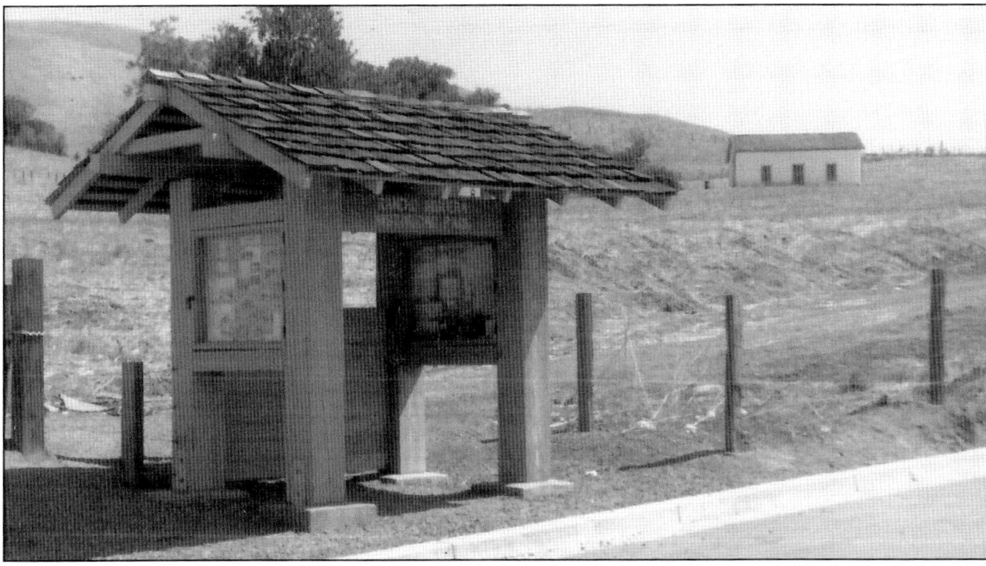

The information kiosk at the entrance to the Higuera Adobe was built by the City of Fremont. It sits outside the park and is accessible to the public. Mission Peak Heritage Foundation, led by Dr. Robert Fisher, prepared the historical documents and drawings and placed them in the kiosk. The Washington Township Historical Society conducted tours through the adobe. (PH.)

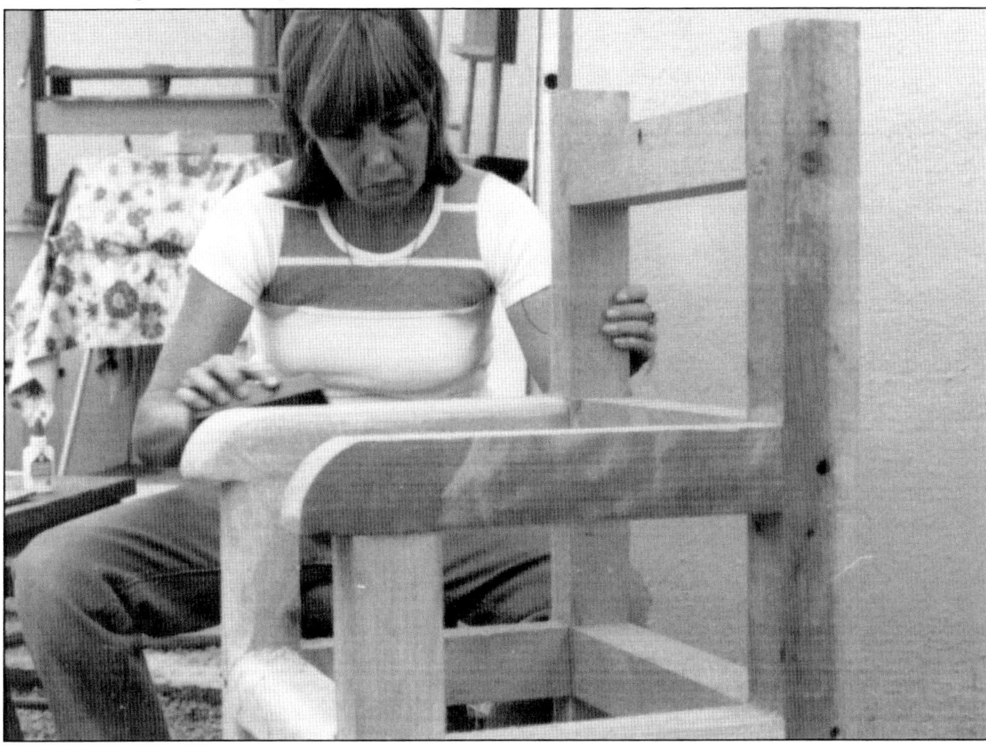

Artisans Alberta George and Jacquee Cook, of the Sand Fleas Workshop, a local artisan business, hand-constructed the period-style furniture for the adobe. Here, Cook puts the finishing touches on one of the chairs. Two Kennedy High School students, Luis Vierra and C.C. Walters, created and donated eight metal candle holders. (Courtesy Alberta Nunes George.)

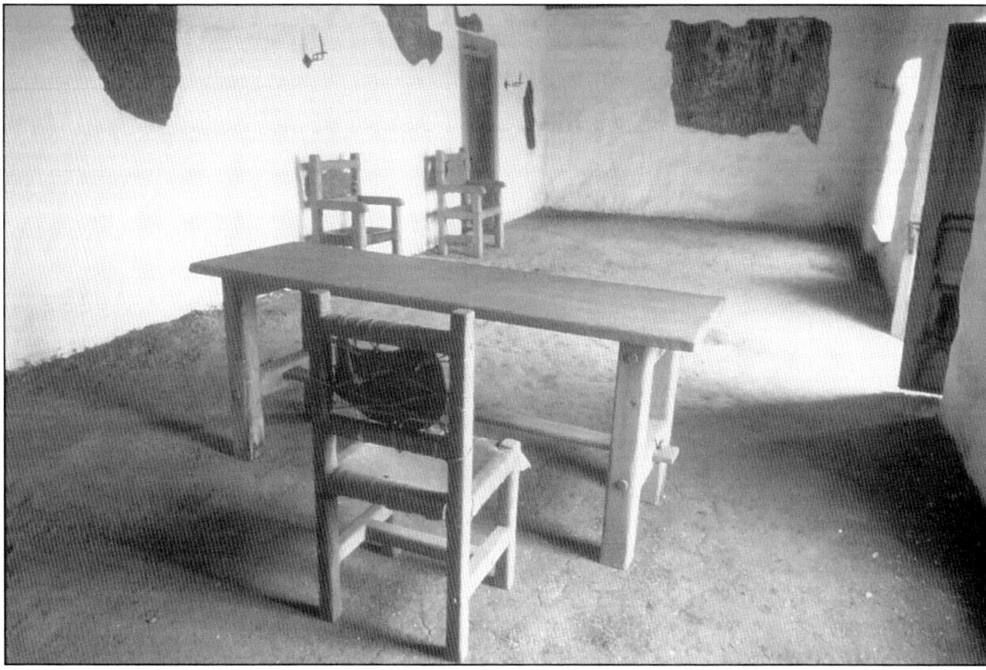

The interior of the Galindo-Higuera Adobe is seen here. The floor was compacted into a very smooth finish. Some areas of the wall were left exposed so visitors could view the adobe brick construction.

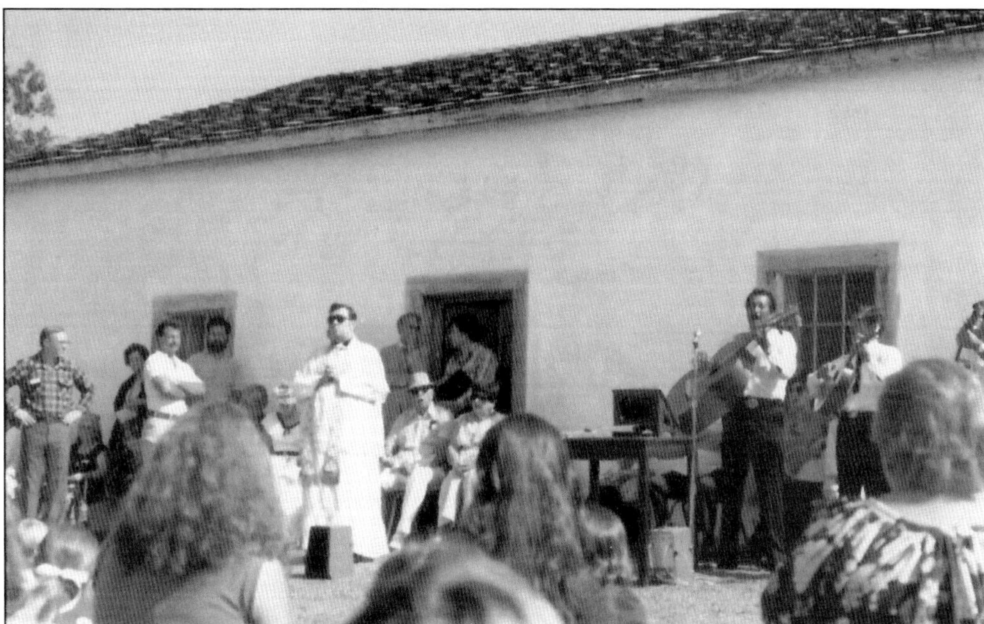

The adobe, with its whitewashed walls, was completed and dedicated on September 30, 1979. Here, a mariachi band led by Larry Lucero performs. Fr. William Abeloe, the pastor of St. Joseph Church in Mission San Jose, blessed the adobe, and the benediction was led by Rev. Peter Adgie of Centerville Presbyterian Church. The program was developed by Al Box and members of the Mission Peak Heritage Foundation and Washington Township Historical Society. John Weed was the master of ceremonies. (PH.)

Ted Harpainter (right) was Fremont's first park superintendent, serving for 19 years until his retirement. Under his management, the system grew from zero parks to 37, as well as more than 30 miles of street landscaping. Harpainter was instrumental in helping to save the giant sycamore tree near the Galindo-Higuera Adobe on Higuera Road. The city required a housing developer to set aside a 10,000-square-foot lot around the tree to preserve it. The tree is 85 feet high and 28 feet 6 inches in circumference and has a 116.25-foot crown spread, giving it a point total of 456 on the California Big Trees scale. It is the second-largest sycamore in the state but has the highest overall point total. Below, Louise Holmes reclines against the base of the historical tree. (Right, courtesy Harpainter Collection; below, PH.)

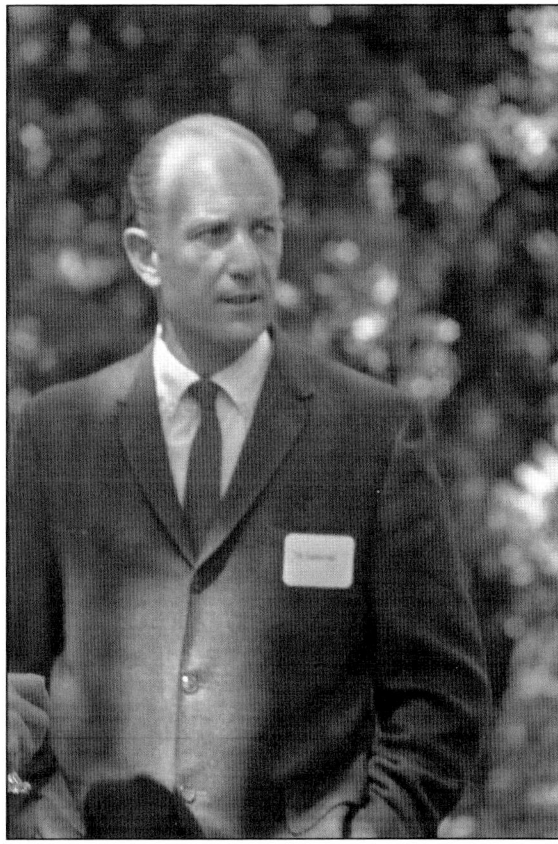

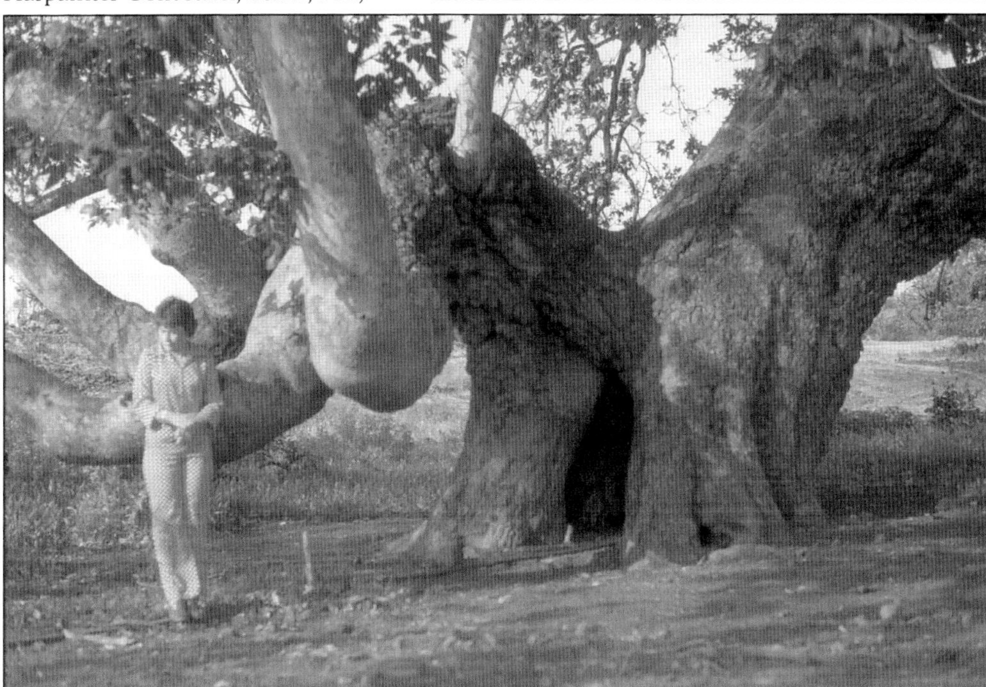

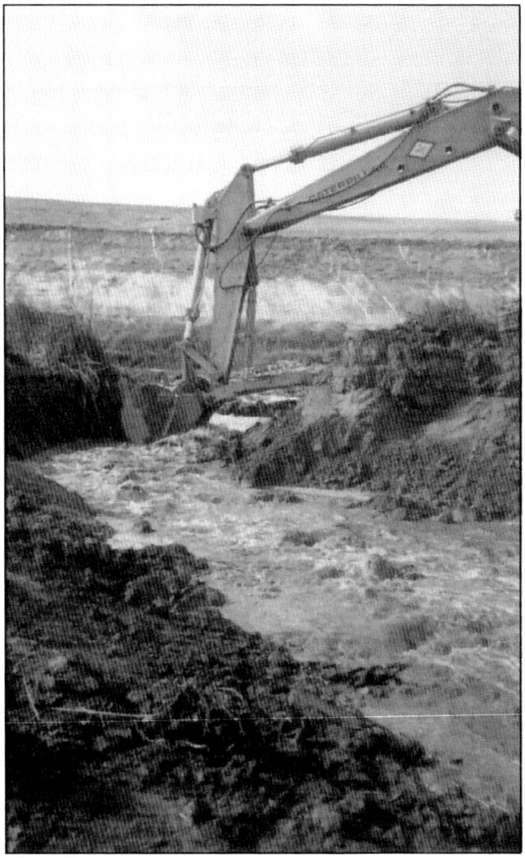

On October 31, 1986, bay water poured onto about 250 acres of former bay lands in the Warm Springs area for the first time in almost a century, marking the return of the largest piece of wetlands ever restored in San Francisco Bay. A backhoe dug a hole through a dike to release the water (left), bringing cheers from both environmentalists and land developers, who united to celebrate the event. Developers King & Lyons agreed to deed the 250 acres of wetlands to the San Francisco Bay National Wildlife Refuge (SFBNWR). In exchange, they received building permits from various state and federal agencies to build on an adjacent 250 acres called Bayside Business Park. Below, a kayaker enjoys the ride as the water pours into the wetlands. (Both, courtesy Donna Olsen.)

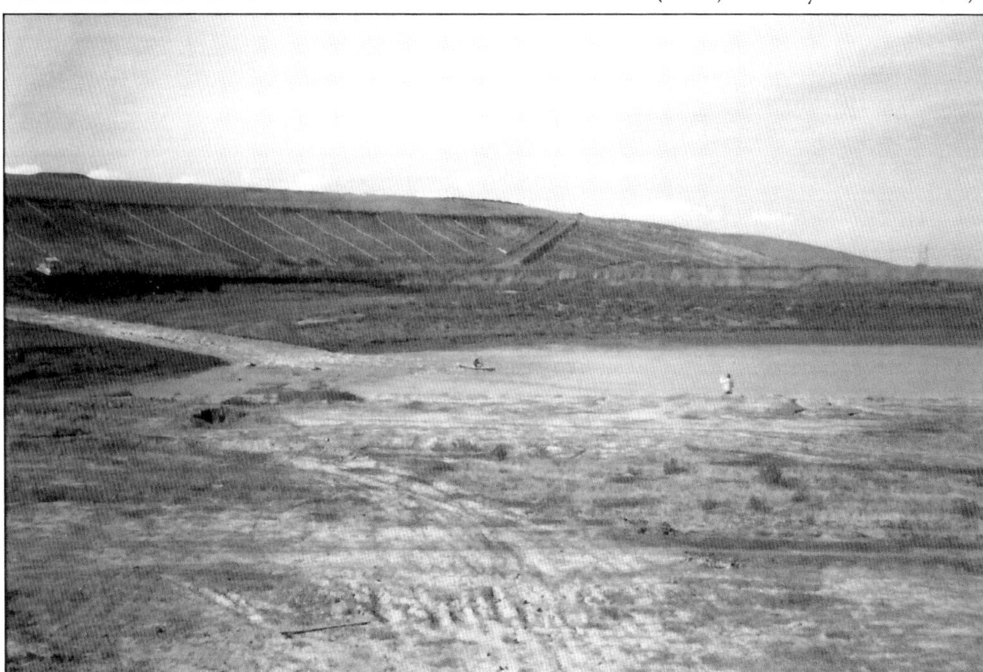

The San Francisco Bay National Wildlife Refuge was founded in 1972 as the first urban refuge in the United States. By 2004, it spanned 30,000 acres of open bay, salt ponds, mudflats, upland, and vernal pool habitats. The areas near Warm Springs were added in sections. Here, Fremont mayor Gus Morrison speaks at the dedication of Warm Springs Seasonal Wetlands in 1992. (Courtesy Donna Olsen.)

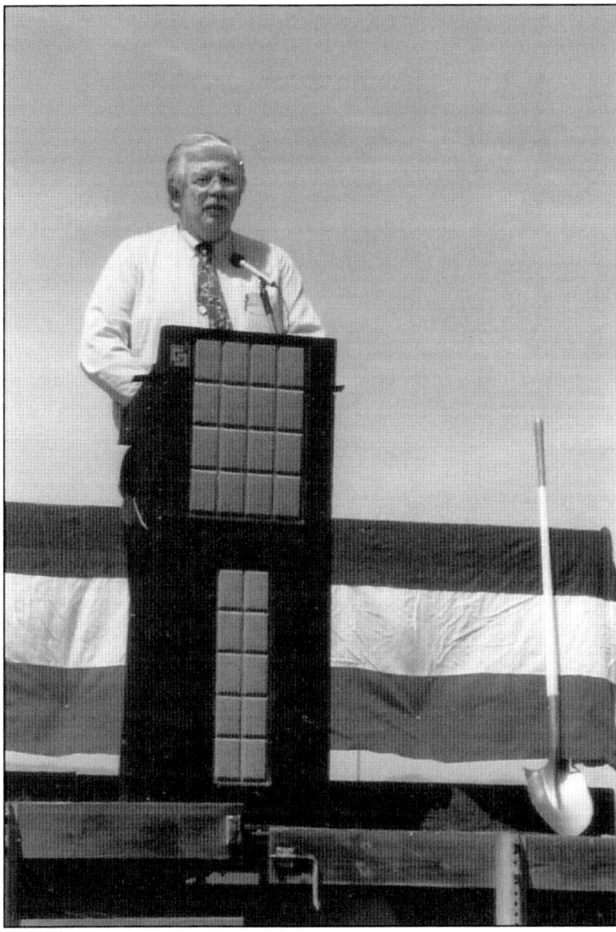

The Cohen Hotel (below) survived the 1906 earthquake intact but did not survive the real estate boom of the 1990s. The handsome building was known by several names, among them the Cohen Hotel, Hidden Valley Ranch, the Stanford Hotel, and Warm Springs Hotel. Last-minute efforts to save the 1869 structure from the wrecker's ball became irrelevant when the structure burned in an early-morning fire in 1993. (Courtesy Paul McGinnis.)

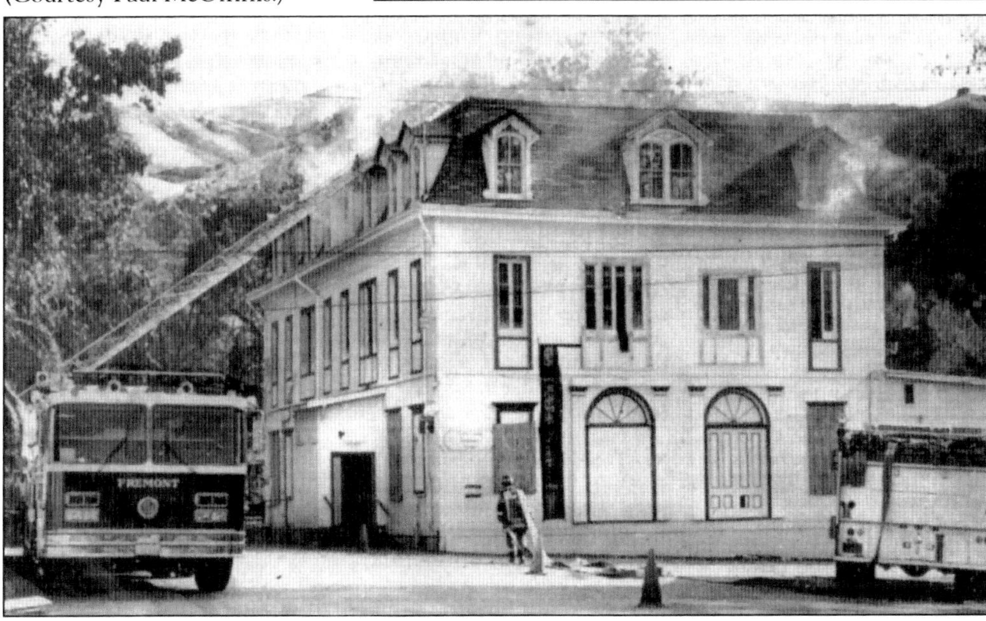

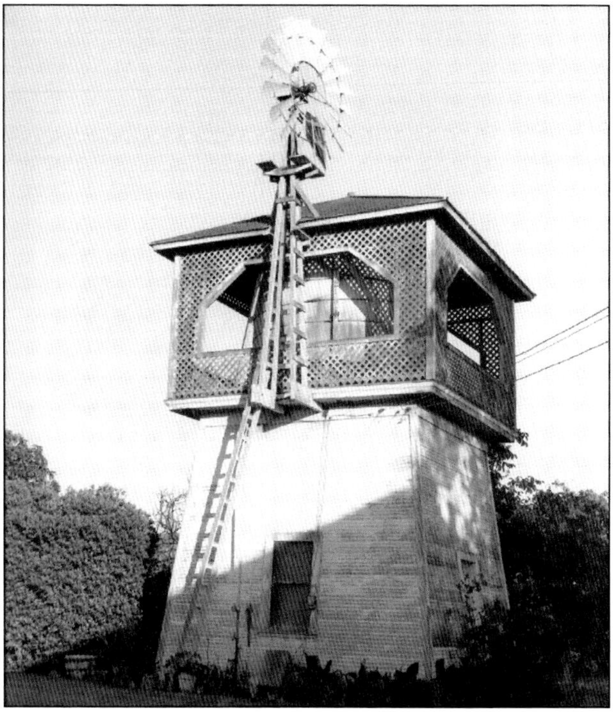

Tank houses were a familiar sight in Warm Springs. Every small farm had a barn, a house, and a tank house. Most were built in a style similar to this, with a windmill, a tank on top, and an enclosed area below. This tank house was on John and Ann Dutra's farm. After being moved a couple of times, it was restored and is now preserved in the Lima Family Cedar Lawn Memorial Park. (TK.)

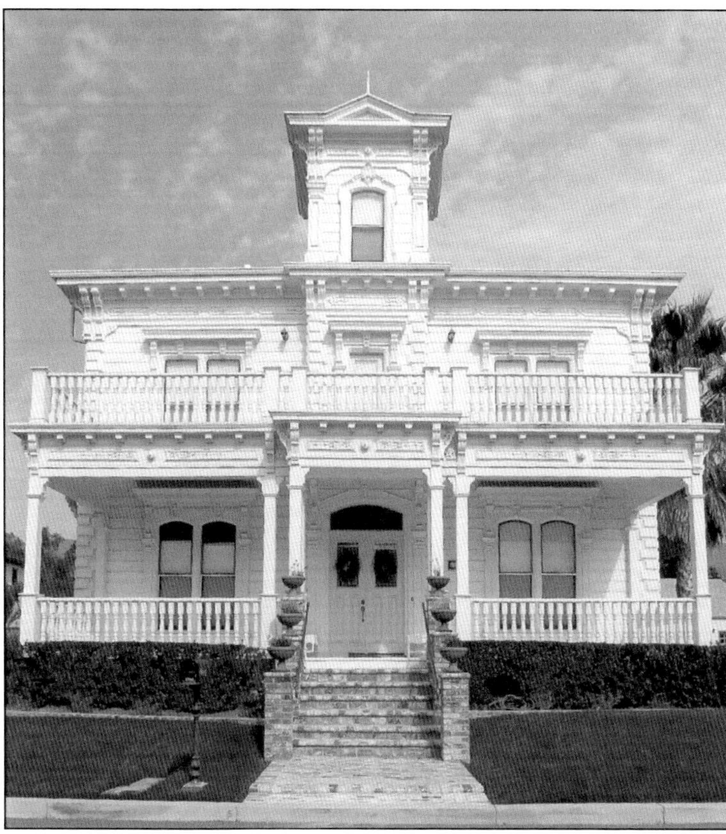

The Curtner home has seen many changes since it was built in 1879. After being owned by the Curtner family, the IDES, and the Bettencourt family, it is now privately owned and has been restored to resemble its original design. The Canary Island palm trees along Wabana Common are believed to have been planted around 1900, when the street was used as the main driveway to the mansion. (GG.)

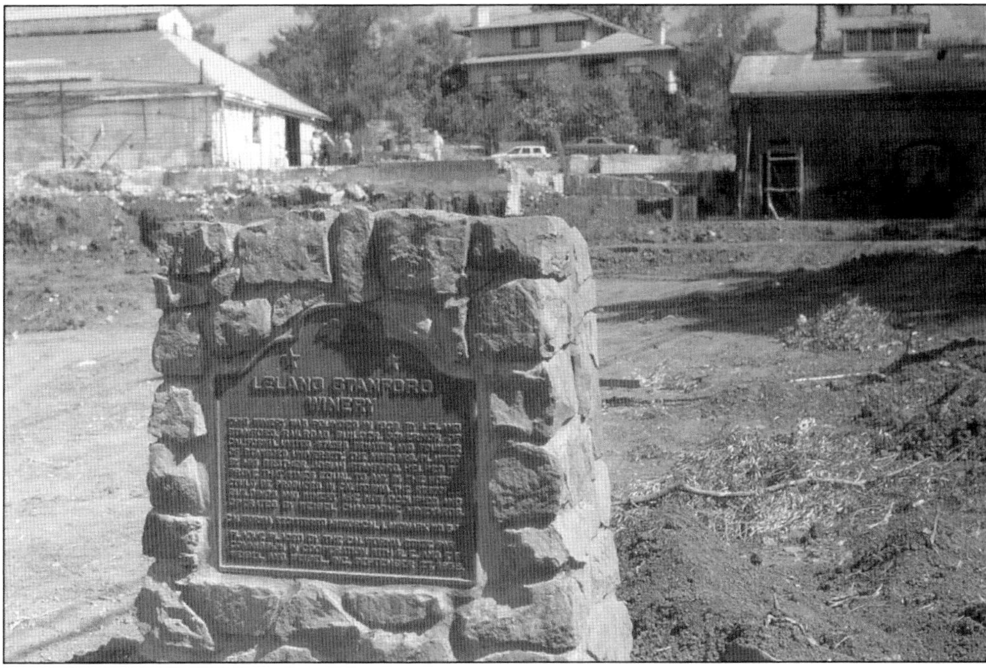


The Leland Stanford Winery is a California Registered Historical Landmark. This plaque was placed at the Weibel Champagne Vineyards in 1958 to commemorate the founding of the winery in 1869. The plaque was later moved from its original position in front of the Weibel Winery and placed beside the brick building in the background on the right. The other two buildings in the background, now demolished, were also part of the original Stanford winery. (PH.)

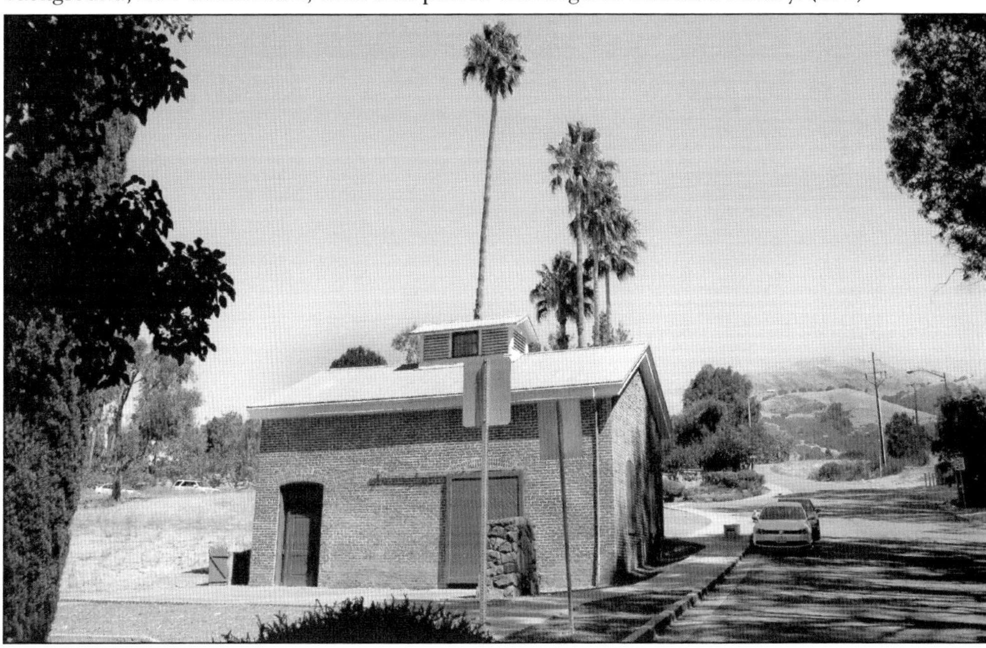

The fully restored brick winery building is on Stanford Avenue. It was constructed by Josiah Stanford in the 1870s and used as a storeroom by the Weibel family. The Mission Peak Regional Preserve staging area is just up the road, with Mission Peak in the background. (GG.)

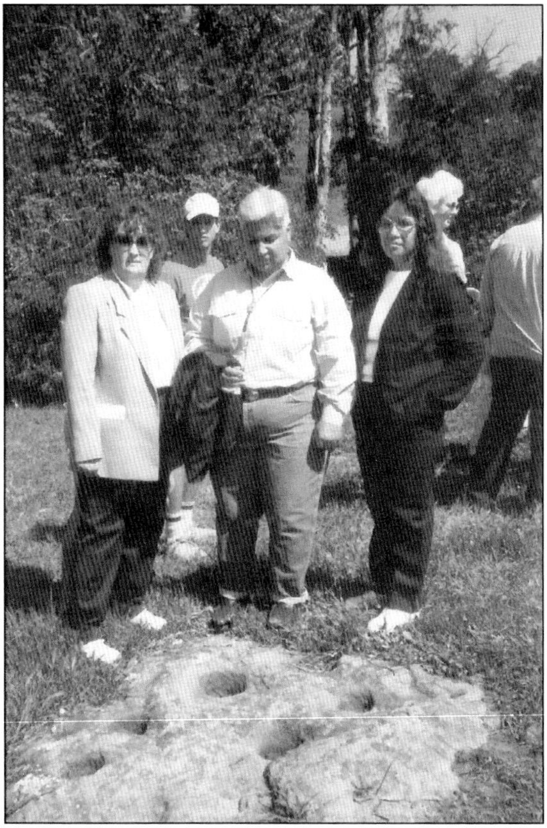

In 1991, a group of vigilant citizens went on a fact-finding walk because of their concerns about a proposed golf course on land that eventually became part of the Mission Peak Regional Preserve, part of East Bay Regional Parks. Participants in the tour included Native Americans from the Muwekma tribe, from left to right, Joan Villa, Rosemarie Cambra, and an unidentified person, who are seen here looking at bedrock mortars. Donna Olsen is in the background. (PH.)

Mission Peak Regional Preserve, part of the East Bay Regional Park District, comprises 2,999 acres. Mission Peak, at an elevation of 2,517 feet, has two main approaches from Fremont, one from the Stanford staging area and the other from Ohlone College. It is common to see hikers like the ones below beginning their ascent to the peak from the Stanford staging area. Plaques commemorating the Anza Expedition, which traveled through the area, were placed at the staging site in 2010. (Courtesy Philip Brazil.)

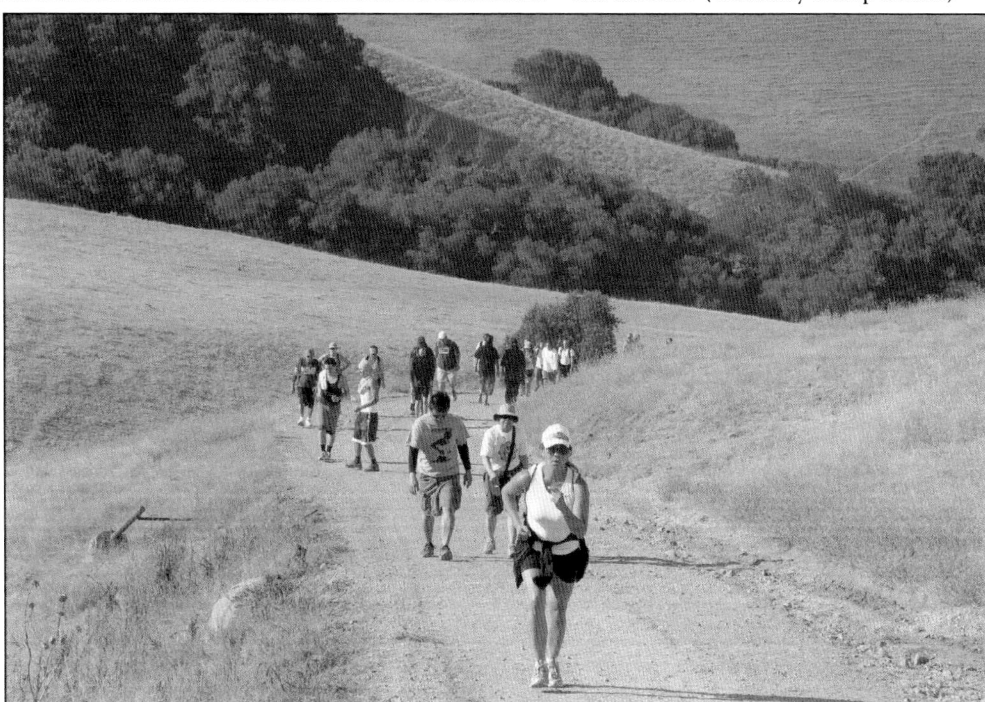

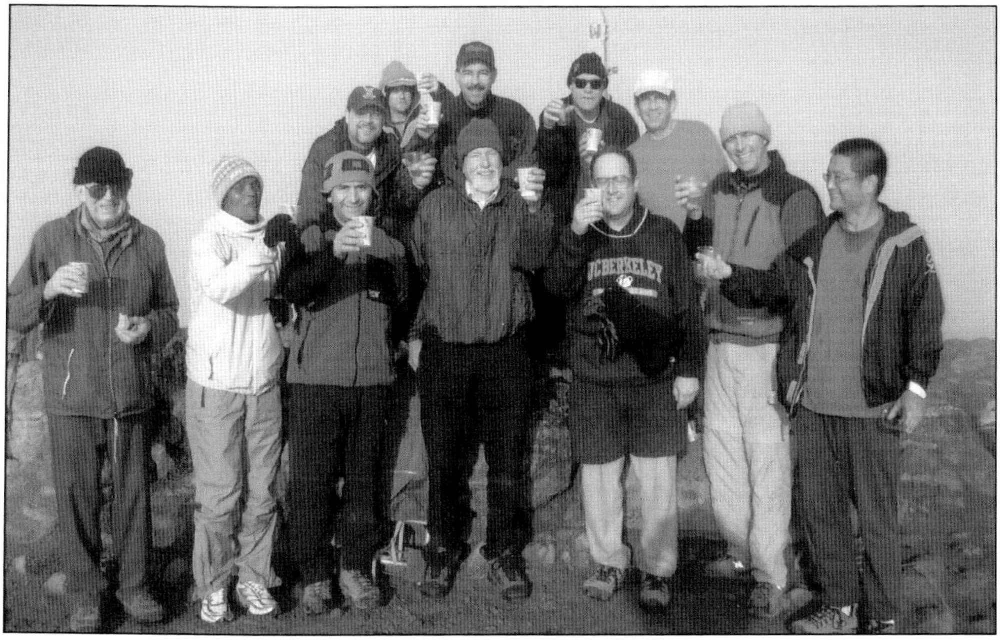

Two avid Mission Peak hikers, John Ogle and Don Eberwine, have each walked to the top of Mission Peak several hundred times. Above, they celebrate Ogle's 77th birthday on the peak in 2006. Ogle is in the middle with the beanie-type hat, and Eberwine (age 84) is on the far left. (Courtesy Celebrate Fremont Collection.)

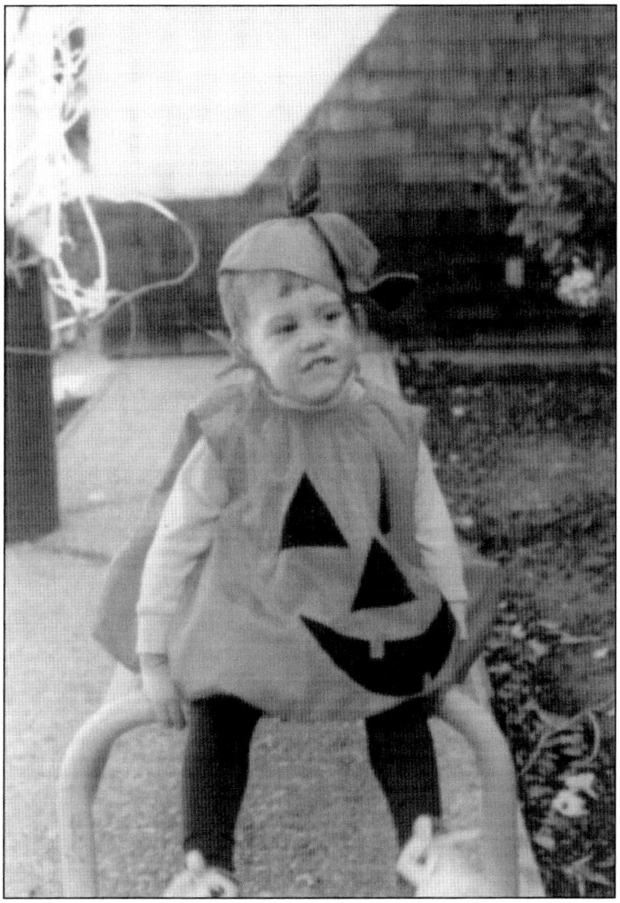

Warm Springs is an area of history, change, and preservation. The area hosts eight parks and preserves: Don Edwards San Francisco Bay National Wildlife Refuge, Mission Peak Preserve, Warm Springs Park, Lone Tree Creek Park, Booster Park, Plomosa Park, and Rancho Higuera Historical Park. Seen here is Max Stephens, age two, who dressed up for a Halloween parade at Warm Springs Park in the 1990s. The Warm Springs Community Center is in the background. (Courtesy Adrienne Stephens.)

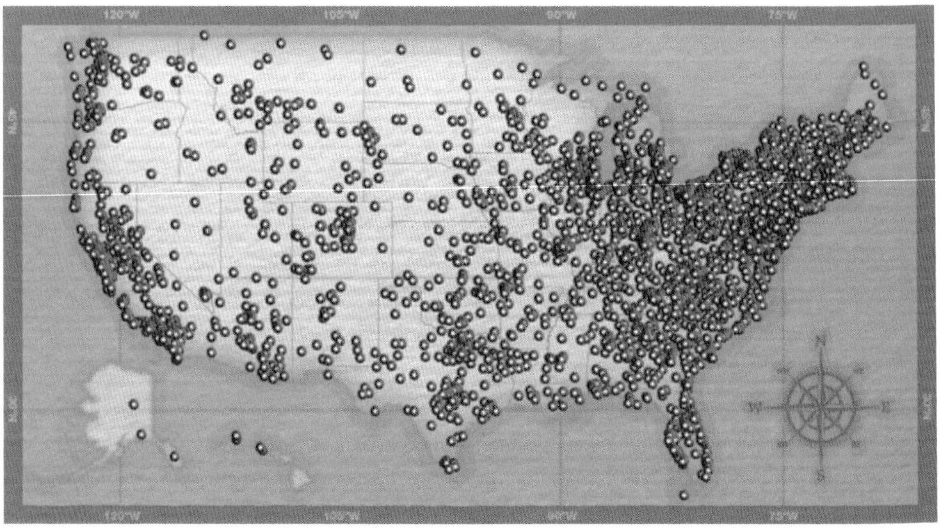



Consistent with our mission to preserve history on a local level, this book was printed in South Carolina on American-made paper and manufactured entirely in the United States. Products carrying the accredited Forest Stewardship Council (FSC) label are printed on 100 percent FSC-certified paper.

MADE IN THE USA